Psychological Interventions in Times of Crisis

Psychological Interventions in Times of Crisis

Laura Barbanel, EdD, ABPP
Robert J. Sternberg, PhD, *Editors*

SPRINGER PUBLISHING COMPANY

Copyright 2006 by Springer Publishing Company, Inc.

Springer Publishing Company, Inc.
11 West 42nd Street, 15th Floor
New York, NY 10036-8002

Acquisition Editor: Sheri W. Sussman
Production Editor: Print Matters
Compositor: Compset
Cover photo by Kevin D. Kupietz

Library of Congress Cataloging-in-Publication Data

Psychological interventions in times of crisis/[edited by] Laura Barbanel, Robert J. Sternberg
    p. cm.
  ISBN 0-8261-3225-1
    1. Crisis intervention (Mental health services) 2. Post-traumatic stress disorder—Prevention.
  I. Barbanel, Laura. II. Sternberg, Robert J.

  RC480.6.P796 2005
  616.89′14—dc22   2005054061

06 07 08 09 10 5 4 3 2 1

Printed in the United States by Bang Printing

CONTENTS

Part II. Community Interventions

Editors

LAURA BARBANEL, EDD, ABPP

Laura Barbanel, Ed.D. ABPP, is a psychologist in private practice in New York. Much of her work focuses on trauma and violence. She is on the faculty of The Manhattan Institute, and is adjunct clinical professor of psychology at Adelphi University and adjunct clinical professor of psychology at Pace University. Dr. Barbanel served as the director of the Graduate Program in School Psychology at Brooklyn College of CUNY for many years.

She was involved in the design and development of the Firehouse Project, whereby clinicians were assigned to firehouses that lost members on September 11, 2001. As a member of the Board of Directors of the American Psychological Association, she co-chaired with Ron Levant the American Psychological Association's Task Force on Psychological Resilience in the Face of Terrorism.

Dr. Barbanel is a fellow of the American Psychological Association and a diplomate of the American Board of Professional Psychology.

ROBERT J. STERNBERG, PhD

Robert J. Sternberg is dean of the School of Arts and Sciences at Tufts University and IBM Professor of Psychology and Education, Professor of Management, and Director of the Center for the Psychology of Abilities, Competencies, and Expertise at Yale. Sternberg was the 2003 President of the American Psychological Association (APA). He has been a member of the APA Board of Directors (2002–2004) and the APA Insurance Trust Board of Trustees (2003), and joined the American Psychological Foundation Board of Directors in 2005. He has been president of the APA Divisions of General Psychology, Educational Psychology,

Psychology and the Arts, and Theoretical and Philosophical Psychology and has served as editor of the *Psychological Bulletin* and the *APA Review of Books: Contemporary Psychology*.

Sternberg received his Ph.D. from Stanford University in 1975 and his B.A. summa cum laude, *Phi Beta Kappa*, with honors with exceptional distinction in psychology, from Yale University in 1972. He also holds five honorary doctorates from European universities.

Sternberg is the author of more than 1000 journal articles, book chapters, and books. He is also a fellow of the American Academy of Arts and Sciences, the American Association for the Advancement of Science, the American Psychological Association (in 15 divisions), the American Psychological Society, the Connecticut Psychological Association, the Royal Norwegian Society of Sciences and Letters, the International Association for Empirical Aesthetics, the Laureate Chapter of *Kappa Delta Pi*, and the Society of Experimental Psychologists. He has won many awards from APA, American Educational Research Association, American Psychological Society, and other organizations.

Contributors

ELENA L. GRIGORENKO, PhD

Dr. Grigorenko holds a Ph.D. in general psychology from Moscow State University (1990) and a Ph.D. in developmental psychology and genetics from Yale (1996). Her professional experiences include conducting research, teaching psychology, and designing educational curricula. Dr. Grigorenko has published more than 150 books and articles. Her main interests are individual differences, child development, and exceptional children. Currently Dr. Grigorenko is Associate Professor at Yale and Moscow State University.

DONNA MACOMBER, MA

Donna Macomber has been a research assistant at the PACE Center at Yale University for 6 years. She received her undergraduate degree in psychology from Albertus Magnus College and her M.A. in psychology from Southern Connecticut State University. Her primary research interests are child development and the testing and assessment of children.

B. HUDNALL STAMM, PhD

B. Hudnall Stamm, received degrees in psychology and statistics at Appalachian State University (B.S., M.A.) and University of Wyoming (Ph.D.). Stamm is a research professor, Director of Telehealth, and director of the Idaho State University Institute of Rural Health. She has been recognized by the International Society for Traumatic Stress Studies for "fundamental contributions to the international public understanding of trauma" and as one of the nation's distinguished researchers by the National Rural Health Association. In her work primarily rural underserved peoples, Stamm's efforts focus on health policy, cultural trauma, and secondary traumatic stress among health care providers where telehealth figures prominently. Her work is used in more than 30 countries and diverse fields including health care, bioterrorism and disaster responding, news media, and the military. For more information, see http://www.isu.edu/irh and http://www.isu.edu/~bhstamm.

AMY C. HUDNALL, MA

Amy C. Hudnall was educated in history (M.A.) and history and German studies (B.A.) at Appalachian State University. She studied at the Goethe Institute and the Bayerische Julius-Maximilians-Universität, Germany. She is a lecturer in the History and Women's Studies Departments, Appalachian State University, and a research assistant professor at the Institute of Rural Health, Idaho State University. Her work focuses on cross-cultural trauma and genocide from a psychological and historical reference and she teaches courses on peace and conflict. She has presented and published on captivity trauma, human rights, secondary trauma, cultural relativism, and cross-cultural conflict.

RACHELLE DATTNER, PhD

Rachelle Dattner is a supervisor in the Relational Orientation division of the New York University Postdoctoral Program in Psychoanalysis and Psychotherapy and a supervisor in the Doctoral Program in Clinical Psychology at the City University of New York. She served as a clinician in the Firehouse Project and is a member of the New York City Disaster Counseling Coalition. In her private practice in Manhattan she continues to work with first responders in individual psychotherapy.

KAREN F. CARR, PhD

Karen Carr is the Clinical Director of the Mobile Member Care Team – West Africa (MMCT), a non-profit organization focusing on training and crisis response for missionaries in West Africa. Carr received her Ph.D. in clinical psychology from Virginia Commonwealth University in 1989. She worked for 8 years in a community mental health center in Henrico County, Virginia, first as a clinical supervisor and then as the program manager of the Emergency Services Unit. In 1998, she left this job to help develop and launch MMCT. She and her two teammates, Darlene Jerome and Marion Dicke, currently live and work in Ghana, West Africa.

NINA K. THOMAS, PhD, ABPP

Nina K. Thomas is a supervisor in and co-chair of the Relational Orientation division of the NYU Postdoctoral Program in Psychotherapy and Psychoanalysis and senior supervisor and faculty in the Contemporary Center for Advanced Psychoanalytic Studies at Fairleigh Dickinson University in Madison, NJ. She is the author of "The Use of the Hero" in the forthcoming *On the*

Ground after September 11: Mental Health Responses and Practical Knowledge Gained, edited by Yael Danieli and Robert Dingman, from Haworth Press. In addition to serving as a clinician in the Firehouse Project, Dr. Thomas also served as co-chair of the American Group Psychotherapy Association's Disaster Outreach Task Force, designing and implementing the multiple training, support, and clinical service groups provided in the greater New York and Washington, DC, metropolitan areas under a grant from the New York Times Company Foundation, 9/11 Neediest Cases Fund.

ESTHER COHEN, PhD

Esther Cohen (Ph.D., Michigan State University, 1973) is a faculty member at the Graduate Program for Educational and Child–Clinical Psychology at the Hebrew University of Jerusalem, Israel. Her publications on trauma are based on 30 years of clinical work with victims of terror and war in Israel. While on sabbatical in New York City during 2001–2, she consulted at various centers as part of the relief efforts in the aftermath of September 11th. Her latest book, with Avigdor Klingman, *School-based Multi-Systemic Interventions for Mass Trauma*, was published by Kluwer Academic/Plenum in 2004.

LAURIE ANNE PEARLMAN, PhD

Laurie Anne Pearlman received her Ph.D. in clinical psychology from the University of Connecticut in 1987. She co-founded the Traumatic Stress Institute in 1986 and the Trauma Research, Education, and Training Institute (TREATI) in 1996. She currently co-chairs the complex trauma task force of the International Society for Traumatic Stress Studies.

Dr. Pearlman has received awards for her clinical and scientific contributions from the Connecticut Psychological Association and the International Society for Traumatic Stress Studies (ISTSS). She has published numerous articles, chapters, and books on psychological trauma and on the deleterious impact of working with survivors known as vicarious traumatization, a term coined in the 1990 article she co-authored on the topic.

IAN S. MILLER, PhD

Ian Miller is a psychologist/psychoanalyst in private practice. He is a faculty member at Columbia University, where he supervises in the Department of Psychiatry. He is also a faculty member at the Manhattan Institute for Psychoanalysis.

Dr. Miller was involved in numerous community interventions following September 11th, 2001. Reflections on these experiences are to be published in the *International Journal for Applied Psychoanalytic Studies* as "Preparation for psychodynamic consultation following community trauma: learning from the 'Firehouse Project'."

ELIZABETH GOREN, PhD

Elizabeth Goren worked with the American Red Cross, New York City Department of Mental Health, and continues to work with the New York City Fire Department in the post–9/11 relief effort. She is affiliated with the New York University Postdoctoral Program in Psychotherapy and Psychoanalysis, where she teaches, supervises, and chairs the interpersonal orientation, and co-chairs the trauma specialization project. She has presented and published on the ethical and clinical considerations for psychoanalysis in disaster community intervention. Currently she is working on a book for the public on living and working as a psychotherapist during and in the aftermath of September 11th.

GEORGE A. BONANNO, PhD

George A. Bonanno is an associate professor of Clinical Psychology in the Department of Counseling and Clinical Psychology, Teachers College, Columbia University. He received his Ph.D. from Yale University in 1991. His research and scholarly interests over the past decade have centered on the question of how human beings cope with extreme adversity, as well as the role in coping played by self-deception, emotion, and emotion regulatory processes. More recently, Dr. Bonanno has focused his empirical and theoretical work on the topic of adult resilience in the context of loss or potential traumatic events. He has also been exploring the salutary role of laugher in coping and is co-editor of the book *Emotion: Current Issues and Future Directions*, published in 2001 by Guilford Press.

Bonanno has recenly been engaged in several longitudinal studies on coping and resilience. These include a recently completed 5-year comparative study of coping with the death of a child or a spouse (funded by the National Institute of Health [NIH]), a mulit-dimensional study of emotion regulation, stressful life events, resilience, and adjustment among college sudents, a study of emotion and well-being among survivors of childhood sexual abuse(in collaboration with researchers at NIH), and a recent study of resilience and adjustment among individuals in or near the World Trade

Center during the 9/11th terrorist attack (funded by the National Science Foundation).

THOMAS J. MC GOLDRICK, PhD

Thomas J. McGoldrick is a clinical psychologist with the U.S. Department of Veterans Affairs Readjustment Counseling Service and in private practice. He served with the counseling service of the FDNY as a firehouse clinician following the 9/11/01 disaster.

ANTHONY D. MANCINI, PhD

Anthony D. Mancini is currently a research scientist in the Bureau of Adult Services and Evaluation Research, New York State Office of Mental Health. In that role, Dr. Mancini conducts research on state mental health services and policies, with a focus on evidence-based practices. He has co-authored a number of articles on psychotherapeutic approaches to bereavement and trauma. Dr. Mancini received his Ph.D. from Columbia University in 2004.

JUDITH L. ALPERT, PhD

Judith L. Alpert is professor of Applied Psychology at New York University. She is also clinical professor and supervisor in the Postdoctoral Program in Psychotherapy and Psychoanalysis at NYU. She has written extensively in the area of trauma. Dr. Alpert maintains a private practice in New York City.

KATHRYN A. DALE

Kathryn A. Dale is a doctoral candidate in the Steinhardt School of Education's School Psychology Program at New York University. She has written about September 11th from the perspectives of New York City school psychologists. She is particularly interested in the impact of trauma on children.

WARREN SPIELBERG, PhD

Dr. Warren Spielberg is a clinical psychologist with more than 15 years of experience working with adults and children of all ages. Over the last 10 years he has conducted research and written about the unique problems of men and boys. He teaches psychology at the New School University, and also works with the Wolfson Center for National Affairs at the same institution. He is co-author, with Kirkland Vaughans, of the upcoming book *Brotherman Rising: Protecting African American Boys From the Culture of Shame*. Since 9/11/01 he has been a consultant to the FDNY, assisting them in the development of the Firehouse Project, for which he was awarded "Practitioner of the Year" by the American Psychological Association (Division 51).

PREETIKA P. MUKHERJEE

Preetika P. Mukherjee is a doctoral student in the School Psychology program at New York University, Steinhardt School of Education. Her two main areas of interests are trauma intervention and parent–child relationships. She has been working on developing and studying the efficacy of intervention for sexually and physically abused inner-city adolescent girls with Dr. Marylene Cloitre at the NYU Child Study Center, Institute for Trauma and Stress. She has also worked with sexually and physically abused girls and women in India. She has presented many papers and posters; papers published online include *Status of Widows of Vrindavan and Varanasi: A Comparative Study.*

GERARD A. JACOBS, PhD

Gerard A. (Jerry) Jacobs is director of the Disaster Mental Health Institute (DMHI) and professor at the University of South Dakota. He is active in field work, training, program development, and consultation nationally and internationally for the Red Cross and the American Psychological Association. He is an author of the World Health Organization *Tool for the Rapid Assessment of Mental Health* (Petevi, Revel, & Jacobs, 2001). Dr. Jacobs served on the Institute of Medicine Committee on Responding to the Psychological Consequences of Terrorism. He works with the Asian Disaster Preparedness Center in psychological support training and program development.

DAVID L. MEYER, MA

David L. Meyer is a doctoral candidate at the University of South Dakota and a Morgan Fellow in the Disaster Mental Health Institute. His primary area of interest is the psychological impact of disaster work on emergency responders and disaster response personnel. He has been an Emergency Medical Technician for 12 years; he is a member of the American Red Cross Disaster Services Human Resources (national disaster team) and a Red Cross disaster response and health and safety instructor. His internship experiences include time at the Asian Disaster Preparedness Center in Bangkok, Thailand, and the national Red Cross Disaster Operations Center in Washington, DC.

ERVIN STAUB, PhD

Ervin Staub is professor of Psychology at the University of Massachusetts, Amherst, and Director of the Ph.D. concentration in "the psychology of peace and the prevention of violence." He has studied helping and altruism in adults and children, genocide and its prevention, and reconciliation. His book include the two volume *Positive Social Behavior and Morality* (1978, 1979); *The Roots of Evil: The Origins of Genocide and Other Group Violence* (1989); and *The Psychology of Good and Evil: Why Children, Adults and Groups Help and Harm* (2003). His awards include the Lifetime Contributions to Peace Psychology Award of the Society for the Study of Peace, Conflict and Violence: Peace Psychology Division of the American Psychological Association, and the Nevitt Sanford Award for Professional Contributions to Political Psychology from the international society for Political Psychology. He is past-President of these Societies. He has worked in varied projects in field settings, such as the development of a training program for the State of California after the Rodney King incident on an ongoing and project in Rwanda on healing, reconciliation, and the prevention of new violence.

Foreword

Psychological Interventions for Victims of Disaster and Trauma

Karen W. Saakvitne, PhD

The world is changing. Our understanding of the world is changing. And, in response, the fields of psychology and mental health are changing. This volume reflects that good news. It is my hope that reading the papers in this book will promote further change.

Some of the key philosophical shifts in our field highlighted in these papers include (1) the adaptation of a trauma framework in place of a traditional pathology model for responding to victims of disaster and traumatic events; (2) the emergence of an integrated understanding of the impact of traumatic events on the physiology, psychology, and spirituality (meaning) of the individual as well as on the community, culture, and society in which s/he lives; (3) a recognition of the importance of cultural and political beliefs in predicting both the effects of and resources necessary to address trauma; (4) the expanding role of the mental health professional outside of his or her office and traditional psychotherapist identity; (5) acknowledgment of and attention to the profound impact of the work on the *self* of the healer; and (6) a reworking of the ethics of psychological intervention in the context of the previous five considerations.

Work with victims of disaster and trauma moves us away from the traditional "us–them" model of mental health taught in medicine and clinical psychology. Trauma work requires us to eschew the compartmentalized approach human health that underlies Western medicine because it is clear that the impact of traumatic events affects the entire self within its community and relationships. We are reaching beyond even the integrative "bio-psycho-social" approaches to theories that integrate the role of spirituality and meaning making and focus on strengths, resources, and resilience. As our understanding of the broad systemic impact of traumatic events increases, we embrace an understanding of human vulnerability and resilience that is based not on psychopathology, but on a complex understanding of human adaptation, psychological needs, spiritual resilience, and community values. This shift to a new paradigm has far-reaching implications for all aspects of our work.

This "trauma framework" gives us a new lens and thus changes our vision. When we look at the distress of a person or community traumatized by disaster or violence, we see (as Staub and Pearlman note) "normal human responses to abnormal events." We see the struggle of the human body, psyche, and spirit to survive, to connect and to make meaning. We see the cost of that struggle and the evidence that the tools of healing exist innately within all people. Our interpretations of what we see change also. For example, we look at grief rather than assuming depression. We understand fear as distinct from anxiety. We understand the desperate struggle to reclaim control and make meaning that can cause a person to behave in ways that seem maladaptive. We understand the terrors of fully knowing, feeling, and integrating (realizing) that drive people to distract, numb, and alter their states of consciousness in order not to know or feel. When we start with the questions, "How does this adaptation help?" and "What problem does it solve?" instead of "What is wrong with you?", we shift our position to stand shoulder to shoulder with the traumatized individual. Only then can we look at the world through their eyes so as to understand what they need to begin to reestablish a sense of self and possibility. This shift in position profoundly changes the nature of the relationship between helper and trauma victim.

Our professional identities and roles have altered. We see ourselves less as the ones with definitive knowledge or answers, but rather as those willing to listen, witness, and offer what information we have as we learn from the experience of those we are helping. Carr says simply that when faced with the inevitable and unanswerable existential questions often raised by traumatic events, "just having the opportunity to ask them in the presence of a non-judging person who can sit in the ambivalence and uncertainty can be very helpful." The value of humility came across in many of the papers in this volume, articulated most explicitly by those authors who worked in countries and cultures different from their own.

For the most part, the papers in this volume address events that affected large numbers of people, whole communities. They reflect public rather than private (or secret) tragedies. In the face of community tragedies, the responses and resources of the individual and the community are intertwined and mutually influence one another. When Carr describes specific aspects of certain African cultures that seem to enhance a person's ability to endure hardship and to promote resilience and community, she highlights the dangers of bringing the cultural assumptions of the United States to work with survivors of these particular African cultures.

Very little of the work reported in the eight chapters on community interventions occurred in psychotherapy offices. As Mukherjee & Alpert note, "The traditional office-based approach of mental health professionals is inconsistent with the needs of individuals after a disaster." As we leave our offices, we will have to abandon some of our discrete formulations and rework our conceptualizations of what "normal" means, what constitutes "health" when human endurance is stretched, and what we have to offer. Our challenge is to make psychology relevant; to take it out of our offices—to the streets, to the field, to the world—and in doing so, to let go and let it be transformed by those to whom we offer it.

The authors who worked in Africa elaborated models of culturally respectful, integrative processes in which they offered their ideas in forums that allowed time, discussion, input, and integration with the lived experience, wisdom, ideas, and beliefs of the people with whom they were working. Their explicit goal was to offer tools to African responders who were already resources within their own communities. The information was given over for the survivors to change, make their own, and carry further if they found it helpful. Again, this approach is a departure from our more familiar identities as experts, authorities, didactic educators, or rescuers.

Constructivism requires we recognize our own constructions, our perceptions and assumptions, and not confuse them with a unitary truth. Trauma work in general, and cross cultural trauma work, in particular, reinforces this caveat. Stamm & Hudnall emphasize, "regardless of the location of the disaster, it is important to understand how the community's culture and historical events combine to create the world in which the people live and in which you will be working."

The need to understand individual and collective trauma responses in the context of sociopolitical environment and beliefs is emphasized repeatedly in these papers. Human-generated trauma occurs in particular social and political contexts that either allow or promote the disenfranchisement and violation of one group by another. Whether the traumatic events are childhood sexual abuse, famine and starvation, acts of war, or genocide, there is a social and political context that has contributed to or failed to prevent the harm. We must understand this reality as we work with survivors to understand what is at stake, what historical truths may be addressed, what dangers empowerment may bring, and what resources are truly available.

In the process of helping, we, the helpers, are also transformed. We become part of the community that has suffered and part of the compassionate community of those who are willing to face the horrors of devastation and violence. In so doing, helpers pay a price. We are forever changed, in both painful and positive ways. Helpers working with trauma survivors lose innocence, illusions, and perhaps idealism. They may experience the shattering of cherished beliefs and feel the heartache of empathy with unthinkable losses. They may feel heartsick and maybe soul sick. Each helper will have to find his or her way to reclaim meaning, learn to tolerate unbearable effects, and find personal resources within and outside him or herself. All helpers need to attend to themselves and accept support as they offer it to others. Throughout this book, authors speak to the vulnerability of workers to secondary or vicarious traumatization, and the importance of systematic attention to self-care and healing for the healers.

Concomitantly, many responders come to this work drawn by a deep sense of commitment, courage, and idealism. It is clear that these qualities can deepen and grow even as they are blended with humility and grief. The work itself is meaningful to the helpers. This sense of meaning is both a source of resilience and an antidote to the impact of vicarious traumatization. As we witness the potential for devastation and human cruelty, we also witness the potential for survival and the strength of the human spirit. When we are willing to face the truth of tragedy, we join those who know the terrible possibilities of nature and humanity, and still hold the capacity to believe in beauty and love, in growth and transformation. We grow from facing devastating loss when we struggle to make meaning from our experience, and we can use it to strengthen our sense of connection to humanity and to a larger purpose. In doing so, we reach outside our comfort zone to feel a part of the larger human community that includes the vulnerable and the bereft. In reading these papers, we become part of that extended community as we witness devastation and trauma and look for hope and healing.

The highest praise one can give for an edited volume is the sincere wish that each author will read the other chapters and try to integrate those ideas into his or her own thinking. I found myself carrying the ideas of each chapter into the reading of the next, leading me into imaginary conversations with authors and a fantasy of extended dialogue among all the contributors. We cannot afford to do this work in isolation. Nor can those we help afford to wait for us each to make the same mistakes and repeatedly learn the same lessons. There is an opportunity here for mutual learning that could significantly deepen our understanding of the challenges of offering psychological interventions in times of crisis, and improve the efficacy of our services. It is my hope that this volume will be a launching pad for many such conversations and debates.

REFERENCES

Levine, P. (2005). *Healing trauma: A pioneering program for restoring the wisdom of your body*. Boulder, CO: Sounds True, Inc.

Saakvitne, K.W., Gamble, S.G., Pearlman, L.A., & Lev, B.T. (2000). *Risking connection: A training curriculum for working with survivors of childhood abuse*. Lutherville, MD: Sidran Foundation & Press.

Introduction

Laura Barbanel and Robert Sternberg

Responding to disaster is not new for psychologists. The field of trauma psychology has existed for some time. But the extent of this response and the participation of psychologists in the recovery efforts in a variety of settings have not been widely visible. Psychologists have responded to the needs of victims of massacres, have set up programs in West Africa for post-traumatic stress disorder (PTSD), have worked in the wake of the war in the former Yugoslavia, and have worked in Chernobyl after its nuclear disaster. The responses of psychologists have been seen, however, as ad hoc and the work generally has not been viewed in a theoretical framework.

In the wake of September 11, the potential of psychologists to respond became a significant force in the recovery. When the tragedy hit, individual psychologists and other mental-health personnel became mobilized in a variety of ways. Disaster Relief Networks that had been in place for years (DRN) activated hundreds of their members to work at the site. Psychologists worked with schools to help them with children's fears, with hospitals, and with other social service agencies. The American Psychological Association developed educational pieces for the public on its website. Public-service ads were developed and launched on radio and TV. The work in this disaster began to be chronicled.

Although psychologists had been working in the midst of disasters for many years, the 9/11 disaster caught the attention of the public and of psychology in a way that had not been the case previously. The breadth of the disaster and its effects had not been studied in quite the same way as in the past. Affected individuals included relatives of victims, rescue workers, people who lived or worked in the area, and people who watched or experienced it in other ways. Psychologists found themselves affected as well, since they lived or worked in the area. They found themselves vicariously traumatized and suffering from compassion fatigue. The effects of a new and more uncertain time have begun to infuse the work that psychologists do. There is clearly a need for more understanding and of greater facility with public response to trauma and of psychological vulnerability to trauma.

The purpose of this book is describe the responses to disaster that psychologists have made in different parts of the world; to discuss the rationale for the particular services; and to provide a theoretical synthesis as it evolves from this work. New models of service delivery have been generated and will be presented.

The first section of the book presents a theoretical framework of trauma response. Mukherjee and Alpert review interventions in disaster from a historical point of view and discuss some of the controversies in the field. Bonanno and Mancini review the literature on bereavement-related depression and PTSD. Jacobs then presents the concept of "Psychological First-Aid" as the kind of treatment that psychologists provide in disasters.

The second section of the book describes specific interventions in particular circumstances. Each of the disasters described has characteristics that are unique to it and has required responses that are different both organizationally and clinically. Specific techniques were developed to suit the context and the culture. Carr's chapter on the mobile care team describes an American psychologist working in West Africa in crisis response. Stamm's chapter describes an intervention that is new to this technology age, that is, telecommuting to the site of the disaster. Interventions have needed to be designed to include the local support staff, which differs widely. In short, each set of responses has had to be designed to suit the needs of the particular circumstance. Staub and Pearlman describe an approach to promoting healing, reconciliation, the prevention of new violence, and the development of positive relations between groups and a peaceful society in the aftermath of the genocide in Rwanda. Dybdhal describes her involvement in Bosnia through projects providing psychosocial assistance to women traumatized by war in cooperation with local health workers. An outcome study was designed to evaluate the effects of an intervention program aimed at helping mothers help their children. Dale and Alpert describe the multiple responses of New York University, a university located in lower Manhattan, to the needs of its community after 9/11. Cohen describes her work looking at the play patterns of children exposed to terrorist attacks in Israel. Grigorenko and Macomber explore the psychological events related to the nuclear disaster in Chernobyl. And finally, a group of seven psychologists (Barbanel, Dattner, Goren, Miller, McGoldrick, Spielberg, & Thomas) describe experiences with the Firehouse Project, which brought psychologists in to serve the counseling needs of firefighters in firehouses affected by 9/11.

Part III is a synthesis by the editors. It will fuse the theoretical work that was discussed in the beginning of the book and the chapters that describe the actual work. What are the principles of trauma and disaster work? Is there a coherence to it that qualifies this work as a specialty in the mental health field or it is simply a potpourri of interventions that have grown up around disaster? The authors seek to make the case that these interventions that have grown up around disaster do indeed constitute a new mental health specialty.

Although each of these efforts has brought to bear all of the clinical and research data available to psychology, responses frequently do not look like traditional psychology. Psychologists have had to stretch their own capabilities and skills. Each response and, therefore, each chapter in this book, is unique and represents the best that psychology has to offer to alleviate the worst of human suffering. It requires tremendous resilience on the part of the psychologists who provide the services. It becomes particularly important to understand the nature of these responses and to learn form them at this point in world history. Are these responses from clinical psychology, community psychology, or something else entirely? Although each contribution is different, as is each disaster, it is important for us to distill the common threads to develop the principles that are operative. The authors and the editors believe that these common principles build a theoretical framework. There is controversy as to whether psychological interventions in the aftermath of disaster are helpful or not. This controversy will be addressed in the book.

Both natural disasters and human made disasters are described. Some of the common threads that are apparent are the following:

1. The work is not in the psychologist's office; it is on the client's turf. What this means is important to address and to understand. Authors will report on their difficulties in keeping traditional boundaries between client and provider, and their struggles to do so. Paradigms for this challenge will be different than in the traditional psychological practice.

2. The issue of culture is extremely important. Typically the psychologists doing the work are from a different background and culture than are the victims of the disaster. The attitude toward psychology and psychological interventions is in itself a cultural consideration that is important to understand to design the work.

3. The work is frequently one of building defenses and empowerment, which for some mental-health providers seems different than the work they ordinarily do. They need to think about this aspect of their work differently.
4. It is important to destigmatize mental-health services and make them as nonthreatening as possible—something the psychologist has to plan for.
5. Time considerations, always important in the work, become even more critical as individuals who are frequently there for only brief periods of time provide services at disaster sites.
6. Clinical work has to be threaded with educational work. In traditional psychological work, the providers of clinical and educational work are typically different people.
7. Ethical considerations may be different than those that are operative in the typical clinical situation. The hope is that in this book we can begin to address these points.
8. The work creates the possibility of secondary traumatization in the mental health worker and this needs to be addressed in any relief effort. Although there is no single chapter that deals with this factor, a number of writers address with it in their chapters.

We wish to acknowledge that there is not much in the book about the tsunami in Southeast Asia, which occurred on Dec. 26, 2004. Only one author even refers to it. That is because the book was conceived and created largely before the tsunami occurred. Psychology has had a presence in the relief efforts. One of the authors, Gerard Jacobs, has served as the American Psychological Association's (APA) liaison to the relief efforts and has worked with CDC and the Asian Preparedness Center.

Furthermore, the APA itself:

1. Made a significant financial contribution to the relief effort.
2. Was in contact with the ARC and DRN (disaster relief network) to advise them on contributions that psychologists can make.
3. Recommended to ARC that it collaborate with APA and its DRN to provide assistance to Southeast Asian people within the U.S. (Dittman, 2005a).

Furthermore, an American psychologist living in Thailand, Ben Weinstein, was on the ground in Southeast Asia helping in the tsunami effort (Dittman, 2005b). He marshaled a great deal of effort from other psychologists as well.

The stories of the mental health efforts in the tsunami have yet to emerge. These stories, as sad as they are likely to be, will add to the trauma literature and will, hopefully, help us further psychological understanding of both the impact of crisis and the impact of mental health interventions. But that is for another volume.

REFERENCES

Dittman M. (2005a). APA joins in tsunami relief efforts. *Monitor on Psychology, 36* (2), 36.
Dittman, M. (2005b). After the wave. *Monitor on Psychology, 36* (3), 36.

Part I

Theoretical Issues

CHAPTER 1

Overview of Psychological Interventions in the Acute Aftermath of Disaster

Preetika P. Mukherjee and Judith L. Alpert

INTRODUCTION

In recent years, disasters occurring throughout the world have devastated communities and individuals. One common link between natural and human-made disasters is their potential to affect many people simultaneously. In addition to people directly affected, many others are emotionally through indirect affects to the disaster. Media and indirect interpersonal exposure offer indirect exposure in the aftermath of a disaster (Pfefferbaum et al., 2000). An example of the latter is knowing someone who lost a relative.

Disasters often have traumatic impact on the community and on individuals. Some dimensions of disasters that are more likely to engender psychological morbidity include: disruption of the experience of safety (Fullerton, Ursano, Norwood, & Holloway, 2003), high perceived threat, low controllability, lack of predictability, high loss, and injury (American Psychiatric Association, 1994; North et al., 1999; Schuster et al., 2001), and exposure to the dead and mutilated (McCarroll, Fullerton, Ursano, & Hermsen, 1996). However, these dimensions are just one aspect of a large set of variables that collectively determine the mental health outcomes of the affected populations. Some additional factors that might predict negative mental health effects following disaster include: individual vulnerabilities (North et al., 1999, 2002; Norris, Byrne, Diaz, & Kaniasty, 2001; Yehuda, 2002), low resilience

(Bonnano, 2004), poor coping strategies (Bonanno & Field, 2001; Bonanno, Noll, Putnam, O'Neill, & Trickett, 2003; Pennebaker, 2000), and other traumatic life events, such as death of a family member or friend (Maes, Delmeire, Mylle, & Altamura, 2001; North et al., 1999).

Within mainstream psychology, disasters have traditionally been conceptualized as abnormal events that overwhelm normal coping responses. With this understanding, mental health professionals have assisted in the recovery of affected communities and individuals. However, the research interest in post-disaster interventions has increased only in the last decade. The majority of these intervention studies have focused on individual trauma and psychosocial distress. The role of community interventions in the recovery process has received relatively little attention. Individual interventions are an integral part of recovery after a disaster; however, such interventions generally do not address the multitude of changing needs that characterize the post-disaster environment. People would find it difficult to heal from the effects of individual trauma if the surrounding community remained devastated (Erickson, 1976). Because the healing of the community and the individual is a mutual process, we will focus on both community and individual interventions and, specifically, on those interventions that are delivered by mental health professionals in the immediate aftermath of a disaster.

COMMUNITY-BASED INTERVENTIONS

A disaster is more than an individual-level event (Bolin, 1985). It is also a community event with potential psychological and social consequences for those who incur direct losses and for those who do not. Although the empirical data on community intervention is limited, there is growing body of research on the overall impact of disasters and risk factors for communities (Norris et al., 2001). Research has indicated that the majority of the mental health problems experienced by disaster survivors are stress-induced symptoms precipitated by numerous problems they encounter in the aftermath (Lima, Pai, Santacruz, Lozano, & Luna, 1987; Norris et al., 2002). These problems include loss of residence and possessions, disruptions to communal support networks (Cronkite & Moos, 1984; Lima et al., 1987), interrupted employment, dissatisfaction with living conditions, and disappointment with care provided by relief organizations (Lima et al., 1987). It has also been indicated that the risk for impairment in the disaster-struck community is greatest when there is: (a) extreme and widespread damage to property, (b) high prevalence of trauma in the form of injuries, threat to life, and loss of life, (c) serious and ongoing financial problems for the community, and/or (d) human carelessness or, especially, human intent in causing the disaster (Norris et al., 2002).

Although psychologists have been a part of community rebuilding in various disaster situations in the past (e.g., Hanlon, 2003; Howes & Hayes, 1999; Parson, 2002; Rousseau, 1996), the literature on their role in community intervention is limited.

Role of Psychologists in Community-Based Intervention

In the immediate aftermath of a disaster, the focus is on basic resources for victims and their families, such as food, water, shelter, safety, and physical health (Gurwitch, Sitterle, Young, & Pfefferbaum, 2002). Past studies have shown that resource loss resulting from disaster appears to account for a significant amount of variance in psychological distress (Freedy, Saladin, Kilpatrick, Resnick, & Saunders, 1994; Gerrity & Steinglass, 1994). Additionally, resource loss leads to a sense of loss of control, which has been shown to be critical in the development of stress after a disaster (Freedy et al., 1994; Parson, 2002; Schuster et al., 2001).

Another damaging aspect of a disaster that aggravates the feeling of helplessness is disruption in social support networks (Kaniasty & Norris, 1993, 1995) and community cohesion. Decreases in social support following disaster account for victims' subsequent declines in mental health (e.g., Brewin, Andrews, & Valentine, 2000; Kaniasty & Norris, 1993).

Provisions of Resources

Based on the needs of the victims, the focus of initial psychological interventions following a disaster has to be on rescue and recovery, the establishment of safety, the provision of food and water, and protection from the environment (Norwood & Ursano, 1997). Kinston and Rosser (1974) noted that in times of disaster the most important aspect of psychological care is the social provision of physical care. Thus, physical care is the prime and essential function of relief organizations. Failure to provide for basic needs can be a potent source of traumatization above and beyond that created by the disaster itself (Ray, 2001).

Psychologists in past disasters have played a key role in the initial recovery operations. For example, in the Swissair Flight 111 tragedy in 1998, many psychologists were involved in helping victims' families and rescue workers (Howes & Hayes, 1999). The process of identifying bodies is one of the major stressors in disasters, regardless of profession or past experience

(Ursano & McCarroll, 1994). Despite the high level of stress, psychologists provided support to the families of victims and the rescue workers in dealing with the remains.

Similar to the Swissair tragedy, in the wake of September 11th many psychologists and other mental-health personnel became mobilized in a variety of ways. Psychologists worked with schools, hospitals, and other social service agencies. The American Psychological Association developed public-service ads that were then launched on radio and television.

In addition to participating in recovery operations, psychologists can also aid in identifying the sections of the community that require additional assistance in disaster aftermath. Disaster literature indicates that preexisting social stratification (by class, caste, gender, urbanicity, etc.) sometimes interferes with providing basic resources to disaster victims (Ray, 2001). In a comprehensive examination of four natural disasters (tornado, flooding, hurricane, and earthquake) that struck four culturally and ethnically diverse sites (Texas, Utah, Hawaii, and California), it was found that the poor and minorities had the greatest difficulties securing adequate assistance (Bolin & Bolton, 1986). For the marginalized section of the community, the level of disruption experienced after a disaster is intensified with personal resources, time, and energy available for recovery activities are limited in comparison because those available to the less marginalized groups (Ray, 2001). Thus, effective disaster intervention requires that needs and priorities of vulnerable groups be taken into account.

Mental health professionals have knowledge of vulnerable groups (e.g., minorities, elderly, and women) and skills in communication. Thus, they can facilitate dialogue across a wide range of professionals, such as community officials, members of disaster response agencies, and rescue personnel. This process might help planners and managers look beyond geographical vulnerability to understand certain social patterns in their communities that result in accentuated risk to some categories of people (Morrow, 1999). Implementing that programs are along more egalitarian and participatory lines may result in serving a far larger group of victims and producing a more integrated, cooperative post-disaster community. Unfortunately, at present, there is little, if any, research on the development of intervention programs that might address the problems of minority sections of the post-disaster community.

Building and Maintaining Social Support Networks

In addition to provisions of basic resources, another basic strategy to reduce psychological distress in disaster victims includes mobilization of support networks. Professionals are important sources of assistance when the level of need is high. However, they cannot supplant natural helping networks (Watson et al., 2003). Hence one important role of the mental health professional is to maintain and support these natural networks (Bland et al., 1997; Geil, 1990). After the September 11th attacks, psychologists helped victims in understanding the necessity for seeking and receiving sustenance from naturally occurring support networks, such as family members, friends, members of the community, the clergy, and others (Parson, 2002).

Research indicates that a low level of social support might lead to mental health problems (e.g., Brewin et al., 2000; Kaniasty & Norris, 1993) whereas maintaining or establishing support for the victims and their families might function to protect victims from acute distress and reduce long-term problems (McNally, Bryant, & Ehlers, 2003). A few approaches have been suggested in different studies that would be helpful in rebuilding social support networks in the community. These include: role of "grief leadership," a term developed by Ingraham (1988) to identify the role of leader in aiding the community to express grief; organizing memorial services; and encouraging participation of neighbors and friends in post-disaster chores (Ingraham, 1987; Raphael, 1986; Watson et al., 2003; Wright & Bartone, 1994).

Research has emphasized the critical role of community leaders in integrating the community and providing support following a disaster (Ingraham, 1987; Raphael, 1986; Wright & Bartone, 1994). It has been suggested that the key commanders' activities as a "grief leader" help affected individuals to focus on identification with the group (Wright & Bartone). In addition, it has been observed in post-impact disaster communities that repeated acknowledgement of the common experience of grief and loss involving the community as a whole established relationships and strengthened bonds among group members (Raphael, 1986). These linkages provide the foundation for developing instrumental and affective layers of support and maintaining the social fabric of the community. The formal roles, relationships, and organizational boundaries within the community shift to more informal linkages. For example, following the Gander plane crash in 1985, in which 8 air crew and 248 U.S. Army soldiers were killed, the key commanders of the army division played a critical role in integrating the families and soldiers. They encouraged people to mourn the loss and supported the families of those who died (Wright & Bartone, 1994). This support from military leaders is believed to have helped in moving the group from a state of initial shock into a mourning process involving the entire community.

Because community leaders have a unique position in establishing a social support network, it is important that they are trained to deal with disaster situations. Mental health professionals can consult and train civic leaders in the process of dealing with grief and loss for victims and families. As grief leadership entails modeling appropriate ways of expressing sorrow and anger (Ingraham, 1987), leaders can be encouraged to express their own grief. Additionally, mental health professionals can assist in organizing memorials to those who have died or to the heroes of a disaster. Recognition of those who have distinguished themselves through extraordinary service is an important component of the recovery process of a community.

Additionally, disaster support groups can be helpful for victims with limited support systems. Groups help to counter isolation, challenge errone-ous beliefs about uniqueness and pathology, provide emotional support, and allow survivors to share information (Grossman, 1973). Some studies have shown that mental health professionals have been involved in organizing and facilitating self-help support groups for survivors and that those survivors who attend these support groups identify the sessions as having been a vital part of their recovery (Zunin, personal communication, 1990). Researchers have also recommended methods for maximizing the success of disaster sup-port groups, such as understanding the needs of the community, establishing trust, acknowledging the loss, expressing empathy and sympathy, and clearly specifying the assistance being offered (Zunin & Zunin, 1991; Zunin).

In addition, when networks have been severely disrupted or destroyed, mental health workers may foster community activities, which bring indi-viduals together at the neighborhood or community level to address con-crete issues of concern. For example, group meetings can be organized in which survivors collectively plan how to rebuild their community, identify and discuss local problems, work together toward achievable goals, canvass the community to learn about others' needs, and emotionally share their in-dividual and collective losses. The process can assist survivors with disaster recovery not only by helping with concrete problems, but by reestablishing feelings of control, competence, self-confidence, and effectiveness. Perhaps most importantly, the process helps to reestablish social bonds and support networks that have been fractured by the disaster (Watson et al., 2003). Mental health professionals, with their expertise in working with groups, can assist the community in developing such social activities.

Another area related to social support, which has not been well investi-gated, is the formation of altruistic communities. Researchers studying public responses to disasters such as hurricanes, floods, or earthquakes describe an outpouring of immediate mutual helping in affected areas and communities. These emergent collective entities, loosely labeled as "altruistic" or "therapeu-tic" communities, are characterized by higher than usual levels of communal fellowship, cooperation, altruism, and solidarity (e.g., Barton, 1969; Fritz, 1961; Geil, 1990). There are many examples of altruistic behavior. For example, in the midst of the September 11 tragedy, some people sacrificed their lives to help others. One New Yorker, Nino Vendome, provided food and water to people fleeing in the streets on September 11th and he continued his services for 3 months. He turned his restaurant into a 24-hour free dining service and spent over $400,000 of his own money. Nino was an inspiration to other people who wanted to support the rescue workers of 9/11. In acknowledgment of his efforts, four trailers full of food were delivered for the workers. Top chefs in New York volunteered to cook and a man from Texas traveled to New York City and volunteered his culinary skills on a truck-sized barbecue (O'Connor, 2003).

It is possible that the formation of altruistic communities has positive effects for both the individuals providing support and those being supported. It has been found that people who actively work to help others in a time of trauma feel in control and hence benefit psychologically (Myers, 1991). Many observers have claimed that, in such states of emergency, the experience of the same fate increases identification among victims and previous, race, ethnic, and social class barriers temporarily disappear (Eranen & Liebkind, 1993). More understanding of the role of altruistic communities is needed to better plan disaster interventions.

Outreach and Information Dissemination

The traditional office-based approach of mental health professionals is inconsistent with the needs of individuals after a disaster, when there are large numbers of people who need help at one time. Mental health professionals must conduct outreach programs in disaster-struck communities (Myers, 1994) and thus flexibility, mobility, and creativity are essential. In some cases, survivors who need mental health intervention can be identified in the process of outreach. In such situations, outreach might be a precursor to individual treatment. However, outreach to individuals can be a beneficial intervention in and of itself. The educational aspect of outreach can promote and enhance healthy adaptation and coping. By providing survivors with anticipatory guidance about normal stress and grief reactions, stress management strategies, and information about resources, outreach may actually prevent a survivor from experiencing mental health problems (Erickson, 1976). For example, outreach provided by mental health professionals following the Swissair flight crash in 1998 (Howes & Hayes, 1999) and the Rhode Island nightclub fire in February 2003 (Hanlon, 2003) aided the victims in understanding their feelings and coping with grief.

Psychologists can provide victims and their families with information about coping resources. A factor closely related to knowledge of resources is the perceived availability of different coping resources. An individual may be aware of a particular option (such as visiting a mental health professional) but feel the option is not readily available. In addition, people may be more likely to make one visit to a physician because it is perceived as less expensive than numerous visits to a mental health counselor. Although the mental health services in the aftermath of a disaster might be available at low or no cost, perceptions about costs might create a barrier.

Research has indicated that many people turn to their primary care physicians for help after a disaster for both psychological and physical symptoms (Yates, Axsom, & Tiedman, 1999). However, physicians typically receive little training in recognizing or treating depression and anxiety and they may fail to correctly diagnose distress-related symptoms (Yates et al.). Physicians are also generally reluctant to discuss psychological issues with patients (Ormel & Tiemens, 1995). The post-disaster role of physicians has received little research attention. Lima, Pai, Santacruz, and Lozano (1991) have argued that physicians need to be trained on the diagnosis and treatment of anxiety and depression. Psychologists can play a vital role in consulting physicians on psychological disorders commonly encountered after disasters, such as somatization (Rundell & Ursano, 1995), anxiety, and depression. Psychologists can also educate physicians about the occurrence of high-risk behaviors and maladaptive reactions (e.g., family violence, substance abuse). Through educational outreach programs to primary care providers, psychologists can aid in early case identification and interventions and can potentially decrease morbidity and mortality.

Another important aspect of outreach involves the role of the media. The media must relay accurate information regarding coping resources to disaster victims. The mass media are commonly seen as indispensable communication tools in dealing with disaster. Many people, even victims who directly experienced the catastrophe, rely on the media to relate the nature of a disaster. Smith (1992) noted the comment of one airline passenger who survived a crash landing near Sioux City, Iowa, in which 112 died. The survivor remarked, "We knew something was wrong. We didn't know it was that bad until we saw it on the news" (p. 1).

The mass media can prepare the public to meet disasters, provide warning and information about how to cope, offer a forum for public reactions, and provide a record of events (Wilkins, 1985). People are much more likely to turn to the mass media for announcements and information after the disaster, particularly if damage is extensive (Mileti & O'Brien, 1992). Therefore, interveners have used the media effectively in disseminating information regarding available resources (Aguilera & Planchon, 1995; Gist & Stolz, 1982). Further, because mental health professionals are aware of the negative effects of the media (McGolerick & Echterling, 1995), they can be more cautious in its use as an information dissemination source.

Conclusion

Psychologists have become increasingly involved in the planning of community interventions in disaster contexts (e.g., Wessells & Monteiro, 2000). With their expertise in working with individuals, families, and systems, they understand the importance of conceptualizing mental health needs within the context of personal coping resources, family functioning, and broader community resources (Hobfoll, 1998). Although there has been limited research on the role of psychologists in community intervention, psychologists have aided in many ways after disasters. They have restored support networks, conducted outreach programs, provided public education, and trained community leaders and other resource personnel (teachers, nurses etc.), for example. The literature also lacks empirical studies on the efficacy of the components of community interventions. Knowledge of effectiveness of different components would aid psychologists in designing improved community intervention programs in the wake of disasters. Education and mutually helpful relationships among clinicians, researchers, and community leaders is essential for furthering our understanding of the nature of the psychological trauma.

INDIVIDUAL INTERVENTIONS

Although many people experience acute stress-related symptoms in the wake of traumatic events, only a minority develop acute stress disorder, PTSD, or both (McNally et al., 2003). However, given that a significant minority of people exposed to trauma develop lasting psychological problems, in the immediate aftermath of a disaster it is important to consider such issues as: (a) what kind of interventions should be offered, (b) when they should be offered, and (c) to whom they should be offered?

There are two different types of individual interventions provided by mental health professionals in the wake of disaster: (1) early interventions (e.g., psychological debriefing, cognitive behavior therapy, eye movement desensitization and reprocessing, and pharmacotherapy), and (2) long-term interventions (e.g., psychotherapy, supportive therapy). In this review we focus on the effectiveness of early interventions. It is beyond the scope of this chapter to discuss long-term interventions.

Early interventions that are delivered within the first few days of the traumatic event focus on: (a) reducing distress, (b) treating specific symptoms, (c) supporting the victims and families in normal healing, and (d) following-up on the progress of victims. Studies on early interventions following exposure to traumatic stress have increased in the past decade. The focus has been on finding ways to prevent psychopathology and deterioration in functioning (Watson et al., 2003). Unfortunately, the evidence for effective early interventions, particularly after disasters, remains very limited. A number of treatment approaches for PTSD have been proposed to be helpful, including: psychological debriefing, cognitive behavior therapy, eye movement desensitization and reprocessing, and pharmacotherapy (Foa, Keane, & Friedman, 2000; Yehuda, 2002). In the following sections we will review the rationale, technique, and effectiveness of these interventions in the disaster context, as they also have shown some promise in preventing psychopathology and reducing distress in early phases of a traumatic event.

Psychological Debriefing

Psychological debriefing (PD) is a brief crisis intervention, usually administered within days of a traumatic event (Raphael & Wilson, 2000). In general, this intervention encourages participants to describe and share both factual and emotional aspects of their disaster experience.

Rationale

Psychological debriefing has its roots in World War I (Litz, Gray, Bryant, & Adler, 2002). Following major battles, commanders met with their men to debrief them. The objective was to boost morale by having combatants share stories about what had happened during the engagement. This historical group debriefing method was also used by American troops during World War II and continues to be used by the Israeli army today (Shalev, Peri, Rogel-Fuchs, Ursano, & Marlowe, 1998).

Drawing parallels between the stress of combat and the stress of emergency medical service, Mitchell (1983) reasoned that a similar approach might diminish stress reactions among firefighters, police officers, emergency medical technicians, and other people exposed to what he referred to as "critical incidents" (i.e., traumatic events). Thus, he developed the most widely used method of psychological debriefing: Critical Incident Stress Debriefing (CISD). By helping trauma-exposed individuals talk about their feelings and reactions to the critical incident, the debriefing facilitator aims to reduce the incidence, duration, and severity of, or impairment from, traumatic stress (Everly & Mitchell, 1999; Mitchell, 1983). The widespread use of this modality in disaster settings derives from the belief that immediate processing gives an individual the ability to cognitively restructure the event so that it is remembered in a less traumatic way.

The CISD framework has been revised recently. It is now considered a part of a more comprehensive Critical Incident Stress Management (CISM) program (Everly & Mitchell, 1999). The CISM program, a comprehensive, integrative, multi-component crisis intervention system, is a series of interventions with high face validity. It is designed to address the needs of emergency service organizations and personnel. The CISM interventions are designed to psychologically prepare or debrief individuals after they have been subjected to a significant traumatic event, meet the support needs of individuals during critical incidents, provide CISD as well as delayed interventions, consult with organization and leaders, work with families of those directly affected by trauma, and facilitate referrals and follow-up interventions to address lingering stress disorders. For detailed discussion of the treatment technique review Mitchell (1983) and Mitchell and Everly (2001).

Research Evidence and Controversy

Although there are numerous anecdotal reports (Mitchell, 1983; Shalev et al., 1998) and research (Nurmi, 1999; Wee, Mills, & Koehler, 1999) suggesting that debriefing those involved in a traumatic experience reduces subsequent psychological morbidity, there continues to be controversy over its use (e.g., Goode, 2001; Herbert et al., 2001). The controversy has grown as increasing numbers of studies have failed to confirm the efficacy of CISD as a method for attenuating posttraumatic distress (Raphael & Wilson, 2000). Critics of debriefing have cited studies that have either failed to show beneficial effect or indicate that debriefing can impede natural recovery from trauma (Bisson, Jenkins, Alexander, & Bannister, 1997; Carlier, Voerman, Gersons, 2000; Conlon, Fahy, & Conroy, 1999; Rose, Brewin, Andrews, & Kirk, 1999).

Some investigators (e.g., McNally et al., 2003; Rose et al., 1999) have also questioned the studies supporting CISD on methodological grounds. The following methodological concerns have been stated: (a) lack of prospective controlled design, (b) random allocation to treatment conditions, (c) lack of pre-intervention data on subjects, and (d) reliance on questionnaire results as opposed to validated interview data.

On the other hand, advocates of debriefing argue that the studies indicating no or negative effects of debriefing are characterized by methodological problems that undermine their accuracy (Everly, Flannery, & Mitchell, 2000; Mitchell, 2002). Some of the problems include: (a) using individual rather than group debriefing; (b) using debriefing as a stand-alone intervention outside of prescribed multi-faceted Critical Incident Stress Management–like context (Everly & Mitchell, 1999); and (c) using inappropriate participants (e.g., auto accident victims, rape victims, industrial accident victims).

The debate on the effectiveness of CISD is ongoing. In the *Cochrane Review*, an independent report of one session debriefing, Wessely, Rose, and Bisson (2001) concluded that there is sufficient empirical evidence to recommend that one-session debriefing should not be provided routinely immediately after trauma. The reviewers also stated that careful randomized control trials of CISD and other forms of psychological debriefing for both individuals and groups are needed. More research is also needed to examine (a) the optimal time-frame and frequency of providing debriefing, (b) appropriate clients for debriefing, (c) causes of symptom exacerbation, when they occur, and (d) effectiveness of group debriefing. Research continues on the effectiveness of debriefing. The International Society for Traumatic Stress Studies, in its practice guidelines (Bisson, McFarlane, & Rose, 2000), state that, if employed, debriefing should be conducted by experienced, well-trained practitioners, should not be mandatory, should utilize some clinical assessment of potential participants, and should be accompanied by clear and objective evaluation procedures.

Individual Psychotherapy

Numerous psychotherapeutic approaches for the treatment of acute trauma have been described, such as psychodynamic (Chertoff, 1998), supportive psychotherapy (Osterman & Chemtob, 1999), and cognitive behavior therapy. Although the long-term effectiveness of psychodynamic and supportive therapy in the treatment of PTSD has been reported (Brom, Kleber, & Defares, 1989), only cognitive behavioral therapy (CBT) has been subjected to rigorous study as an early intervention after a disaster. It is also the technique that lends itself most readily to rigorous research. Thus, the focus in this chapter is the techniques and effectiveness of CBT.

Cognitive Behavior Therapy

Cognitive-behavioral therapy (CBT) is an action-oriented form of psychosocial therapy. It combines two effective forms of psychotherapy: (1) cognitive therapy and (2) behavioral therapy. Underlying CTB is the belief that maladaptive, or faulty, thinking patterns cause maladaptive behavior and "negative" emotions. The treatment focuses on changing an individual's thoughts (cognitive patterns) in order to change his/her behavior and emotional state.

A number of different techniques may be employed in cognitive behavioral therapy to help patients with PTSD. They include education about the nature and universality of symptoms, exposure procedures, cognitive processing procedures, and anxiety management programs (Foa & Meadows, 1997).

Exposure procedures. The procedures promote symptom reduction by allowing patients to realize that, contrary to their mistaken ideas: (a) being in objectively safe situations that remind one of the trauma is not dangerous; (b) remembering the trauma is not equivalent to experiencing it again; (c) anxiety decreases even without avoidance or escape; and (d) experiencing anxiety/PTSD symptoms does not lead to loss of control (Foa & Jaycox, 1996).

These procedures, which involve patients confronting their fears, vary on the dimensions of exposure medium (imaginal vs. in vivo), exposure length (short vs. long), and arousal level during exposure (low vs. high). Systematic desensitization (SD), for example, is at the extreme of imaginal, brief, and minimally arousing exposure, and in vivo is at the other extreme on each dimension. (For more details, see Foa, Steketee, & Rothbaum, 1989.)

Cognitive processing therapy. This treatment, developed by Resick and Schnicke (1992, 1993), incorporates components of cognitive therapy and exposure. The cognitive component includes training clients in challenging problematic cognitions, particularly self-blame, and attempts to mentally undo the event. The exposure component consists of writing a detailed account of the trauma and reading it.

Anxiety management programs. Underlying anxiety management treatments (AMT) (e.g. Suinn, 1974) is the belief that pathological anxiety stems from skill deficits and that AMT provides patients with a repertoire of strategies to handle anxiety. Strategies include relaxation training, positive self-statements, breath retraining, biofeedback, social skills training, and distraction techniques. Unlike exposure therapy (Foa & Kozak, 1986) and cognitive therapy (Beck, Emery, & Greenberg, 1985), which are designed to correct the mechanisms underlying pathological anxiety, AMT aims to provide ways to manage anxiety when it occurs. Foa (1995) noted that one of the most commonly used anxiety management treatments for PTSD is stress inoculation training (SIT) (Meichenbaum, 1975).

Research Evidence

In general, psychological treatments for early PTSD symptoms have been adapted from CBT programs (e.g., Foa & Meadows, 1997; Foa & Rothbaum, 1998). As in the case of psychological debriefing, early attempts to apply CBT techniques in the first few weeks following trauma failed to demonstrate efficacy (Frank et al., 1988; Veronen & Kilpatrick, 1983). Although the patients receiving CBT showed substantial improvement in psychological symptoms, the studies did not establish that these changes were greater than those occurring with natural recovery. However, more recent studies, including several random control trials, suggest that CBT may be effective in treating PTSD symptoms and accelerating recovery in people recently exposed to trauma (Bryant, Sackville, Dang, Moulds, & Guthrie, 1999; Foa, Hearst-Ikeda, & Perry, 1995). Some of the studies have shown that early CBT treatments reduce the risk of long-term PTSD (see reviews by Ehlers & Clark, 2003; Litz, Gray, Bryant, & Adler, 2002). Case reports likewise indicate the efficacy of CBT in treating PTSD (Difede et al., 2002; Gidron et al., 2001). These acute studies are consistent with studies of chronic PTSD, in which both cognitive therapy and imaginal exposure have been found to be effective (Tarrier et al., 1999).

Although the brief cognitive behavioral interventions described above represent encouraging attempts to prevent the development of chronic posttraumatic pathology in recent victims, some studies have not shown any difference in the improvement between CBT and assessment only groups (Brom, Kleber, & Hofman, 1993; Foa, Zoellner, & Feeny, 2002). This pattern of results (no difference between CBT and assessment only) supports the conclusion that detailed assessments with an empathic clinician immediately after a traumatic event have a positive impact on recovery. Future research is needed to investigate the role of the clinician in the immediate aftermath of a disaster and also to elucidate which specific components of CBT are necessary to achieve positive change following recent traumatic exposure.

Possible Contraindications for Exposure Therapy

It has been suggested that one of the elements of cognitive behavioral interventions (i.e., prolonged exposure) might not be appropriate for everyone (Bryant & Harvey, 2000). The investigators stated that exposure technique might be contraindicated when the acutely traumatized client exhibits extreme anxiety, suicide risk, marked ongoing stressors, or acute bereavement. In such cases where exposure methods may be contraindicated, other techniques, including anxiety management, supportive therapy, or pharmacological intervention, may be used (Bryant & Harvey). More research is needed to explore the issue of contraindication.

Eye Movement Desensitization and Reprocessing

Eye movement desensitization and reprocessing (EMDR) is used to decrease distressing thoughts or memories. In this desensitization procedure, clients are asked to think of a troublesome thought while tracking finger movements across their visual field. This process is believed to foster cognitive and emotional changes in the participant resulting in thoughts becoming less distressing.

Rationale

EMDR was developed by Dr. Francine Shapiro in 1987 and has been used for more than a decade (Shapiro, 1995). Although EMDR evolved from cognitive behavioral therapy, it is not theory-driven. It originated from Dr. Shapiro's observation that her own troublesome thoughts were reduced when her eye movements went back and forth while walking. She then developed a model based on this technique to account for the resolution of traumatic memories. She called it "accelerated information-processing" (Foa et al., 2000).

Shapiro postulated that trauma blocks the information system and leads to the development of pathologies, including distortions in perception, feeling and response. By accessing traumatic material and activating information processing with EMDR, people are able to adapt traumatic memories into a normalized form. The stimulation of eye movements (taps or tones) activates a "self-healing mechanism" (Foa et al., 2000) that enables people to process traumatic memories quickly. According to Wilson, Becker, and Tinker (1995), positive results are reported after one to four 90-minute sessions.

According to Shapiro (2002), as an integrative approach EMDR aims to (a) facilitate resolution of memories (e.g., elicitation of insight, cognitive reorganization, adaptive affects, and physiological responses), (b) desensitize stimuli that trigger present distress as a result of second-order conditioning, and (c) incorporate adaptive attitudes, skills, and behaviors for enhanced functioning within larger social systems. These comprehensive treatment goals are attained through EMDR's standardized procedures and protocols (Shapiro, 1995, 1999, 2001), which incorporate aspects of a wide range of theoretical orientations (Shapiro, 2002). These include psychodynamic (Neborsky & Solomon, 2001; Wachtel, in press cognitive behavioral (Smyth & Poole, in press; Wolpe, 1990; Young, Zangwill, & Behery, in press), physiological

(Siegel, in press; van der Kolk, in press), experiential (Bohart & Greenberg, in press), and interactional therapies (Kaslow, Nurse, & Thompson, in press). For a detailed discussion of the treatment technique review, see Foa and colleagues (2000).

Research Evidence and Controversy

Shapiro conducted the first randomized experiment on EMDR in 1989. She found substantial treatment effects (e.g., reduced self-reported distress) with EMDR (then called "EMD") after only one session. The positive effects reported in the Shapiro study attracted little attention until they were supplemented by Joseph Wolpe's editorial footnote regarding his own success with the method (Shapiro, 1989) and his publication of a case using the procedures (Wolpe & Abrams, 1991). These events precipitated the publication of over 100 case studies (e.g., Marquis, 1991; Page & Crino, 1993; Puk, 1991). These studies typically found a significant reduction of symptoms. However, some early critics (Acierno, Hersen, Van Hasselt, Tremont, & Mueser, 1994) stated that the results were usually based on subjective measures and no standardized or objective dependent measures were obtained. Further, in these published case reports, EMDR was combined with other interventions, such as relaxation training, real life exposure, and cognitive restructuring (Acierno et al.). As a result one cannot determine whether the apparent improvement reported in such cases is attributable to EMDR, the ancillary treatment, or the combination of treatments. Critics also reported that lack of experimental control drastically limits the drawing of any conclusions regarding treatment efficacy in these case studies. The improvement in these cases might be due to variables other than EMDR (Gastright, 1995), such as placebo effects and spontaneous remission.

Foa and colleagues (2000) reviewed the literature on EMDR and found that more recent research (Edmond, Rubin, & Wambach, 1999; Ironson, Freund, Strauss, & Williams, 2002; Lee, Gavriel, Drummond, Richards, & Greenwald, 2002; Wilson et al., 1995; Wilson, Silver, Covi, & Foster, 1996) has overcome many of the limitations of earlier studies and provides stronger support for the efficacy of EMDR. These studies assessed the clients clinically prior to treatment; utilized random assignment either to EMDR, comparison treatment, or control; used standardized measures and scored with independent assessors. Each study found EMDR to be significantly more effective than the comparison treatment or control. Recently, two meta-analyses supported the efficacy of EMDR in treating single-trauma PTSD (Van Etten & Taylor, 1998; Davidson & Parker, 2001). Additionally, research using brain scans has found that neurobiological problems in brain asymmetry among traumatized individuals appeared to be corrected after EMDR treatment (van der Kolk, Burbridge, & Suzuki, 1997). More controlled studies have been done supporting the effectiveness of EMDR with PTSD than has been the case for any other psychotherapy for PTSD (Spector & Read, 1999).

The Division of Clinical Psychology of the American Psychological Association identifies EMDR as one of three empirically validated treatment approaches (along with exposure therapy and stress-inoculation therapy) that are probably efficacious in treating PTSD (Chambless et al., 1998). EMDR was also designated as an effective treatment for PTSD in the treatment guidelines of the International Society for Traumatic Stress Studies (Chemtob, Tolin, van der Kolk, & Pitman, 2000).

Despite the foregoing support for the effectiveness of EMDR in treating PTSD, its clinical procedures continue to be debated. Some of the ongoing controversies include that: (a) EMDR is not different from exposure therapy; (b) the integral component of EMDR, eye movement, is not necessary; and (c) there are problems with inadequately trained therapists.

It is important to mention here that none of the studies on the effectiveness of EMDR mentioned above were conducted within the first 4 weeks of traumatic exposure. Thus, research is needed to determine the effectiveness of EMDR in the immediate aftermath of a traumatic event.

Conclusion

The quality of research on EMDR has improved over the years. Many of the recently published studies have tried to address the weaknesses identified by critics of EMDR (Cahill, Carrigan, & Freuh, 1999). Future studies should examine the role of individual differences in participants when studying treatments and should look for factors affecting individual outcomes (Sikes & Sikes, 2003). Studies should also investigate practitioner characteristics that are associated with outcomes to ascertain the conditions under which EMDR might be more or less effective than exposure therapies (Ironson et al., 2002).

Pharmacotherapy

If symptoms are severe enough to prevent effective trauma-focused therapy, pharmacotherapy is often utilized. Pharmacotherapy has been shown to alleviate the three clusters of PTSD symptoms: reexperiencing, avoidance and hypervigilance (Friedman, 1998b). Some of the useful pharmacological treatments for PTSD are described below:

Serotonergic Agents

Studies have consistently shown that serotonergic dysregulation can create avoidance, hypervigilance, and other associated symptoms (Brady, Sonne, & Roberts, 1995). Selective serotonin reuptake inhibitors (SSRIs) have the broadest range of efficacy in reducing all three clusters of PTSD symptoms (Brady et al., 1995). In addition, these agents are used to treat many disorders that often coexist with PTSD. For example, patients taking sertraline (Zoloft) have reduced alcohol consumption, and those taking fluvoxamine (Luvox) have had a reduction in obsessive thoughts and the elimination of insomnia (Brady et al.; Marmar et al., 1996).

Recent studies with sertraline (Davidson, Rothbaum, van der Kolk, Sikes, & Farfel, 2001; Davidson, Pearlstein, et al., 2001; Londborg et al, 2001; Rapaport, Endicott, & Clary, 2002) and paroxetine (Marshall, Beebe, Oldham, & Zaninelli, 2001; Tucker et al., 2001) indicate not only that these medications may reduce PTSD symptoms and produce global improvement in functioning, but also that they are effective against comorbid disorders and associated symptoms and have few side effects.

Tricyclic Antidepressants

The effectiveness of tricyclic antidepressants in relieving symptoms of PTSD has been mixed. In several studies, their use resulted in modest lessening of the symptoms of reexperiencing and minimal or no effect on avoidance or arousal symptoms. Patients treated with tricyclic antidepressants have not shown greater improvement than those treated with SSRIs (Davidson et al., 1990).

Monoamine Oxidase Inhibitors

Monoamine oxidase (MAO) inhibitors have been used primarily as an effective antidepressant for refractory depression, but their use has been curtailed because of the dangerous side effect of hypertensive crisis in patients whose diets contain tyramine. Patients with PTSD who have received phenelzine (Nardil) have shown moderate to good improvement in reexperiencing and avoidance symptoms, but the drug has had little effect on the symptoms of hyperarousal. Insomnia ceases to be a problem in these patients, and they also have a modest reduction in the frequency of nightmares (DeMartino, Mollica, & Wilk, 1995). However, there are substantial risks with the use of these agents because patients with PTSD frequently ingest alcohol and other contraindicated or illegal substances, which may cause serious and possibly life-threatening reactions.

Antiadrenergic Agents

Because autonomic hyperactivity may be a problem in patients with PTSD, antiadrenergic agents may be effective pharmacotherapy. Three agents in particular, clonidine (Catapres), propanolol (Inderal), and guanfacine (Tenex), have successfully reduced nightmares, hypervigilance, startle reactions, and outbursts of rage (Blank, 1994).

Benzodiazepines

Historically, benzodiazepines were the primary agent in PTSD treatment. Alprazolam (Xanax) and clonazepam (Klonopin) have been used extensively, but the efficacy of benzodiazepines against the major PTSD symptoms has not been proven in controlled studies (Friedman, 1998). These agents are effective against anxiety, insomnia, and irritability, but they should be used with great caution because of the high frequency of comorbid substance dependence in patients with PTSD.

Early Pharmacological intervention studies

Although pharmacological research in the area of PTSD is growing, only a few studies have examined the effects of medications in the early phases after trauma.

Tricyclic antidepressant. Robert, Blakeney, Villarreal, Rosenberg, and Meyer (1999) used a randomized, double-blind design to test whether children with burn and acute stress disorder symptoms might benefit from imipramine treatment (tricyclic antidepressant) administered for 7 days or more after they were injured. Imipramine was significantly more effective than chloral hydrate (a sleep-inducing depressant): 83% of children who received low-dose imipramine treatment showed a reduction in acute stress disorder symptoms, in contrast to 38% of the chloral hydrate group.

Antiadrenergic agent. One study tested whether PTSD could be prevented among adult survivors of acute trauma who were given a 10-day, double-blind course of the β-adrenergic antagonist propranolol (40 mg 4 times/day) versus a 10-day course of placebo (Pitman et al., 2002). Forty-one emergency room patients who had just experienced a traumatic event were recruited for this randomized double-blind study. The treatment group and the control group did not differ in terms of PTSD symptoms at either a 1-month or 3-month assessment. Despite the fact that the groups did not differ in concentration of PTSD cases, 0% of the propranolol patients versus 43%

of the placebo patients were classified as physiologic responders 3 months after the event. This study suggests that more studies with a long-term follow-up are warranted.

Benzodiazepines. Gelpin, Bonne, Peri, Brandes, and Shalev (1996) conducted a small pilot study in which the benzodiazepines, lonazepam and alprazolam, were prescribed approximately 7 days after the patients visited an emergency room for treatment related to potentially traumatic life events. At 6-month assessment, nine participants in the benzodiazepines group (69%), versus two in the control group (15%), met the diagnostic criteria for PTSD. This suggests that benzodiazepines treatment may have worsened the outcomes. This result is consistent with other negative results involving benzodiazepines treatment for chronic PTSD (Friedman, Davidson, Mellman, & Southwick, 2000). There is still no evidence indicating whether benzodiazepines are an effective pharmacological intervention for those with either acute or chronic post-traumatic reactions.

Anti-psychotics. Stanovic, James, and Vandevere (2001) reported that burn victims treated with a low dose of resperidone (anti-psychotic) experienced diminished nightmares and flashbacks and decreased hyperarousal and sleep disturbances 1–2 days after starting treatment. There have been no studies on the efficacy of anti-psychotics in treating early traumatic stress symptoms. More studies are warranted more studies to better understand the efficacy of resperidone.

Conclusion

Although pharmacotherapy can have positive effects on acute traumatic symptoms, more research is needed to understand the effectiveness of the drugs on global improvement and functional improvement. SSRIs are the only drugs that have shown some promise in global improvement and have fewer side effects. It is possible that there might not be one drug that will help in alleviating all traumatic symptoms. For example, it has been suggested that MAO inhibitors/tricyclic antidepressant are best for reexperiencing symptoms, SSRIs for avoidant/numbing symptoms, and clodine/propranolol for hyperarousal symptoms (Friedman & Southwick, 1995). Thus, antidepressant research needs to be conducted to increase the understanding of the efficacy of an array of drugs with complementary actions rather than only studying the efficacy of one drug. In addition to effectiveness studies on drugs, another issue that needs to be addressed is the effectiveness of the combination of pharmacotherapy and psychological intervention in the aftermath of a disaster.

Research (Lin, Poland, Anderson, & Lesser, 1996) indicates that ethnocultural aspects might have an affect on victims' response to drugs. Lin and colleagues found that Caucasian versus Asian patients exhibit different pharmacokinetic responses to the same dose of the same drug. This finding suggests that social/familial factors must be researched in relation to the effectiveness of pharmacotherapy in treatment of acute responses to traumatic events.

CONCLUDING COMMENTS

Disasters are complex events that affect a large number of people simultaneously. The effects of disasters are diverse and require mental health responses that address myriad outcomes, including psychological disorders, generalized distress, physical illness, and various interpersonal problems. Thus, after a disaster, multiple levels of intervention (community, individual, family) with varying degrees of intensity (maintaining support network, psychoeducation, short-term and long-term treatment) are required. Disaster intervention needs to take a more balanced perspective than presently afforded by mainstream psychology (Kenardy & Carr, 2000; Wesseley, Rose, & Bisson, 1998). Although crisis intervention, supportive counseling, and education have their place in disaster response, these practices are in many cases linked to other kinds of intervention, such as tangible assistance, advice, and information (Salzer & Bickman, 1999). Mental health professionals need to respond to community and individual requirements. In addition, interventionists must tread lightly so as not to disrupt natural social networks of healing and support (Gist & Devilly, 2002; Herbert et al., 2001). For example, in many war-torn regions, such as Iraq, the main goal for victims is first to establish safety and restore their community and culture (e.g., Giller, 1998). Offering individual interventions, whether psychological debriefing or CBT, is likely to puzzle the victims, who often regard psychotherapy as foreign to their experience. The development of palatable interventions, cognizant of a wide array of needs and demands associated with recovery, can be critical in ensuring that persons experiencing difficulties are identified and linked to appropriate services and resources.

Although there are numerous studies on early interventions after disasters, there are limited studies that focus on terrorist attacks. Pre-September 11th literature on post-traumatic interventions examined the effects of psychological services on veterans, police, burn victims, and victims of rape, assault, shootings, and auto accidents. Unlike traumatic events associated with terrorism, natural disasters tend to have a clear beginning and end, and are characterized by a rapid return to a more familiar sense of predictability and control of the environment and a diminishment of feelings of vulnerability and insecurity. Fear, unpredictability, and pervasive experience of loss of safety are much more extensive after a terrorist attack compared with other disasters. Thus, the type of interventions required immediately after a terrorist attack might differ from that in other disasters. Implementing controlled treatment and preventative trials at the time of any disaster is difficult. During a terrorist attack it becomes almost impossible. For example, in the aftermath of the events of September 11, 2001, any prospective research became secondary to the crucial clinical efforts of mental health professionals (Katz, Pellegrino, Pandya, Ng, & DeLisi, 2002).

It is important to recognize disaster intervention as an interdisciplinary process. Disasters have substantial social and psychological impacts on preexisting social and economic vulnerabilities, which intensifies loss and disruption. Effective disaster intervention, therefore, needs to ensure that the diverse interests and priorities of communal life are integrated into planning and response, especially those of vulnerable persons and groups. Thus, disaster mental health is in need of a comprehensive model to help develop focused interventions and follow-ups. The literature contains a wealth of information with many varied approaches. A comprehensive, coherent body of knowledge the underlies and defines a general model with tested planning, approaches, and interventions can help improve on the useful and helpful information we already have.

REFERENCES

Acierno, R., Hersen, M., Van Hasselt, V.B., Tremont, G., & Mueser, K.T. (1994). Review of the validation and dissemination of eye movement desensitization and reprocessing: A scientific and ethical dilemma. *Clinical Psychology Review, 14,* 287–299.

Aguilera, D. M., & Planchon, L. A. (1995). The American Psychological Association—California Psychological Association Disaster Response Project: Lessons from the past, guidelines for the future. *Professional Psychology Research and Practice, 26,* 550–557.

American Psychiatric Association. (1994). *Diagnostic and statistical manual of mental disorders* (4th ed.). Washington, DC: American Psychiatric Press.

Barton, A.H. (1969). *Communities in disaster. A sociological analysis of collective stress situations.* New York: Doubleday and Company Inc.

Beck, A.T., Emery, G., & Greenberg, R.L. (1985). *Anxiety disorders and phobias: A cognitive perspective.* New York: Basic Books.

Bisson, J.I., Jenkins, P.L., Alexander, J., & Bannister, C. (1997). Randomised controlled trial of psychological debriefing for victims of acute burn trauma. *British Journal of Psychiatry, 171,* 78–81.

Bisson, J., McFarlane, A., & Rose, S. (2000). Psychological debriefing. In E. Foa, T. Keane, & M. Friedman (Eds.), *Effective treatments for PTSD: Practice guidelines from the International Society for Traumatic Stress Studies* (pp. 39–59). New York: Guilford Press.

Bland, S., O'Leary, E., Farinaro, E., Jossa, F., Krogh, V., Violanti, J., et al. (1997). Social network disturbances and psychological distress following earthquake evacuation. *Journal of Nervous and Mental Disease, 185,* 188–194.

Blank, A.S. Jr. (1994). Clinical detection, diagnosis, and differential diagnosis of posttraumatic stress disorder. *Psychiatric Clinic of North America, 17,* 351–383.

Bohart, A., & Greenberg, L. (in press). EMDR and experiential psychotherapy. In F. Shapiro (Ed.), *EMDR and the paradigm prism.* Washington, DC: American Psychological Association Press.

Bolin, R. (1985). Disaster characteristics and psychosocial impacts. In B. J. Sowder (Ed.), *Disasters and Mental Health: Selected Contemporary Perspectives* (pp. 3–28). Rockville, MD: National Institute of Mental Health.

Bolin, R., & Bolton, P. (1986). *Race, religion, and ethnicity in disaster.* Boulder: University of Colorado.

Bonnano, G.A. (2004). Loss, trauma, and human resilience: Have we underestimated the human capacity to thrive after extremely aversive events? *American Psychologist, 59,* 20–28.

Bonanno, G. A., & Field, N. P. (2001). Examining the delayed grief hypothesis across five years of bereavement. *American Behavioral Scientist, 44,* 798–806.

Bonanno, G. A., Noll, J. G., Putnam, F. W., O'Neill, M., & Trickett, P. (2003). Predicting the willingness to disclose childhood sexual abuse from measures of repressive coping and dissociative experiences. *Child Maltreatment, 8,* 1–17.

Brady, K.T., Sonne, S.C., & Roberts, J.M. (1995). Sertraline treatment of comorbid posttraumatic stress disorder and alcohol dependence. *Journal of Clinical Psychiatry, 56,* 502–505.

Brewin, C.R., Andrews, B., & Valentine, J.D. (2000). Meta-analysis of risk factors for posttraumatic stress disorder in trauma-exposed adults. *Journal of Consulting and Clinical Psychology, 68,* 748–766.

Brom, D., Kleber, R. J. & Defares, P. B. (1989). Brief psychotherapy for post-traumatic stress disorders. *Journal of Consulting and Clinical Psychology, 57,* 607–612.

Brom, D., Kleber, R., & Hofman, M. (1993). Victims of traffic accidents: Incidence and prevention of posttraumatic stress disorder. *Journal of Clinical Psychology, 49*(2), 131–140.

Bryant, R.A., & Harvey, A.G. (2000). *Acute stress disorder: A handbook of theory, assessment, and treatment.* Washington, DC: American Psychological Association.

Bryant, R.A., Sackville, T., Dang, S.T., Moulds, M., & Guthrie, R. (1999). Treating acute stress disorder: An evaluation of cognitive behavior therapy and supportive counseling techniques. *American Journal of Psychiatry, 156,* 1780–1786.

Cahill, S., Carrigan, M.H., & Freuh, B.C. (1999). Does EMDR work? And if so, why?: A critical review of controlled outcome and dismantling research. *Journal of Anxiety Disorders, 13,* 5–33.

Carlier, I.V.E., Voerman, A.E., & Gersons, B.P.R. (2000). The influence of occupational debriefing on post-traumatic stress symptomatology in traumatized police officers. *British Journal of Medical Psychology, 73,* 87–98.

Chambless, D.L., Baker, M.J., Baucom, D.H., Beutler, L.E., Calhoun, K.S., Crits-Christoph, P., et al. (1998). Update on empirically validated therapies. *Clinical Psychologist, 51,* 3–16.

Chemtob, C.M., Tolin, D.F., van der Kolk B.A., & Pitman, R.K. (2000). Eye movement desensitization and reprocessing. In E. B. Foa, T. M. Keane, & M. J. Friedman (Eds.), *Effective treatments for PTSD: Practice guidelines from the International Society for Traumatic Stress Studies* (pp. 139–155, 333–335). New York: Guilford Press.

Chertoff, J. (1998). Psychodynamic assessment and treatment of traumatized patients. *Journal of Psychotherapy Practice and Research, 7,* 35–46.

Conlon, L., Fahy, T.J., & Conroy, R. (1999). PTSD in ambulant RTA victims: A randomized controlled trial of debriefing. *Journal of Psychosomatic Research, 46,* 37–44.

Cronkite, R. & Moos, R. (1984). The role of predisposing and moderating factors in the stress illness relationship. *Journal of Health and Social Behavior, 25,* 372–393.

Davidson, J., Kudler, H., Smith, R., Mahorney, S.L., Lipper, S., Hammett, E., et al. (1990). Treatment of posttraumatic stress disorder with amitriptyline and placebo. *Archives of General Psychiatry, 47,* 259–266.

Davidson J. R., Pearlstein, T., Londborg, P., Brady, K.T., Rothbaum, B.O., Bell, J., et al. (2001). Efficacy of Sertraline in preventing relapse of posttraumatic stress disorder. *American Journal of Psychiatry, 158,* 1974–1980.

Davidson, J.R., Rothbaum, B.O., van der Kolk, B.A., Sikes, C.R., & Farfel, G.M. (2001). Multicenter, double-blind comparison of sertraline and placebo in the treatment of posttraumatic stress disorder. *Archives of General Psychiatry, 58,* 485–492.

Davidson, P. R., & Parker, K. C. H. (2001). Eye movement desensitization and reprocessing (EMDR): A meta-analysis. *Journal of Consulting and Clinical Psychology, 69,* 305–316.

DeMartino, R., Mollica, R.F., & Wilk, V. (1995). Monoamine oxidase inhibitors in posttraumatic stress disorder. *Journal of Nervous and Mental Disease, 183,* 510–515.

Difede, J., Ptacek, J.T., Roberts, J.G., Barocas, D., Rives, W., Apfeldorf, W.J., et al. (2002). Acute stress disorder after burn injury: A predictor of posttraumatic stress disorder. *Psychosomatic Medicine, 64,* 826–834.

Edmond, T., Rubin, A., & Wambach, K.G. (1999). The effectiveness of EMDR with adult female survivors of childhood sexual abuse. *Social Work Research, 23,* 103–116.

Ehlers, A., & Clark, D.M. (2003). Early psychological interventions for adult survivors of trauma: A review. *Biological Psychiatry, 53,* 817–826.

Eranen, L., & Liebkind, K. (1993). Coping with disaster: The helping behavior of communities and individuals. In J.P. Wilson & B. Raphael (Eds.), *International Handbook of Traumatic Stress Syndromes* (pp. 957–964). New York: Plenum.

Erickson, K. (1976). *Everything in its path.* New York: Simon & Schuster.

Everly, G.S., Flannery, R., & Mitchell, J.T. (2000). Critical Incident Stress Management (CISM): A review of the literature. *Aggression and Violent Behavior: A Review Journal, 5,* 23–40.

Everly, G.S., Jr., & Mitchell, J.T. (1999). *Critical Incident Stress Management (CISM): A new era and standard of care in crisis intervention* (2nd ed.). Ellicott City, MD: Chevron.

Foa, E.B. (1995). *PDS (Posttraumatic Stress Diagnostic Scale) manual.* Minneapolis: National Computer System.

Foa, E.B., Hearst-Ikeda, D., & Perry, K.J. (1995). Evaluation of a brief cognitive-behavioral program for the prevention of chronic PTSD in recent assault victims. *Journal of Consulting and Clinical Psychology, 63,* 948–955.

Foa, E.B., & Jaycox, L.H. (1996). Cognitive-behavioral treatment of post-traumatic stress disorder. In D. Spiegel (Ed.), *The practice of psychotherapy.* Washington, DC: American Psychiatric Press.

Foa, E.B., Keane, T.M., & Friedman, M.J. (2000). *Effective treatments for PTSD: Practice guidelines from the International Society for Traumatic Stress Studies.* Guilford Press, Guilford Press.

Foa, E.B., & Kozak, M.J. (1986). Emotional processing of fear: exposure to corrective information. *Psychological Bulletin, 99,* 20–35.

Foa, E.B., & Meadows, E.A. (1997). Psychosocial treatments for posttraumatic stress disorder: A critical review. *Annual Review of Psychology, 48,* 449–80.

Foa, E.B., & Rothbaum, B.O. (1998). *Treating the trauma of rape: Cognitive-behavioral therapy for PTSD.* New York: Guiford Press.

Foa, E.B., Steketee, G., & Rothbaum, B.O. (1989). Behavioral/cognitive conceptualizations of post-traumatic stress disorder. *Behavior Therapy, 20,* 155–176.

Foa, E.B., Zoellner, L.A., & Feeny, N.C. (2002). *An evaluation of three brief programs for facilitating recovery.* Manuscript submitted for publication.

Frank, E., Anderson, B., Stewart, B.D., Dancu, C., Hughes, C., & West, D. (1988). Efficacy of behavior therapy and systematic desensitization in the treatment of rape trauma. *Behavior Therapy, 19,* 479–489.

Freedy, J., Saladin, M., Kilpatrick, D., Resnick, H., & Saunders, B. (1994). Understanding acute psychological distress following natural disaster. *Journal of Traumatic Stress, 5,* 441–454.

Friedman, M.J. (1998). Pharmacotherapy for posttraumatic stress disorder: A status report. *Psychiatry and Clinical Neurosciences, 52,*115–121.

Friedman, M.J., Davidson, J.R.T., Mellman, T.A., & Southwick, S.M. (2000). Pharmacotherapy. In E.B. Foa, T.M. Keane, & M.J. Friedman (Eds.), *Effective treatments for PTSD: Practice guidelines from the International Society for Traumatic Stress Studies* (pp. 84–105). New York: Guilford Press.

Friedman, M.J., & Southwick, S.M. (1995). Towards pharmacotherapy for post traumatic stress disorder. In M.J. Friedman, D.S. Charney, & A.Y. Deutch (Eds.), *Neurobiological and clinical consequences of stress: From normal adaptation to posttraumatic stress disorder* (pp. 465–481). Philadelphia: Lippincott-Raven.

Fritz, C. (1961). Disasters. In R. Merton & R. Nisbet (Eds.), *Social problems* (pp. 651–694). New York: Harcourt Brace.

Fullerton, C. S., Ursano, R. J., Norwood, A. E., & Holloway, H. C. (2003) Trauma, terrorism, and disaster. In R. J. Ursano, C. S. Fullerton, & A. E. Norwood (Eds.), *Terrorism and disaster: Individual and community mental health interventions* (pp. 1–20). Cambridge, MA: Cambridge University Press.

Gastright, J. (1995). EMDR works! Is that enough? *Cincinnatti Skeptic, 4,* 1–3.

Geil, R. (1990). Psychosocial processes in disasters. *International Journal of Mental Health, 19,* 7–20.

Gelpin, E., Bonne, O., Peri, T., Brandes, D., & Shalev, A. (1996). Treatment of recent trauma with benzodiazepines: A prospective study. *Journal of Clinical Psychiatry, 57,* 390–394.

Gerrity, E.T., & Steinglass, P. (1994). Relocation stress following natural disasters. In R.J. Ursano, B.G. McCaughey, & C.S. Fullerton (Eds.), *Individual and community responses to trauma and disaster: The structure of human chaos* (pp. 220–247). London: Cambridge University Press.

Gidron, Y., Gal., R., Freedman, S., Twiser, I., Lauden, A., Snir, Y., et al. (2001). Translating research findings to PTSD prevention: Results of a randomized-controlled pilot study. *Journal of Traumatic Stress, 14,* 773–780.

Giller, J. (1998). Caring for "victims of torture" in Uganda: Some personal reflections. In P.J. Bracken & C. Petty (Eds.), *Rethinking the trauma of war* (pp. 128–145). London: Free Association Books.

Gist, R., & Devilly, G.J. (2002). Post-trauma debriefing: The road too frequently travelled. *Lancet, 360,* 741–742.

Gist, R., & Stolz, S.B. (1982). Mental health promotion and the media: Community response to the Kansas City Hotel disasters. *American Psychologist, 37,* 1136–1139.

Goode, E. (2001, September 16). Some therapists fear services could backfire. *New York Times,* p. 21.

Grossman, L. (1973). Train crash: Social work and disaster services. *Social Work, 18,* 38–44.

Gurwitch, R.H., Sitterle, K.S., Young, B.H., & Pfefferbaum, B. (2002). Helping children in the aftermath of terrorism. In A. LaGreca, W. Silverman, E. Vernberg, and M. Roberts (Eds.), *Helping children cope with disasters* (pp. 327–357). Washington, DC: American Psychological Association.

Hanlon, P. (2003, April). Psychologists respond to Rhode Island club fire. *New England Psychologist.* Retrieved July 16, 2004, from http://www.nepsy.com/leading/0304_ne_rifire.html

Herbert, J. D., Lilienfeld, S., Kline, J., Montgomery, R., Lohr, J., Brandsma, L., et al. (2001, November). Letter of caution for psychologists. *Monitor on Psychology, 32,* 4. Retrieved July 26, 2004, from http://www.apa.org/monitor/nov01/letters.html

Hobfoll, S. (1998). *Stress, culture, and community: The psychology and philosophy of stress.* New York: Plenum.

Howes, J.L., & Hayes, C.J.A. (1999, Winter). Psychologists respond to the Swissair flight 111 tragedy. *Psynopsis.* Retrieved July 16, 2004, from http://www.cpa.ca/Psynopsis/Swissair.html

Ingraham, L.H. (1987). Grief leadership. In *The human response to the Gander military air disaster: A summary report.* Division of Neuropsychiatry Report No. 88–12.

Ingraham, L. H. (1988, October). *Grief leadership in work groups.* Paper presented at the Fourth Annual Conference on Military Medicine, Uniformed Services University of the Health Sciences, Bethesda, MD.

Ironson, G.I., Freund, B., Strauss, J.L., & Williams, J. (2002). A comparison of two treatments for traumatic stress: A community based study of EMDR and prolonged exposure. *Journal of Clinical Psychology, 58,* 113–128.

Kaniasty, K., & Norris, F. (1993). A test of the support deterioration model in the context of natural disaster. *Journal of Personality and Social Psychology, 64,* 395–408.

Kaniasty, K., & Norris, F.H. (1995). In search of altruistic community: Patterns of social support mobilization following Hurricane Hugo. *American Journal of Community Psychology, 23,* 447–477.

Kaslow, F.W., Nurse, A.R., & Thompson, P. (in press). Utilization of EMDR in conjunction with family therapy. In F. Shapiro (Ed.), *EMDR and the paradigm prism.* Washington, DC: American Psychological Association Press.

Katz, C. L., Pellegrino, L., Pandya, A., Ng, A., & DeLisi, L. E. (2002). Research on psychiatric outcomes and interventions subsequent to disasters: A review of the literature. *Psychiatry Research, 110,* 201–217.

Kenardy, J., & Carr, V. (2000). Debriefing post disaster follow-up after a major earthquake. In B. Raphael & J. Wilson (Eds.), *Psychological debriefing: Theory, practice and evidence* (pp. 174–181). Cambridge, U.K.: Cambridge University Press.

Kinston, W., & Rosser, R. (1974). Disaster: Effects on mental and physical state. *Journal of Psychosomatic Research, 18,* 437–456.

Lee, C., Gavriel, H., Drummond, P., Richards, J. & Greenwald, R. (2002). Treatment of post-traumatic stress disorder: A comparison of stress inoculation training with prolonged exposure and eye movement desensitisation and reprocessing. *Journal of Clinical Psychology, 58,* 1071–1089.

Lima, B.R., Pai, S., Santacruz, H., & Lozano, J. (1991). Psychiatric disorders among poor victims following a major disaster: Armero, Colombia. *Journal of Nervous and Mental Disease, 179,* 420–427.

Lima, B., Pai, S., Santacruz, H., Lozano, J., & Luna, J. (1987). Screening for the psychological consequences of a major disaster in a developing country: Armero, Colombia. *Acta Psychiatrica Scandinavica, 76,* 345–352.

Lin, K., Poland, R.E., Anderson, D., & Lesser, I.M. (1996). Ethnopsychopharmacology and the treatment of PTSD. In A.J. Marsella, M.J. Friedman, E.T. Gerrity, & R.M. Scurfield (Eds.), *Ethnocultural aspects of posttraumatic stress disorder: Issues, research, and clinical applications* (pp. 505–526). Washington, DC: American Psychological Association.

Litz, B.T., Gray, M.J., Bryant, R.A., & Adler, A.B. (2002). Early intervention for trauma: Current status and future directions. *Clinical Psychology: Science and Practice, 9,* 112–134.

Londborg, P. D., Hegel, M. T., Goldstein, S., Goldstein, D., Himmelhoch, J.M., Maddock, R., et al. (2001). Sertraline treatment of posttraumatic stress disorder: Results of 24 weeks of open-label continuation treatment. *Journal of Clinical Psychiatry, 62,* 325–331.

Maes, M., Delmeire, L., Mylle, J., & Altamura, C. (2001). Risk and preventive factors of posttraumatic stress disorder (PTSD): Alcohol consumption and intoxication prior to a traumatic event diminishes the relative risk to develop PTSD in response to that trauma. *Journal of Affective Disorder, 63,* 113–121.

Marmar, C.R., Schoenfeld, F., Weiss, D.S., Metzler, T., Zatzick, D., Wu, R., et al. (1996). Open trial of fluvoxamine treatment for combat-related posttraumatic stress disorder. *Journal of Clinical Psychiatry, 57,* 66–72.

Marquis, J.N. (1991). A report on seventy-eight cases treated by eye movement desensitization. *Journal of Behavior Therapy and Experimental Psychiatry, 22,* 187–192.

Marshall, R.D., Beebe, K.L., Oldham, M., & Zaninelli, R. (2001). Efficacy and safety of paroxetine treatment for chronic PTSD: A fixed-dose, placebo-controlled study. *American Journal of Psychiatry, 158,* 1982–1988.

McCarroll, J.E., Fullerton, C.S., Ursano, R.J., & Hermsen, J.M. (1996). Posttraumatic stress symptoms following forensic dental identification: Mt. Carmel, Waco, Texas. *American Journal of Psychiatry, 153,* 778–782.

McGolerick, R., & Echterling, L.G. (1995, August). *Vicarious impact of a public trauma.* Poster session presented at the annual meeting of the American Psychological Association Annual Convention, New York.

McNally, R.J., Bryant, R.A., & Ehlers, A. (2003). Does early psychological intervention promote recovery from posttraumatic stress? *Psychological Science in Public Interest, 4,* 45–79.

Meichenbaum, D. (1975). Self-instructional methods. In F.H. Kanfer & A.P. Goldstein (Eds.), *Helping people change* (pp. 357–391). New York: Pergamon.

Mileti, D.S., & O'Brien, P.W. (1992). Warnings during disaster: Normalizing communicated risk. *Social Problems, 39,* 40–57.

Mitchell, J.T. (1983). When disaster strikes. The Critical Incident Stress Debriefing process. *Journal of Emergency Medical Services, 8,* 36–39.

Mitchell, J.T. (2002, November 11). *CISM research summary.* Retrieved from http://www.icisf.org/articles/cism_research_summary.pdf

Mitchell, J.T., & Everly, G.S., Jr. (2001). *Critical Incident Stress Debriefing: An operations manual for CISD, defusing and other group crisis intervention services* (3rd ed.). Ellicott City, MD: Chevron.

Morrow, B. (1999). Identifying and mapping community vulnerability. *Disasters, 12,* 1–18.

Myers, D. (1991). Emotional recovery from the Loma Prieta earthquake. *Networks: Earthquake Preparedness News, 6,* 6–7.

Myers, D. G. (1994). Psychological recovery from disaster: Key concepts for delivery of mental health services. *National Center of PTSD Clinical Quarterly, 4,* 3–5.

Neborsky, R.J., & Solomon, M.F. (2001). The challenge of short-term psychotherapy. In M.F. Solomon & R.J. Neborsky (Eds.), *Short-term therapy for long-term change* (pp. 1–15). New York: Norton.

Norris, F. H., Byrne, C. M., Diaz, E., & Kaniasty, K. (2001). *50,000 disaster victims speak: An empirical review of the empirical literature, 1981–2001.* Report prepared for the National Center for PTSD and the Center for Mental Health Services (SAMHSA). Retrieved April 5, 2004, from http://obssr.od.nih.gov/Activities/911/disaster-impact.pdf

Norris, F., Friedman, M., Watson, P., Byrne, C., Diaz, E., & Kaniasty, K. (2002). 60,000 disaster victims speak: Part I. An empirical review of the empirical literature, 1981–2001. *Psychiatry, 65*(3), 207–239.

North C.S., Nixon S.J., Shariat S., Mallonee, S., McMillen, J. C., Spitznagel, E. L., et al. (1999). Psychiatric disorders among survivors of the Oklahoma City bombing. *Journal of American Medical Association, 282,* 755–762.

North, C.S., Tivis, L., McMillen, J.C., Pfefferbaum, B., Spitznagel, E.L., Cox, J., et al. (2002). Psychiatric disorders in rescue workers after the Oklahoma City bombing. *American Journal of Psychiatry, 159,* 857–859.

Norwood, A.E., & Ursano, R.J. (1997). Psychiatric interventions in post-disaster recovery. *The Hatherleigh Company, Ltd.* Retrieved July 16, 2004, from http://www.hatherleigh.com/disaster.pdf

Nurmi, L.A. (1999). The sinking of the Estonia: The effects of Critical Incident Stress Debriefing (CISD) on rescuers. *International Journal of Emergency Mental Health, 1,* 23–31.

O'Connor, K. (2003). *Acts of kindness.* Unpublished manuscript.

Ormel, J., & Tiemens, B. (1995). Recognition and treatment of mental illness in primary care: Towards a better understanding of a multifaceted problem. *General Hospital Psychiatry, 17,* 160–164.

Osterman, J.E., & Chemtob, C.M. (1999). Emergency intervention for acute traumatic stress. *Psychiatric Services, 50,* 739–740.

Page, A.C., & Crino, R.D. (1993). Eye-movement desensitization: A simple treatment for posttraumatic stress disorder? *Australian and New Zealand Journal of Psychiatry, 27,* 288–293.

Parson, E.R. (2002). Victims of disasters: Helping people recover from acute distress to healing and integration. *Gift from within.* Retrieved July 16, 2004, from http://www.giftfromwithin.org/html/victims.html

Pennebaker, J. W. (2000). The effects of traumatic disclosure on physical and mental health: The values of writing and talking about upsetting events. In J.M. Violanti & D. Paton (Eds.), *Posttraumatic stress intervention: Challenges, issues, and perspectives* (pp. 97–114). Springfield, IL: Charles C Thomas.

Pfefferbaum, B., Seale, T., McDonald, N., Brandt, E., Rainwater, S., Maynard, B., et al. (2000). Posttraumatic stress two years after the Oklahoma City bombing in youths geographically distant from the explosion. *Psychiatry, 63,* 358–370.

Pitman, R.K., Sanders, K.M., Zusman, R.M., Healy, A.R., Cheema, F., Lasko, N.B., et al. (2002). Pilot study of secondary prevention of posttraumatic stress disorder with propranolol. *Biological Psychiatry, 51,* 189–192.

Puk, G. (1991). Treating traumatic memories: A case report on the eye movement desensitization procedure. *Journal of Behavior Therapy and Experimental Psychiatry, 22,* 149–151.

Rapaport, M.H., Endicott, J., & Clary, C.M. (2002). Posttraumatic stress disorder and quality of life: results across 64 weeks of sertraline treatment. *Journal of Clinical Psychiatry, 63,* 59–65.

Raphael, B. (1986). *When disaster strikes: How individuals and communities cope with catastrophe.* New York: Basic Books.

Raphael, B., & Wilson, J.P. (Eds.). (2000). *Psychological debriefing: Theory, practice and evidence.* Cambridge, U.K.: Cambridge University Press.

Ray, A. (2001). From relief work to sustainable community development. *Journal Changemakers.net.* Retrieved May 15, 2004, from http://changemakers.net/journal/01october/ray.cfm

Resick, P.A., & Schnicke, M.K. (1992). Cognitive processing therapy for sexual assault victims. *Journal of Consulting and Clinical Psychology, 60,* 748–56.

Resick, P.A., & Schnicke, M.K. (1993). *Cognitive processing therapy for rape victims. A treatment manual.* Newbury Park, CA: Sage.

Robert, R., Blakeney, P.E., Villarreal, C., Rosenberg, L., & Meyer, W.J. (1999). Imipramine treatment in pediatric burn patients with symptoms of acute stress disorder: A pilot study. *Journal of the American Academy of Child and Adolescent Psychiatry, 38,* 873–878.

Rose, S., Bisson, J.I., Wessely, S. (2001). Psychological debriefing for preventing post traumatic stress disorder (PTSD) (Cochrane Review). In *The Cochrane Library,*

4. Oxford, England: Update Software. Abstract retrieved July 11, 2004, from http://www.update-software.com/abstracts/AB000560.htm

Rose, S., Brewin, C.R., Andrews, B., & Kirk, M. (1999). A randomized controlled trial of individual psychological debriefing for victims of violent crime. *Psychological Medicine, 29,* 793–799.

Rousseau, A.W. (1996, May 8). *Oklahoma City's recovery: A district branch perspective.* Paper presented at the American Psychiatric Association's Annual Meeting, New York.

Rundell, J.R., & Ursano, R.J. (1995). Psychiatric responses to trauma. In R.J. Ursano & A.E. Norwood (Eds.), *Emotional aftermath of the Persian Gulf war: Veterans, families, communities, and nations* (pp. 43–81). Washington, DC: American Psychiatric Press.

Salzer, M., & Bickman, L. (1999). The short- and long-term psychological impact of disasters: Implications for mental health intervention and policy. In R. Gist & B. Lubin (Eds.), *Response to disaster: Psychosocial, community, and ecological approaches* (pp. 63–82). Ann Arbor, MI: Braun-Brumfield.

Schuster, M., Stein, B., Jaycox, L., Collings, R., Marshall, G., Elliot, M., et al. (2001). A national survey of stress reactions after the September 11, 2001, terrorist attacks. *New England Journal of Medicine, 345* (20), 1507–1512.

Shalev, A.Y., Peri, T., Rogel-Fuchs, Y., Ursano, R., & Marlowe, D. (1998). Historical group debriefing after combat exposure. *Military Medicine, 163,* 494–498.

Shapiro, F. (1989). Eye movement desensitization: A new treatment for post-traumatic stress disorder. *Journal of Behavior Therapy and Experimental Psychiatry, 20,* 211–217.

Shapiro, F. (1995). *Eye Movement Desensitization and Reprocessing: Basic principles, protocols, and procedures.* New York: Guilford.

Shapiro, F. (1999). Eye movement desensitization and reprocessing (EMDR) and the anxiety disorders: Clinical and research implications of an integrated psychotherapy treatment. *Journal of Anxiety Disorders, 13,* 35–67.

Shapiro, F. (2001). *Eye Movement Desensitization and Reprocessing, Basic principles, protocols and procedures* (2nd ed.). New York: Guilford Press.

Shapiro, F. (2002). EMDR 12 years after its introduction: Past and future research. *Journal of Clinical Psychology, 58,* 1–22.

Siegel, D.J. (in press). The developing mind and the resolution of trauma: Some ideas about information processing and an interpersonal neurobiology of psychotherapy. In F. Shapiro (Ed.), *EMDR and the paradigm prism.* Washington, DC: American Psychological Association.

Sikes, C., & Sikes, V. (2003). EMDR: Why the controversy? *Traumatology, 9,* 169–181.

Smith, C. (1992). *Media and apocalypse: News coverage of the Yellowstone forest fires, Exxon Valdez oil spill, and Loma Prieta earthquake.* Westport, CT: Greenwood Press.

Smyth, N.J., & Poole, D.A. (in press). EMDR and cognitive behavior therapy: Exploring convergence and divergence. In F. Shapiro (Ed.), *EMDR and the paradigm prism*. Washington, DC: American Psychological Association.

Spector, J., & Read, J. (1999). The current status of eye movement desensitisaton and reprocessing (EMDR). *Clinical Psychology and Psychotherapy, 6,* 165–174.

Stanovic, J.K., James, K.A., & Vandevere, C.A. (2001). The effectiveness of risperidone on acute stress symptoms in adult burn patients: A preliminary retrospective pilot study. *Journal of Burn Care Rehabilitation, 22,* 210–213.

Suinn, R. (1974). Anxiety management training for general anxiety. In R. Suinn & R. Weigel (Eds.), *The innovative therapy: Critical and creative contributions* (pp. 66–70). New York: Harper & Row.

Tarrier, N., Pilgrim, H., Sommerfield, C., Faragher, B., Reynolds, M., Graham, E., et al. (1999). A randomized trial of cognitive therapy and imaginal exposure in the treatment of chronic post traumatic stress disorder. *Journal of Consulting and Clinical Psychology, 67,* 13–18.

Tucker, P., Zaninelli, R., Yehuda, R., Ruggiero, L., Dillingham, K., & Pitts, C.D. (2001). Paroxetine in the treatment of chronic posttraumatic stress disorder: Results of a placebo-controlled, flexible-dosage trial. *Journal of Clinical Psychiatry, 62,* 860–868.

Ursano, R.J., & McCarroll, J.E. (1994). Exposure to traumatic death: The nature of stressor. In R.J. Ursano, B. G. McCaughey, & C. S. Fullerton (Eds.), *Individual and community responses to trauma and disaster: The structure of human chaos* (pp. 46–71). Cambridge, U.K.: Cambridge University Press.

van der Kolk, B.A. (in press). Beyond the talking cure: Somatic experience and subcortical imprints in the treatment of trauma. In F. Shapiro (Ed.), *EMDR and the paradigm prism*. Washington, DC: American Psychological Association.

van der Kolk, B.A., Burbridge, B.A., & Suzuki, J. (1997). The psychobiology of traumatic memory: Clinical implications of neuroimaging studies. In R. Yehuda & A. C. McFarland (Eds.), *Annals of the New York Academy of Sciences (Vol. 821): Psychobiology of Posttraumatic Stress* Disorder (pp. 99–113). New York: New York Academy of Sciences.

Van Etten, M.L., & Taylor, S. (1998). Comparative efficacy of treatments for posttraumatic stress disorder: A meta-analysis. *Clinical Psychology & Psychotherapy, 5,* 126–144.

Veronen, L.J., & Kilpatrick, D.G. (1983). Stress management for rape victims. In D. Meichenbaum & M.E. Jaremko (Eds.), *Stress reduction and prevention* (pp. 341–374). New York: Plenum.

Watson, P.J., Friedman, M.J., Gibson, L.E., Ruzek, J.I., Norros, F.H., & Ritchie, E.C. (2003). Early intervention for trauma-related problems. In R.J. Ursano & A.E. Norwood (Eds.), *Trauma and disaster responses and management* (pp. 97–124). Arlington, VA: American Psychiatric Publishing.

Wee, D.F., Mills, D.M., & Koehler, G. (1999). The effects of Critical Incident Stress Debriefing (CISD) on emergency medical services personnel following the Los Angeles civil disturbance. *International Journal of Emergency Mental Health, 1,* 33–37.

Wessells, M.G., & Monteiro, C. (2000). Healing wounds of war in Angola: A community-based approach. In D. Donald, A. Dawes, & J. Louw (Eds.), *Addressing childhood adversity* (pp. 176–201). Cape Town, South Africa: David Philip.

Wessely, S., Rose, S., & Bisson, J. (1998). A systematic review of brief psychological interventions ('debriefing') for the treatment of immediate trauma related symptoms and the prevention of posttraumatic stress disorder (Cochrane Review). *The Cochrane Library,* 3. Oxford, England: Update Software.

Wilkins, L. (1985). Television and newspaper coverage of a blizzard: Is the message helplessness? *Newspaper Research Journal, 6,* 51–65.

Wilson, S. A., Becker, L. A., & Tinker, R. H. (1995). Eye movement desensitization and reprocessing (EMDR) treatment for psychologically traumatized individuals. *Journal of Consulting and Clinical Psychology, 63,* 928–937.

Wilson, S.A., Silver, S.M., Covi, W.G., & Foster, S. (1996). Eye movement desensitization and reprocessing: Effectiveness and automatic correlates. *Journal of Behavior Therapy and Experimental Psychiatry, 27,* 219–229.

Wolpe, J. (1990). *The practice of behavior therapy* (4th ed.). New York: Pergamon.

Wolpe, J., & Abrams, J. (1991). Post-traumatic stress disorder overcome by eye movement desensitization: A case report. *Journal of Behavior Therapy and Experimental Psychiatry, 22,* 39–43.

Wright, K.M., & Bartone, P.T. (1994). Community response to disaster: the Gander plane crash. In R.J. Ursano, B.G. McCaughey, & C.S. Fullerton (Eds.), *Individual and community responses to trauma and disaster: The structure of human chaos* (pp. 267–284). Cambridge, U.K.: Cambridge University Press.

Yates, S., Axsom, D., & Tiedman, K. (1999). The help seeking process for distress after disasters. In R. Gist & B. Lubin (Eds.), *Response to disaster: Psychological, community, and ecological approaches* (pp. 133–165). Philadelphia: Brunner/Mazel.

Yehuda, R. (2002). Post-traumatic stress disorder. *New England Journal of Medicine, 346,* 108–114.

Young, J., Zangwill, W., & Behery, W.E. (in press). EMDR and schema-focused therapy. In F. Shapiro (Ed.), *EMDR and the paradigm prism.* Washington, DC: American Psychological Association.

Zunin, L.M., & Zunin, H.S. (1991). *The art of condolence: What to write, what to say, what to do at a time of loss.* New York: HarperCollins.

CHAPTER 2

Bereavement-Related Depression and PTSD

Evaluating Interventions

George A. Bonanno and Anthony D. Mancini

Coping with the death of a close friend or relation can be one of the most highly stressful experiences a person might endure (Holmes & Rahe, 1967). Losses that result from violence and other types of potentially traumatic circumstances appear to be even more difficult for bereaved survivors (Bonanno & Kaltman, 1999). Although many bereaved individuals will recover from such losses within 1 to 2 years and most even sooner, a small but significant subset will experience unremitting distress and depression and in some cases the symptoms of post-traumatic stress disorder (PTSD) for years after the loss (Bonanno & Kaltman, 2001).

Bereaved persons exhibiting chronic grief reactions would be obvious candidates for clinical intervention (Jordan & Neimeyer, 2003; Mancini, Pressman, & Bonanno, in press; Schut, Stroebe, van den Bout, & Terheggen, 2001). Unfortunately, however, despite the voluminous literature on therapeutic techniques and interventions for bereavement, the research evidence suggests the rather sobering conclusion that *existing clinical interventions for bereavement have been generally inefficacious* (Allumbaugh & Hoyt, 1999; Kato & Mann, 1999; Neimeyer, 2000). For example, two recent meta-analytic studies compared randomly assigned grief treatment and control groups. In contrast to the generally robust effect sizes typically observed for psychotherapeutic outcomes, grief-specific therapies produce only small and relatively inconsequential effects (Allumbaugh & Hoyt, 1999; Kato & Mann, 1999; Neimeyer, 2000). Importantly, in one of these analyses, an alarming 38% of the individuals receiving grief treatments grew worse relative to no-treatment controls (Neimeyer, 2000). As seems to be the case with psychotherapy generally, bereaved persons who self-selected grief therapy benefited more from the intervention did than bereaved participants recruited by investigators (Allumbaugh & Hoyt, 1999). And the clearest benefits were evidenced with bereaved individuals experiencing chronic grief reactions, although the effect size in this case was still smaller than is normally observed for psychotherapy outcome (Neimeyer).

Why have grief therapies been so ineffective in controlled studies? There are several possibilities. One explanation is that the apparent symptoms of chronic grief may reflect a long-standing depressive disorder and other difficulties that pre-dated the loss (Bonanno, Wortman, et al., 2002; Bonanno, Moskowitz, Papa, & Folkman, 2004). Indeed, because interventions in controlled studies usually occur at relatively late stages of grief (more than 2 years post-loss, on average; Allumbaugh & Hoyt, 1999), it is likely that a sizable proportion of the participants identified as having chronic grief were in fact suffering from chronic depression. Indeed, in a recent prospective study that tracked participants' adjustment beginning on average 3 years prior to the death of their spouse, about one third of the bereaved persons with chronic symptoms following loss were in fact suffering from chronic depression (Bonanno, et al., 2002). At 18 months of bereavement, the chronically depressed individuals had similar levels of depression and distress as did bereaved individuals more clearly exhibiting chronic grief reactions. A recent follow-up of this study showed, however, that by 4 years of bereavement the chronically grieving participants had exhibited considerable recovery and had reliably lower levels of depression than bereaved participants who were depressed did both pre- and post-bereavement (Boerner, Wortman, & Bonanno, in press). It seems likely then, and the evidence strongly suggests, that a grief-focused intervention would prove particularly ineffective for persons whose chronic symptoms probably have less to do with grief and more to do with pre-existing psychopathology (Bonanno et al., 2002; Bonanno, Moskowitz, et al., 2004; Mancini et al., in press).

Another and perhaps even more compelling explanation for the lack of efficacy found for grief therapies is the over-inclusion of bereaved individuals who have moderate or minimal symptoms and thus probably have no clear need for treatment (Bonanno, 2004; Jordan & Neimeyer, 2003). Because of the smaller scope for improvement for this group, the inclusion of persons with moderate or minimal symptomatology in efficacy studies of bereavement interventions would almost certainly diminish the overall effect size.

Finally, a third reason, noted above, may be that some bereaved individuals suffer from both chronic depressive symptoms and trauma reactions associated with the nature of the loved one's death (e.g., death due to violence; Kaltman & Bonanno, 2003). For these individuals, traditional forms of grief counseling may fail to address or may even exacerbate the traumatic nature of their grief reactions (Shear & Frank, in press).

To address these issues in this chapter, we first review the evidence and theoretical rationale for the primary patterns of trajectories of grief reaction. Next, we consider some of the common clinical assumptions about bereavement and note ways in which these assumptions fail to account for individual differences in grief course. We then consider the more specific case of bereavement following potentially traumatic events. Finally, we propose a number of specific recommendations for the assessment and treatment of bereaved individuals.

FROM RESILIENCE TO CHRONIC GRIEF: THE VARIETIES OF GRIEF REACTION

The experience of grief following the death of a loved one has been associated with a number of difficulties and disruptions in normal functioning. These may include transient *cognitive disorganization*, such as confusion and preoccupation with the deceased, identity disturbances ("a piece of me is missing"), feelings of uncertainty about the future, and a compromised sense of life's underlying meaning or purpose; *dysphoric emotions*, including sadness, anger, anxiety, irritability, fear, hostility, and guilt, as well as intense loneliness and pining or yearning for the lost loved one; *health problems*, such as somatic difficulties, new or worsened illnesses, and additional or increased use of medications; and *disrupted social and occupational functioning*, including social withdrawal and isolation, and the temporary inability to fulfill normal social and occupational roles (for a review, see Bonanno & Kaltman, 2001).

As had been shown with acute stressors generally (e.g., Lucas, Clark, Georgellis, & Denier, 2003), bereaved persons vary greatly in their reactions to loss (Bonanno & Kaltman, 1999, 2001; Wortman & Silver, 1989, 2001). Recent reviews of the longitudinal and descriptive studies on bereavement conducted over the past several decades revealed three primary trajectories of individual differences in grief reaction: *chronic or complicated grief* (persistent and disabling grief symptoms for several years or longer), *recovery* (acute symptoms that gradually subside over the course of 1 or 2 years), and *minimal grief or resilience* (mild, transient symptoms lasting up to several weeks followed by a stable pattern of healthy functioning across time) (Bonanno,

2004; Bonanno & Kaltman, 2001). Although bereavement theorists have often described a fourth pattern representing delayed grief reactions (e.g., Parkes & Weiss, 1983; Rando, 1993), a number of studies that have directly attempted to measure this pattern have failed to find evidence of its existence (e.g., Bonanno & Field, 2001; Bonanno et al., 2002; Middleton, Burnett, Raphael, & Martinek, 1996).

Chronic Grief versus the Recovery Pattern

Somewhere between 10% to 15% of bereaved persons, suffer from chronic disruptions in functioning that may endure for years after the loss. For many of these individuals, the various disruptions in functioning wrought by the loss often coalesce in what appears to be a chronic depression reaction. When the loss occurs in the context of disasters and other potentially traumatic events, such as homicides, accidents, or terrorist attacks, however, bereaved individuals must contend not only with sadness and remorse over the loved one's absence, but often horrific, recurrent images of the loved one's suffering, fear, and anguish. Not surprisingly, bereavement following such events tends to result in more chronic depressive reactions AND considerably greater levels of symptoms of PTSD relative to bereavement following death by natural causes (Kaltman & Bonanno, 2003; Zisook, Chentsova-Dutton, & Shuchter, 1998).

A number of investigators have advocated the adoption of new diagnostic criteria for what has been variously described as traumatic, complicated, or pathologic grief (e.g., Horowitz et al., 1997; Kim & Jacobs, 1991; Prigerson et al., 1995; Prigerson et al., 1999). Although potentially useful, these efforts are largely based on consensus (Prigerson et al., 1999) and have yet to culminate in empirically-based criteria that might be widely endorsed in the field. In the absence of this type of evidence, perhaps complicated grief is best understood in terms of symptoms associated with existing diagnostic categories for anxiety, depression, and, in some cases, PTSD (Bonanno & Kaltman, 2001). Consistent with this conceptualization, the DSM-IV classifies bereavement as a "V code," or a stressor that may be a focus of clinical concern but that is not considered a diagnosis in and of itself, even in its most severe and chronic forms (American Psychiatric Association, 1994).

How, then, should clinicians identify persons suffering from chronic grief? An obvious but perhaps principal difference between the conventional recovery pattern and chronic grief reactions is the duration of symptoms and their impact on functioning. However, duration of symptomatology does not appear to be the only factor to distinguish chronic reactions; severity of symptoms even in the initial months of bereavement also appears to inform such reactions. Recent research has shown, for example, that bereaved individuals who ultimately developed chronic reactions struggle with acute symptom levels in the early months of bereavement. This distinction is illustrated by comparing the chronic grief with the recovery pattern (Bonanno et al., 2002). Bereaved persons who show the recovery pattern may experience moderate levels of symptoms as well as difficulties carrying out their normal tasks at work or in the care of loved ones, but they somehow manage to struggle through these tasks and slowly but gradually begin to return to their pre-loss or baseline level of functioning, usually over a period of 1 or 2 years (Bonanno, 2004). By contrast, chronic grievers evidence substantial symptomatology and a dramatically reduced ability to perform well at work, to maintain relationships with friends or intimates, and to meet parenting obligations. These difficulties may persist for years after the loss, but at a minimum should endure for at least 1 year after bereavement to warrant the label "chronic grief." Here it is again important to return to the distinction, discussed earlier, regarding chronic depression symptoms. Although this issue is not considered in relation to bereavement in the DSM-IV, it is apparent that for some bereaved individuals the symptoms of chronic grief may, in fact, represent an unresolved depression that predated the loss (Bonanno et al., 2002; Mancini et al., in press). We will return to the issue of chronic grief versus chronic depression and also consider other conceptualizations of chronic or complicated grief reactions in greater detail later in this article.

Resilience to Loss

Although many bereaved persons experience at least some of the difficulties described above, it is important to emphasize that *most bereaved persons experience only minimal disruptions in functioning* and *regain psychological equilibrium relatively quickly* (e.g., within a few weeks) after the loss (Bonanno, 2004). And it has become increasingly clear that such individuals are not likely to require and may even be harmed by clinical intervention (Jordan & Neimeyer, 2003; Raphael, Minkov, & Dobson, 2001). Although estimates in the literature vary, the available evidence suggests that approximately 80% of bereaved persons experience either moderate or minimal grief symptoms that will resolve on their own by the end of the first year (for a review, see Bonanno & Kaltman, 2001).

Traditionally, bereavement theorists have considered the recovery pattern to be the most common or "modal" response to loss, whereas the absence of distress during bereavement has been viewed as both rare and pathological (Bowlby, 1980; Deutsch, 1937; Jacobs, 1993; Lindemann, 1944; Rando, 1993; Worden, 1991). Bereavement theorists have also tended to assume that bereaved individuals who do not exhibit overt signs of grieving will eventually manifest delayed grief reactions (for a review see Bonanno & Field, 2001), a phenomenon that is widely endorsed among clinicians and researchers in the field (Middleton, Moylan, Raphael, Burnett, 1993). And, as would not be surprising given these assumptions, bereavement theorists have historically viewed the absence of grief as a form of denial that also necessitates clinical intervention (Bowlby; Deutsch; Jacobs; Lindemann; Rando; Worden). Indeed, in a recent survey of self-identified bereavement experts (Middleton et al., 1993), a majority (65%) endorsed beliefs that "absent grief" usually stems from denial or inhibition, and that it is generally maladaptive in the long run.

Despite the strength with which these views appear to be represented in the bereavement literature, recent research studies that have mapped the different types or trajectories of grief reaction suggest a dramatically different picture (for reviews see Bonanno, 2004, in press; Mancini et al., in press). Bonanno (2004) defined a resilient trajectory following the death of a close relation or other forms of potentially traumatic events as "the ability . . . to maintain relatively stable, healthy levels of psychological and physical functioning . . . as well as the capacity for generative experiences and positive emotions" (p. 20–21). Several recent bereavement studies have in fact demonstrated that this type of resilient response pattern occurs with greater frequency than any other type of outcome during bereavement (e.g., Bonanno, Keltner, Holen, & Horowitz, 1995; Bonanno, Znoj, Siddique, & Horowitz, 1999; Bonanno, Wortman et al., 2002; Bonanno, Moskowitz, et al., 2004). What's more, there has been no indication in these studies that bereaved people showing the resilient pattern are maladjusted or have less capacity for intimacy and social interaction than do other individuals (Bonanno et al., 2002; Bonanno, Wortman, and Nesse, 2004a,b). To the contrary, when resilient individuals have been distinguished from other bereaved individuals, they have tended to score higher on factors that suggest resilience (e.g., acceptance of death, Bonanno et al., 2002; comfort from positive memories of the deceased, Bonanno, Wortman, and Nesse, 2004). Finally, there has been no support in these studies for the assumption that the absence of distress eventually leads to delayed grief reactions (Bonanno & Field, 2001; Bonanno et al., 2002; Boerner, Wortman, et al., in press), and this was true even where the researchers fully expected to demonstrate delayed reactions (e.g., Middleton et al., 1996).

COMMON CLINICAL ASSUMPTIONS ABOUT BEREAVEMENT

A particularly widespread assumption in the bereavement literature is that active efforts are required to cope with loss, a process commonly referred to as "grief work" (W. Stroebe & Stroebe, 1991). Rooted in this perspective, traditional models for grief counseling have typically employed procedures designed to promote the bereaved person's efforts to work through the loss. For example, bereaved persons are implored to accept the reality of the loss, to review specific memories and express feelings (particularly negative ones) associated with the lost loved one, and to make active efforts to relinquish their attachment to the deceased (e.g., Rando, 1993).

A related clinical assumption is that the absence of overt distress in response to bereavement is itself indicative of pathology, because it suggests that the person is inhibiting or dissociating from negative feelings (Middleton et al., 1993) or lacked a strong attachment to the deceased (Fraley & Shaver, 1999). For example, bereaved persons who do not display overt distress have been assumed to be avoiding the "tasks" of grieving (Worden, 1991). Such responses to loss have often been thought to portend later and much more severe difficulties that could be avoided by engaging in "grief work" processes.

Despite widespread endorsement of the "grief work" perspective (and the concomitant pathologizing of those who fail to evince grief symptoms), startlingly little empirical evidence exists to support these assumptions about bereavement (Wortman & Silver, 1989). Indeed, a number of bereavement theorists have argued in recent years that *traditional models of coping with loss are not supported by the empirical data* (Bonanno, 2001, 2004; Bonanno & Kaltman, 1999; Murphy, Johnson, & Lohan, 2003; Wortman & Silver, 1989, 2001). Of greater potential concern, there is growing evidence that not only are processes associated with grief work incompatible with the evidence; engaging in such processes to a significant degree may actually exacerbate grief reactions (Bonanno & Kaltman, 1999; Bonanno, Papa, Lalande, Nanping, & Noll, in press).

Although bereavement researchers and theorist have widely endorsed the importance of the working-through process, empirical examination of these processes or their purported role during bereavement has been slow in coming. One reason for this delay is that the griefwork assumption and its components have never been clearly defined (Archer, 1999; W. Stroebe & Stroebe, 1993). Psychoanalytically oriented theorists have, for example, emphasized the quality or depth of the working-through process (e.g., emotional acceptance of the loss, Parkes & Weiss, 1983). Yet this type of theorizing blurs the distinction between grief processing and grief outcome and does not readily lend itself to prospective empirical research.

In an attempt to obviate this problem, researchers have more recently attempted to measure various aspects of grief processing hypothesized to underlie successful working through (e.g., thinking about and expressing the thoughts, memories, and emotions associated with the loss). The results of these studies came as something of a surprise, at least to traditional theorists; these studies consistently failed to support and even contradicted the presumed salutary role of extensive grief processing (for a review see Bonanno & Kaltman, 1999). For example, a series of our own studies focused on the presumed necessity of experiencing and expressing negative emotions associated with loss. These studies consistently linked negative emotions earlier in bereavement with a more protracted grief course, regardless of whether the emotion was experienced, expressed nonverbally, or described in naturally occurring discourse (Bonanno & Keltner, 1997; Bonanno et al., 1995; Bonanno, Mihalecz, & LeJeune, 1999; Bonanno, Znoj, et al., 1999). Similarly, M. Stroebe, Stroebe, Shut, Zech, E., and van den Bout (2002) examined written and verbal forms of emotional disclosure during bereavement and found no evidence that the disclosure of grief-related thoughts and emotions improved adjustment.

Another study recently documented this detrimental effect of grief processing using a psychometrically robust questionnaire measure (Bonanno, Papa, et al., in press). Of particular note, this study compared the prospective relationship of grief processing to adjustment among matched bereaved samples from two dramatically different countries, the United States and the People's Republic of China, and revealed potentially important cultural differences. Consistent with previous research, the negative effects of excessive grief processing were clearly evidenced in the American sample. However, for the bereaved in China, grief processing was virtually unrelated to adjustment. One implication of these results is that the personal experience of grief and the processes involved in its expression may be radically different in Eastern or collectivist and Western or individualistic cultures. Nonetheless, it is important to note that in both countries there was no apparent support for the assumed usefulness of processes associated with psychological working through the loss. In our section on assessment and treatment below, we discuss alternate conceptualizations of grief counseling that stand in contrast to traditional grief work assumption.

BEREAVEMENT-RELATED TRAUMA REACTIONS

Although there is as yet a paucity of research on PTSD symptoms during bereavement, several studies have clearly indicated that loss due to violent or unnatural death increases risk for PTSD symptoms. Initial support for this idea came from indirect evidence, such as studies comparing grief reactions after violent death and natural death across non-matched samples (e.g., Rynearson & McCreery, 1993). More recently, however, two studies provided direct evidence for the association of violent deaths with trauma symptoms. Zisook and colleagues (1998) examined data from a large sample of conjugally bereaved adults at the 2-month point in bereavement. The criterion for PTSD was met by about 10% of the participants whose spouses had died of natural causes, regardless of whether the death was expected or not. In contrast, over one third of the participants whose spouses had died of suicide or accidents met the PTSD criteria. More recently, Kaltman and Bonanno (2003) measured symptoms of depression and PTSD symptoms prospectively among a sample of midlife conjugally bereaved individuals. Bereaved participants whose spouses had died from violent deaths (suicide, accident, homicide) exhibited significantly greater PTSD symptoms across the 25 months of the study compared with other participants. As in the study by Zisook and colleagues, the expectedness of the loss, by itself, was unrelated to trauma symptoms. Additionally, although both the violent- and natural-death bereaved groups showed elevated depression, for natural-death participants depression decreased over time, whereas for the violent-death participants depression remained elevated through 25 months. Together, these findings suggest that bereavement following violent death may lead to a particularly thorny combination of trauma reactions and chronic depression.

As noted earlier, a growing number of bereavement researchers and theorists have argued that complicated or traumatic grief reactions represent a separate and unique diagnostic entity characterized by both depressive symptoms, such as dysphoria and social withdrawal, and PTSD symptoms, such as intrusive thoughts and images and avoidant behaviors, as well as symptoms of acute separation distress, such as intense pining or yearning for the deceased, that are not represented in the DSM-IV (e.g., Prigerson, Shear, Bierhals, et al., 1997; Prigerson, Shear, Jacobs, et al., 1999). The primary arguments put forth for the creation of a unique diagnostic category to represent complicated grief have been that it does not precisely match any single existing DSM-IV diagnosis, that the symptoms thought to comprise complicated grief do not completely overlap with the symptoms used to define major depressive disorder or PTSD, and that existing treatments for either depression or PTSD do not appear to be efficacious for cases of traumatic grief (Shear & Frank, in press). The question of whether or not a new diagnostic category is needed, or whether simply the combination of depression and PTSD diagnoses would suffice (see Bonanno & Kaltman, 2001), goes beyond the scope of the present chapter. However, the issue of treatment inefficacy is of obvious relevance. We return to this issue below.

RECOMMENDATIONS FOR ASSESSMENT OF BEREAVED PERSONS

Assessment Recommendation 1: Conduct a Thorough Assessment

Among the areas that should be assessed but are often ignored in the treatment of bereaved persons are personality organization, prior psychiatric or trauma history and specifically depressive reactions contiguous with the loss event, internalized or externalized coping style, support network, and general pre-loss levels of functioning and symptomatology (Bonanno et al., 2002; Jordan & Neimeyer, 2003).

Assessment Recommendation 2: Distinguish Chronic Grief from Chronic Depression

Bereaved persons who exhibit symptoms of apparent chronic grief may instead be experiencing a chronic depression that existed before the loss (Bonanno et al., 2002). Because the etiology of chronic depression and chronic grief is so divergent, each symptom pattern is likely to require a different treatment approach. For this reason, it is essential to distinguish chronic grief from chronic depression among bereaved persons presenting for treatment. At a superficial level, chronic grief reactions may be indistinguishable from chronic depressive reactions predating the loss. Fortunately, however, a number of characteristics have been identified that should help to distinguish these two patterns. For example, persons with chronic depression, when compared with chronic grievers, have been found to have greater perceived deficits in coping efficacy, more difficulty managing troubling feelings, and less positive affect (Bonanno, Wortman, & Nesse, 2004). In addition, those suffering from chronic depression, by definition, experience higher levels of pre-loss distress than do chronic grievers. Although patients' self-report of their pre-bereavement functioning may be unreliable, more accurate histories can be obtained from records, if available, and from other informants, such as close friends or relatives (Bonanno, Rennicke, & Dekel, 2004). On the other hand, chronic grief, when compared with chronic depression, has been associated with more active efforts to understand the loss, including higher levels of processing and searching for meaning during the first 6 months of bereavement (Bonanno, Wortman, and Nesse, 2004). These differences suggest that routine assessment of bereaved patients should include the degree to which the bereaved person is searching for meaning about the loss, pre-loss level of functioning, and perceived coping skills.

Assessment Recommendation 3: Identify Symptoms of Bereavement-Related Trauma

Another critical area of assessment is the existence of trauma symptoms associated with the loss, particularly when the death was due to suicide, accident, or other any other factor that might be considered unnatural or excessively violent in nature. In the case of such losses, symptoms of bereavement-related trauma may include recurrent and intrusive images of the bereaved person's suffering; avoidance of places, activities, or personal objects associated with the lost loved one; difficulties sleeping; trouble concentrating; irritability; and agitation (Kaltman & Bonanno, 2003; Zisook et al., 1998), all symptoms that are diagnostic of PTSD (American Psychiatric Association, 1994).

Assessment Recommendation 4: Take Account of Additional Risk Factors

A number of other factors may predispose bereaved persons to more adverse outcomes and should, therefore, be borne in mind by clinicians (Jordan & Neimeyer, 2003; W. Stroebe & Schut, 2001). Among the categorical risk factors are spousal loss for men (particularly when older and isolated) and the loss of a child for mothers. Other characteristics that pose additional risk include prior psychiatric and trauma histories, perceived coping deficits, and high levels of dependency on the lost loved one. This latter factor in particular may predispose bereaved individuals toward chronic grief reactions (Bonanno et al., 2002). In addition, severe levels of distress at early stages of bereavement may be prognostic of later difficulties.

RECOMMENDATIONS FOR TREATMENT OF BEREAVED PERSONS

Treatment Recommendation 1: Treat Traumatic Symptoms First

Although only a small subset of bereaved individuals will evidence PTSD-like symptoms or the constellation of depression and PTSD symptoms sometimes referred to as traumatic grief, the difficulties these individuals struggle with have proved particularly resistant to traditional grief treatments (Shear & Frank, in press). The most plausible explanation for the lack of treatment effectiveness in this case is that traditional grief treatments are oriented toward the amelioration of depressive symptoms but not trauma symptoms. Accordingly, a number of new interventions for traumatic grief reactions have been proposed or are currently in development that incorporate elements from treatments with demonstrated efficacy for PTSD symptoms, such as prolonged exposure (e.g., Foa, Dancu, Hembree, Jaycox, Meadows & Street, 1999). Preliminary reports for such treatments are encouraging (Shear, 2001). Although much research is needed in this area, the most logical protocol would appear to require addressing trauma symptoms as an initial stage of treatment before proceeding to subsequent grief-focused intervention techniques.

Treatment Recommendation 2: Facilitate Emotional Disclosure Without Giving Priority to Negative Feelings

Traditional grief therapies have emphasized the importance of expressing negative emotions associated with the loss, but research examining this question has found that expressing negative emotions (Bonanno & Keltner, 1997), confronting feelings of anger or sadness (Bonanno et al., 1995), and focusing on emotions associated with the loss (Nolen-Hoeksema, Parker, & Larson, 1994) are generally associated with more persistent grief symptoms and worse outcomes. On the other hand, the expression of positive feelings, and the modulation of negative emotions, has been consistently associated with a more rapid improvement and reduction in grief symptoms (Keltner & Bonanno, 1997; Moskowitz, Folkman, & Acree, 2003; Ong, Bergman, & Bisconti, 2004). These findings strongly argue against a principal focus of traditional grief counseling therapies—the presumed salutary effects of confronting, focusing on, and expressing negative emotions associated with the loss.

One explanation for these findings on negative emotional expression can be derived from research on the benefits of verbal disclosure. Ample research has identified the adaptive consequences of talking about acute stressors or trauma (e.g., Pennebaker, 1993), a process that appears to promote important processes of cognitive integration and restructuring (Greenberg, Wortman, & Stone, 1996). In the context of bereavement, however, the positive effects have been less clear (Kelly & McKillop, 1996). Indeed, Stroebe, Stroebe, Schut, Zech, and van den Bout (2002) recently examined the effects of written and verbal forms of emotional disclosure during bereavement and found no evidence that the disclosure of grief-related emotion improved adjustment. Given such findings, it is worthwhile to consider an important moderating factor in disclosure, demonstrated by Lepore, Silver, Wortman, and Wayment, (1996): the extent to which others are seen as available and willing to listen to expressed feelings. Without a supportive environment, the benefits of disclosure are diluted (Kelly & McKillop, 1996; Lepore, Ragan, & Jones, 2000).

Taken together, these findings suggest that, rather than seeking to promote the disclosure of negative feelings about the loss and discount the expression of positive ones, clinicians should adopt a neutral, non-directive stance with regard to the content of the bereaved person's disclosures; instead, we believe clinicians' focus should be on providing a safe environment in which disclosure is supported when volunteered by the patient. In sum, there is *virtually no evidence* that encouraging the expression of negative feelings about the loss, a basic therapeutic technique in traditional models of grief counseling, will facilitate the resolution of grief, whereas *evidence does support* the beneficial effects of positive emotional expression. It should also be noted that there are a number of positive aspects of grieving that have often been ignored in the literature (Bonanno & Kaltman, 2001); these include feelings of self-growth, greater focus on future goals, and comforting memories of the deceased (Bonanno et al., 1995; Stein, Folkman, Trabasso, & Christopher-Richards, 1997; Zisook, Paulus, Shuchter, & Judd, 1997).

Treatment Recommendation 3: Rely on Principles of Sound Clinical Practice More than Bereavement-Specific Procedures to Address Grief

Recent recommendations for clinical practice underscore the importance of tailoring treatments to the patient's coping style, symptom constellation, and degree of functional impairment (Beutler, 2000). However, investigators have noted the signal failure of traditional grief counseling models to account for differences in mourners (Jordan & Neimeyer, 2003). Moreover, the techniques recommended by traditional grief therapies—expressing negative emotions, reviewing memories of the deceased, and active efforts to relinquish attachment—have received almost no support in the literature (Wortman & Silver, 1989, 2001). For this reason, it is recommended that clinicians rely to a greater extent on therapeutic principles that are broadly applicable rather than procedures specifically designed to treat grief (see Beutler, 2000, for a review of cross-cutting therapeutic principles).

It may also prove useful, although little data is yet available on this issue, to incorporate global interventions designed to foster improved social functioning and a general expansion and broadening of the self. Resilient individuals appear to cope effectively during bereavement, at least in part, because they are able to maintain a sense of identity constancy from pre- to post-bereavement (Bauer & Bonanno, 2001; Bonanno, Papa, & O'Neill, 2001). The mechanisms by which they achieve this type of continuity are at this point only speculative, as no research has yet addressed this question. However, we have elsewhere speculated that resilient individuals are able to function effectively after loss because they have a broader, more multifaceted sense of self that allows them to absorb a major loss without the accompanying sense of identity loss, and also because they have a well-developed and active social milieu from which they might draw supportive resources (Bauer & Bonanno, 2001; Bonanno et al., 2001). We are currently exploring the compelling possibility that interventions for bereaved individuals might include generalized components designed to improve or facilitate development of resilience factors of this type. It may even be possible to enact such interventions without focusing on bereavement.

Treatment Recommendation 4: Persons with Moderate, Minimal or Absent Grief Symptoms Should Not Receive Grief-Focused Treatment

As discussed earlier, recent empirical studies and reviews have clearly indicated that the relative absence of grief is *not* an appropriate rationale for clinical intervention (Bonanno, 2004; Bonanno et al., 2002; Jordan & Neimeyer, 2003; Raphael et al., 2001). Despite suggestions by some theorists (e.g., Worden, 1991), the notion that absent or minimal grief should be treated prophylactically, in an effort, for example, to forestall a more severe grief reaction down the road, has received no empirical support. Rather, consistent with a growing body of evidence, persons with absent or minimal symptoms of grief appear to be displaying genuine resilience and manifesting effective coping mechanisms (Bonanno, 2004). Moreover, although persons with moderate symptoms of grief do experience some disruptions in functioning and may appear to be candidates for intervention, available evidence does not support a grief-focused intervention for this group either. Rather, such persons can be expected gradually to emerge from their difficulties on their own, a process that should generally be allowed to unfold without clinical intervention, unless symptoms worsen or are excessively protracted. In summary, only persons who evince particularly severe symptoms of grief soon after loss or whose symptoms persist unabated for a long period of time after loss (at least 1 year) are likely to benefit from a grief-focused intervention.

DIRECTIONS FOR FUTURE RESEARCH

The bereavement field now faces something of a dual dilemma; not only have historically dominant assumptions about the necessity of engaging in grief work consistently failed to generate convincing empirical support, but standard grief-focused interventions, based largely on this assumption, have also shown a sobering lack of efficacy. Our analysis of the bereavement literature suggests that this lack of efficacy is at least partly due to three factors: (1) inattention to the distinction between chronic grief and chronic depression, (2) failure to identify and treat trauma symptoms when they occur independently from grief reactions, and (3) the inclusion of bereaved persons with mild to moderate levels of grief symptoms in treatment studies.

Another important question is whether a thoroughgoing focus on grief is therapeutic even for persons with severe and persistent grief symptoms. One way to address this question would be a controlled trial where bereaved participants are randomly assigned to either a grief-focused or a symptom-focused intervention. An alternate approach would be to investigate qualities of the therapeutic alliance in relation to the perceived emphasis and usefulness of a grief-focused intervention. In addition, researchers might profitably employ designs that examine the effectiveness of grief interventions in routine clinical settings, eschewing rigorous controls. In real-world settings, clinicians might rely on more generic therapeutic procedures that are less indebted to grief work and that may be more effective. Indeed, investigators have argued that research on grief interventions should take greater account of the broader literature on psychotherapy outcomes, in which nonspecific, relational, and contextual aspects are widely regarded as the active ingredient in psychotherapy (Jordan & Neimeyer, 2003). In this broader framework, grief counseling would be based not on specific therapeutic procedures but on more generally accepted principals of sound clinical practice (Beutler, 2000). It may also be useful to consider taking this idea still further, as discussed earlier, by exploring the efficacy of interventions that are explicitly not about bereavement or grief. Rather, such interventions would focus on building personal strengths and expanding the self, and on ameliorating deficits in social functioning that may have previously blocked patients from obtaining the type of social support that could buffer negative reactions to loss. Our recommendations for practice are consistent with these alternate conceptualizations of grief counseling.

REFERENCES

Allumbaugh, D.L., & Hoyt, W.T. (1999). Effectiveness of grief therapy: A meta-analysis. *Journal of Counseling Psychology, 46,* 370–380.

American Psychiatric Association. (1994). *Diagnostic and statistical manual of mental disorders* (4th ed.). Washington, DC: Author.

Archer, J. (1999). *The nature of grief: The evolution and psychology of reactions to loss.* New york: Routledge.

Beutler, L. E. (2000). David and Goliath: When empirical and clinical standards of practice meet. *American Psychologist, 55,* 997–1007.

Boerner, K., Wortman, C. B., & Bonanno, G. A. (in press). Resilient or at risk?: A four-year study of older adults who initially showed high or low distress following conjugal loss. *Journal of Gerontology: Psychological Science.*

Bonanno, G. A. (2001). The crucial importance of empirical evidence in the development of bereavement theory: Reply to Archer (2001). *Psychological Bulletin, 127,* 561–564.

Bonanno, G. A. (2004). Loss, trauma, and human resilience: Have we underestimated the human capacity to thrive after extremely aversive events? *American Psychologist, 59,* 20–28.

Bonanno, G. A. (in press). Resilience in the face of extreme adversity. *Current Directions in Psychological Science.*

Bonanno, G. A., & Field, N. P. (2001). Examining the delayed grief hypothesis across 5 years of bereavement. *American Behavioral Scientist, 44,* 798–816.

Bonanno, G. A., & Kaltman, S. (1999). Toward an integrative perspective on bereavement. *Psychological Bulletin, 125,* 760–776.

Bonanno, G. A., & Kaltman, S. (2001). The varieties of grief experience. *Clinical Psychology Review, 21,* 705–734.

Bonanno, G. A., & Keltner, D. (1997). Facial expressions of emotion and the course of conjugal bereavement. *Journal of Abnormal Psychology, 106,* 126–137.

Bonanno, G. A., Keltner, D., Holen, A., & Horowitz, M. J. (1995). When avoiding unpleasant emotions might not be such a bad thing. *Journal of Consulting and Clinical Psychology, 69,* 975–989.

Bonanno, G. A., Mihalecz, M. C., & LeJeune, J. T. (1999). The core emotion themes of conjugal bereavement. *Motivation and Emotion, 23,* 175–201.

Bonanno, G. A., Moskowitz, J. T., Papa, A., & Folkman, S. (2004). *Resilience to loss in bereaved spouses, bereaved parents, and bereaved gay men. Journal of Personality and Social Psychology,* 88, 827–843.

Bonanno, G. A., Papa, A., Lalande, K., Nanping, Z., & Noll, J. G. (in press). Grief processing and deliberate grief avoidance: A prospective comparison of bereaved spouses and parents in the United States and China. *Journal of Consulting & Social Psychology, 83,* 1150–1164.

Bonanno, G. A., Rennicke, C., & Dekel, S. (2004). *Self-enhancement among high-exposure survivors of the September 11th terrorist attack: Resilient or socially maladjusted? Journal of Personality and Social Psychology,* 88, 984–998.

Bonanno, G. A., Wortman, C. B., Lehman, D. R., Tweed, R. G., Haring, M., Sonnega, J., et al. (2002). Resilience to loss and chronic grief: A prospective study from preloss to 18-months postloss. *Journal of Personality & Social Psychology, 69,* 975–989.

Bonanno, G. A., Wortman, C. B., & Nesse, R. M. (2004). Prospective patterns of resilience and maladjustment in widowhood. *Psychology & Aging, 19,* 260–271.

Bonanno, G. A., Znoj, H. J., Siddique, H., & Horowitz, M. J. (1999). Verbal-autonomic response dissociation and adaptation to midlife conjugal loss: A follow-up at 25 months. *Cognitive Therapy and Research, 23,* 605–624.

Bowlby, J. (1980). *Loss: Sadness and depression (Attachment and loss, Vol. 3).* New York: Basic Books.

Deutsch, H. (1937). Absence of grief. *Psychoanalytic Quarterly, 6,* 12–22.

Fraley, R. C., & Shaver, P. R. (1999). Loss and bereavement: Attachment theory and recent controversies concerning "grief work" and the nature of detachment. In J. Cassidy & P. R. Shaver (Eds.), *Handbook of attachment: Theory, research, and clinical applications* (pp. 735–759). New York: Guilford Press

Greenberg, M. A., Wortman, C. B., & Stone, A. A. (1996). Emotional expression and physical heath: Revising traumatic memories or fostering self-regulation? *Journal of Personality & Social Psychology, 71,* 588–602.

Holmes, T., & Rahe, R. (1967). The social readjustment scale. *Journal of Psychosomatic Research, 11,* 213–218.

Horowitz, M. J., Siegel, B., Holen, A., Bonanno, G. A., Milbrath, C., & Stinson, C. H. (1997). Diagnostic criteria for complicated grief disorder. *American Journal of Psychiatry, 154,* 904–910.

Jacobs, S. (1993). *Pathologic grief: Maladaptation to loss.* Washington, DC: American Psychiatric Press.

Jordan, J. R., & Neimeyer, R. A. (2003). Does grief counseling work? *Death Studies, 27,* 765–786.

Kaltman, S., & Bonanno, G.A. (2003). Trauma and bereavement: Examining the impact of sudden and violent deaths. *Journal of Anxiety Disorders, 17,* 131–147.

Kato, P. M., & Mann, T. (1999). A synthesis of psychological interventions for the bereaved. *Clinical Psychology Review, 19,* 275–296.

Kelly, A. E., & McKillop, K. J. (1996). Consequences of revealing personal secrets. *Psychological Bulletin, 120,* 450–465.

Keltner, D., & Bonanno, G. A. (1997). A study of laughter and dissociation: Distinct correlates of laughter and smiling during bereavement. *Journal of Personality & Social Psychology, 73,* 687–702.

Kim, K., & Jacobs, S. (1991). Pathologic grief and its relationship to other psychiatric disorders. *Journal of Affective Disorders, 21,* 257–263.

Lepore, S. J., Ragan, J. D., & Jones, S. (2000). Talking facilitates cognitive-emotional processes of adaptation to an acute stressor. *Journal of Personality & Social Psychology, 78,* 499–508.

Lepore, S. J., Silver, R. C., Wortman, C. B., & Wayment, H. A. (1996). Social constraints, intrusive thoughts, and depressive symptoms among bereaved mothers. *Journal of Personality & Social Psychology, 70,* 271–282.

Lindemann, E. (1944). Symptomatology and management of acute grief. *American Journal of Psychiatry, 101*, 1141–1148.

Lucas, R. E., Clark, A. E., Georgellis, Y., & Diener, E. (2003). Reexamining adaptation and the set point model of happiness: Reactions to changes in marital status. *Journal of Personality & Social Psychology, 84*, 527–539.

Mancini, A. D., Pressman, D. L., & Bonanno, G. A. (in press). Clinical interventions with the bereaved: What clinicians and counselors can learn from the CLOC study. In D. Carr, R. M. Nesse, & C. B. Wortman (Eds.), *Late life widowhood: New directions in theory, research, and practice.* New York: Springer Publishing.

Middleton, W., Burnett, P., Raphael, B., & Martinek, N. (1996). The bereavement response: A cluster analysis. *British Journal of Psychiatry, 169*, 167–171.

Middleton, W., Moylan, A., Raphael, B., Burnett, P., et al. (1993). An international perspective on bereavement related concepts. *Australian & New Zealand Journal of Psychiatry, 27*, 457–463.

Moskowitz, J.T., Folkman, S., & Acree, M. (2003). Do positive psychological states shed light on recovery from bereavement? Findings from a 3-year longitudinal study. *Death Studies, 27*, 471–500.

Murphy, S. A., Johnson, L. C., & Lohan, J. (2003). Challenging myths about parents' adjustment after the sudden, violent death of a child. *Journal of Nursing Scholarship, 35*, 359–364.

Neimeyer, R. A. (2000). Searching for the meaning of meaning: Grief therapy and the process of reconstruction. *Death Studies, 24*, 541–558.

Nolen-Hoeksema, S., Parker, L. E., & Larson, J. (1994). Ruminative coping with depressed mood following loss. *Journal of Personality & Social Psychology, 67*, 92–104.

Ong, A. D., Bergeman, C. S., & Bisconti, T. L. (2004). The role of daily positive emotions during conjugal bereavement. *Journal of Gerontology: Psychological Sciences, 59B*, 168–176.

Parkes, C. M., & Weiss, R. S. (1983). *Recovery from bereavement.* New York: Basic Books.

Pennebaker, J. W. (1993). Social mechanisms of constraint. In D. Wegner & J.W. Pennebaker (Eds.), *Handbook of mental control. Century psychology series* (pp. 200–219). Englewood Cliffs, NJ: Prentice Hall.

Prigerson, H. G., Maciejewski, P. K., Reynolds, C. F., III, Bierhals, A. J., Newsom, J. T., Fasiczka, A., et al. (1995). Inventory of complicated grief: A scale to measure maladaptive symptoms of loss. *Psychiatry Research, 59*, 65–79.

Prigerson, H. G., Shear, K., Beirhals, A. J., Pilkonis, P. A., Wolfson, L., Hall, M., et al. (1997). Case histories of traumatic grief. *Omega—Journal of Death & Dying, 35*(1), 9–24.

Prigerson, H. G., Shear, K., Jacobs, S. C., Reynolds, C. F., Maciejewski, P. K., Rosenheck, R., et al. (1999). Consensus criteria for traumatic grief: A rationale and preliminary empirical test. *British Journal of Psychiatry, 174*, 67–73.

Rando, T. A. (1993). *Treatment of complicated mourning.* Champaign, IL: Research Press.

Raphael, B., Minkov, C., & Dobson, M. (2001). Psychotherapeutic and pharmacological intervention for bereaved persons. In M.S. Stroebe, R.O. Hansson, W. Stroebe, & H. Schut (Eds.), *Handbook of bereavement research: Consequences, coping, and care* (pp. 587–612). Washington, DC: American Psychological Association.

Rynearson, E. K. & McCreery, J. M. (1993). Bereavement after homicide: A synergism of trauma and loss. *American Journal of Psychiatry, 150,* 258–261.

Schut, H.A., Stroebe, M.S., van den Bout, J., & Terheggen, M. (2001). The efficacy of bereavement interventions: Determining who benefits. In M.S. Stroebe, R.O. Hansson, W. Stroebe, & H. Schut (Eds.), *Handbook of bereavement research: Consequences, coping, and care* (pp. 705–738). Washington, D.C: American Psychological Association.

Shear, M. K., & Frank, E. (in press). Traumatic grief treatment. In J. Ruzek (Ed.),

Shear, M. K, Frank, E., Foa, E., Cherry, C., Reynolds, C. F., III, Vander, J., et al. (2001). Traumatic grief treatment: A pilot study. *American Journal of Psychiatry, 158,* 1506–1508.

Stein, N. L., Folkman, S., Trabasso, T., & Christopher-Richards, A. (1997). Appraisal and goal processes as predictors of well-being in bereaved caregivers. *Journal of Personality & Social Psychology, 63,* 980–988.

Stroebe, M. S., Stroebe, W., Schut, H., & van den Bout, J. (2002). Does disclosure of emotions facilitate recovery from bereavement? Evidence from two prospective studies. *Journal of Consulting & Clinical Psychology, 70,* 169–178.

Stroebe, W., & Schut, H. (2001). Risk factors in bereavement outcome: A methodological and empirical review. In M.S. Stroebe, R.O. Hansson, W. Stroebe, & H. Schut (Eds.), *Handbook of bereavement research: Consequences, coping, and care* (pp. 349–371). Washington, DC: American Psychological Association.

Stroebe, W., & Stroebe, M. S. (1991). Does "grief work" work? *Journal of Consulting & Clinical Psychology, 59,* 479–482.

Worden, J. W. (1991). *Grief counseling and grief therapy: A handbook for the mental health practitioner* (2nd ed.). New York: Springer Publishing.

Wortman, C. B., & Silver, R. C. (1989). The myths of coping with loss. *Journal of Consulting & Clinical Psychology, 57,* 349–357.

Wortman, C. B., & Silver, R. C. (2001). The myths of coping with loss revisited. In M.S. Stroebe, R.O. Hansson, W. Stroebe, & H. Schut (Eds.), *Handbook of bereavement research: Consequences, coping, and care* (pp. 405–429). Washington, DC: American Psychological Association.

Zisook, S., Chentsova-Dutton, Y., & Shuchter, S. R. (1998). PTSD following bereavement. *Annals of Clinical Psychiatry, 10,* 157–163.

Zisook, S., Paulus, M., Shuchter, S. R., & Judd, L. L. (1997). The many faces of depression following spousal bereavement. *Journal of Affective Disorders, 45*(1–2), 85–94.

CHAPTER 3

Psychological First Aid

Clarifying the Concept

Gerard A. Jacobs and David L. Meyer

INTRODUCTION

"Psychological first aid" (PFA) is a term whose meaning has been both murky and complex in the professional literature. The concept of PFA has come into wide use in much of the world. The term is used in newspaper articles, on television news stories, and in the professional literature. Having a discussion of this topic with colleagues, however, brings to mind the often-cited allegory of a group of people who are blindfolded and trying to describe an elephant only by holding on to one portion of it, with one describing the legs, one the trunk, one the tail, etc. Each produces a very different description of the elephant. PFA is a term that is understood differently by many different people in the mental health professions. The purpose of this chapter is to advocate for a common professional understanding of the term, with the purpose of facilitating greater clarity in communication and the more rapid and effective development of PFA, including a more efficient scientific appraisal of its usefulness and refinement of its design and implementation.

It is frequently assumed that PFA is a term recently coined. In fact, the history of the term itself originates at least as early as the closing days of World War II (Blain, Hoch, & Ryan, 1945).

PFA AS A VAGUE OR GENERIC TERM

PFA has often been used in a vague way (Remke & Schroder, 1993) or as a generic term in referring to immediate or early psychological support (Raphael, 2003). Sometimes authors have merely pointed out that "it" (PFA) was needed without defining what "it" was (Streufert, 2004). Wilson, Raphael, Meldrum, Bedosky, and Sigman (2000) refer to PFA in passing, recommending that it be taught as part of physical first aid. There are also studies that use terms similar to PFA. For example, Lundin (1994) discussed strategies for reducing post-traumatic stress disorder in the context of preventive psychiatry, and referred matter-of-factly to "emotional first aid."

CONFUSING PFA WITH CRITICAL INCIDENT STRESS DEBRIEFING OR DISASTER MENTAL HEALTH

The term "psychological first aid" has frequently been used informally, often without definition, or as a substitute for other terminology. This has certainly contributed to confusion about PFA.

A number of articles have essentially equated the terms PFA and Critical Incident Stress Management (CISM; Taylor, 2002) or debriefing (Litz, Gray, Bryant, & Adler, 2002; Macy, Behar, Paulson, Delman, Schmid, & Smith, 2004; Taylor). Mitchell and Everly (1994) defined Critical Incident Stress Debriefing (CISD) as "a group meeting in which a traumatic event is discussed in a non threatening and structured manner. . . . A CISD is structured in that it follows a specific seven phase outline" (pp. 5–6). Mitchell and Everly also refer to the broad range of activities that have evolved around CISD as Critical Incident Stress Management (CISM).

These techniques were originally developed for use with firefighters and law enforcement officers, but they are widely used with many different audiences both the United States and internationally. There has been significant controversy over the use of debriefing techniques in recent years (National Institute of Mental Health [NIMH], 2002; Institute of Medicine, 2003), and using PFA as a substitute term for CISM or CISD or debriefing only serves to create confusion and contribute to misunderstanding in the field.

A number of articles have also equated PFA with disaster mental health or have alluded to PFA as the early stage of disaster mental health (e.g., Leach, 1995; Taylor, 2002; Weissberg, 2002). Jacobs (1995) defined disaster mental health as a field that "focuses on the mental health needs of those directly affected by disaster, or disaster relief personnel, and of those indirectly affected by disaster (secondary victims)" (p. 544). It is a comparatively recent field of study and practice, and has generally referred to services provided by mental health professionals, including crisis intervention, education, advocacy, problem solving, and referral to more traditional mental health services when there is a need.

PFA AS A DISTINCT STRATEGY
FOR PSYCHOLOGICAL SUPPORT

It is the experience of the present authors that a conceptualization has been emerging internationally in which "psychological support" is seen as a more overarching term, and disaster mental health and PFA are components of psychological support. Disaster mental health refers to services provided by mental health professionals in preparation for and during the emergency phase of a disaster operation. It is also sometimes used to refer to some of the long-term professional mental health services provided specifically to those directly affected by disaster.

PFA, on the other hand, is more akin to the concept of physical first aid. First aid refers to preliminary physical care provided by members of the general population, not by medical professionals. In minor cases of physical injury, first aid may suffice to provide the care an individual needs for recovery. There is often no need for follow-up with a medical professional. Similarly, PFA is basic "grassroots" psychological support provided for family, friends, neighbors, and colleagues by members of the general population, not by mental health professionals. Just as physical first aid can be used for injuries ranging from minor scratches to serious wounds, PFA can be used to provide psychological support for experiences ranging from minor stressors in daily life to traumatic events. Just as physical first aid teaches participants how to know when an injury requires professional medical attention, PFA teaches providers when and how to make referrals for professional mental health care.

With this view of PFA in mind the development of the model across time is described. More detail regarding PFA is provided later in the chapter.

Preparation for War

In the era of the cold war the American Psychiatric Association published a pamphlet on PFA to assist civil defense workers in preparing for reactions of the citizenry to a nuclear attack (Mental Health Materials Center, 1955). The pamphlet's descriptions of stress reactions (which included "wild running around," p. 37) seem outmoded. But the booklet encouraged civil defense workers to speak gently with those who were overwhelmed by the situation, and help them to become involved in the response efforts in simple and manageable ways. It also encouraged the workers to monitor their own emotions to ensure that they would not become overwhelmed, and offered some simple principles for self-care. Much of this advice would still seem on-target today.

Preparation for war was also the theme of Von Greyerz (1962), the Chief Medical Officer of the Swedish Civil Defense, whose book encouraged Europe to prepare for World War III. One of the book's four sections focused on PFA. It encouraged civil defense workers to recognize that most people will recover emotionally on their own, and that PFA needed to focus on those who were "loosing [sic] their emotional footing" (p. 86).

Von Greyerz cited four principles for effective PFA: (1) Permit everyone to have their own emotions. This included providing support with few words, not judging or pitying the individual, and allowing the affected individuals to experience their emotions. (2) Consider the patient's psychological incapacity as an injury. This required accepting that the person does not *want* to feel the way he or she does. It also advised the civil defense worker to find tasks for those affected that are within their capacity so that they can contribute to the recovery effort. (3) Try to judge the patient's capacity. This would involve allowing the person to talk about his or her experience, and asking questions about their background, education, and profession. This is similar to current concepts of active listening, albeit with a fairly limited focus. The dialogue was intended both to learn more about the patients and how they could contribute to the response. But Von Greyerz suggested that the dialogue itself was also therapeutic, in that the questioning showed respect for the patients by the civil defense worker, thus encouraging self-esteem on the part of the patients. (4) It was noted that a good helper needed to know him or herself well in order to help others. Knowledge of one's own emotional triggers and vulnerabilities was noted as an important skill. The worker was also admonished to realize the limitations of the help that could be offered in an emergency setting, and to come to an acceptance of those limitations before an event occurs (pp. 81–84). The model promoted by Von Greyerz seems to parallel to a fair degree portions of some current models of PFA.

EARLY MODELS OF PFA

Singer (1982) provided some early thoughts on the nature of disaster mental health, and discussed PFA as a part of that conversation. He suggested nine steps in providing PFA: "1) adopting a sensitive, sympathetic, and flexible attitude towards the wide variety of reactions that may be encountered; 2) ensuring that injured and frightened survivors are not left alone and children in particular are not separated from their parents; 3) making gestures and providing 'tokens' of a simple, practical nature which communicate psychologically that the survivors are being cared for (e.g., providing blankets, food and drinks); 4) encouraging the verbal expression of feelings associated with the disaster experience; 5) offering reassurance; 6) conveying accurate and responsible information to survivors, their loved ones, and the media, and dispelling rumors as they emerge; 7) referring individuals who are showing grossly abnormal, violent, or self-destructive behavior to psychiatric personnel and transferring such persons to a special treatment center so as to minimize their potentially disturbing influence on others; 8) issuing instructions in a confident, easy-to-follow manner; and 9) encouraging survivors to participate in simple, useful tasks as soon as possible—which, from the practical standpoint, means extra help when there are mass casualties" (p. 248).

Raphael (1986) in her pioneering book on disaster mental health, described PFA in the context of services provided in the first hours after a disaster. She saw PFA as including 11 components:

- *Comforting and consoling.* Within this discussion Raphael points out that sometimes the best way to communicate your compassionate care is to sit quietly with the person who has been affected. In our own authors' work in PFA *and* in disaster mental health this is referred to as "being present to" the individual.
- *Protect from further threat.* This may be particularly important if the individual is stunned and having difficulty processing; a common effect of traumatic stress.
- *Immediate care for physical necessities.* In both PFA and disaster mental health, the provision of food, shelter, and warmth are integrally linked with psychological support.
- *Helping affected individuals to become involved in goal-directed behavior.* Some gentle guidance may help the individual to shake off a sense that the experience is unreal. The principle of psychological recovery by caring for the needs of others was important to Alfred Adler's theories (Rychlak, 1981).
- Promote reunion with loved ones separated in the event. In Raphael's model this includes providing psychological support while the dead are identified if the loved ones have not been found among the living.
- In addition to the previous bullet, however, Raphael suggests that supporting individuals while they identify the body of a loved one is a process that merits its own category. Although genetic analysis has reduced the need for such activity, at the time of this writing it is still common in mass casualty events for survivors to need to identify the personal effects of the loved one, such as jewelry, clothing, luggage, and identification. This process shares many of the difficulties identified by Raphael as being associated with the identification of the loved one's body.

- *Accepting the ventilation of feelings.* Note that this does not mean trying to get everyone to talk about their experience, but rather listening when someone feels the need to talk. Raphael notes that this is a stage that may involve intense emotions and may require additional steps to be taken to provide adequate and safe support.
- *Structuring the routine of the individual to give a sense of order in the aftermath of the event.*
- *Promotion of groups' support networks.* Raphael recommends providing opportunities for individuals who have shared the event to get together, whether in family groups, with friends, or with neighbors.
- *Identify and refer individuals who need more traditional mental health care.*
- *Ensure* that the individual is linked to an ongoing system of care and support (pp. 257–260).

Walker (1990) wrote of PFA in a more general manner than did Raphael (1986), suggesting that stress be diffused through PFA. But Walker also offered a list of suggested components for PFA that reflect some common basic strategies for early psychological support and that largely overlap Raphael's model components:

- Understand the event and significant stressors
- Assess the participant's response
- Educate the participant about stress and grief reactions
- Provide the participant with realistic coping responses
- Develop a response plan that mobilizes the individual
- Encourage good physical self-care
- Encourage use of the participant's social support network
- Make appropriate referrals
- Provide follow-up (p. 128).

A somewhat more detailed conceptualization was offered by Ritchie (2003), who classified PFA as a distinct form of early intervention and as a component of disaster mental health. She proposed that PFA consisted of activities to be conducted in the first 48 hours after an event and included the following components:

- Protect survivors from further harm
- Reduce physiological arousal
- Mobilize support for those who are most distressed

- Keep families together and facilitate reunion with loved ones
- Provide information, foster communication and education
- Use effective risk communication techniques (p. 45).

Although these various authors discuss some components of PFA and portray it as a separate entity, reading most of these articles leaves an impression of vagueness and a poorly formed concept. Much greater clarity and detail were brought to PFA in the Red Cross movement.

PSYCHOLOGICAL FIRST AID WITHIN THE RED CROSS MOVEMENT

Danish Red Cross

The Danish Red Cross began a national program of PFA in 1990 (Knudsen, Høgsted, & Berliner, 1997). With a full time staff, there is a continuous program of training, continually construction of a network that is ready to support family, friends, and neighbors when difficult moments occur in life. The Danish model includes three general components: crisis intervention, human support, and the role of professionals. The latter component includes knowing when to make referrals to mental health professionals, as well as emphasizing the importance of self-care and psychological support for the PFA volunteers.

International Federation of Red Cross and Red Crescent Societies

The International Federation of Red Cross and Red Crescent Societies (IFRC) began to develop a psychological support program in 1991 (Simonsen & Reyes, 2003). An International Working Group was formed to explore strategies for psychological support within the Red Cross movement. The group selected PFA as the best form of psychological support to promote in assisting developing countries. The IFRC has supported the development of PFA programs in a number of countries, beginning with Bulgaria in 1996. The IFRC trained an International Roster for Psychological Support in 1998, and expanded that roster with additional training in 2000. IFRC-sponsored programs now operate in countries in Africa, Asia, Europe, and the Caribbean. The IFRC Reference Centre for Psychological Support has also provided Red Cross and Red Crescent national societies with resources and consultation to assist them in developing additional independent programs.

The IFRC published a manual for the training of trainers in psychological support (Simonsen & Reyes, 2003), which is being used in countries around the world. It contains a fairly detailed guide to conducting a week-long training in psychological support for future trainers. The model promoted by the manual includes six modules: (1) an introduction to psychological support; (2) basic concepts of stress, including coping skills and crisis intervention; (3) supportive communication; (4) promoting community involvement; (5) psychological support for special needs populations; and (6) providing psychological support for the helper. This model is built on 7 years of international experience in Europe, Asia, and Africa. It is modified to build on the strengths of each culture within which it is used. It provides a framework of techniques that have proven fairly universally effective. This framework is intended to be explored by local providers and expatriate consultants to develop a custom adaptation for each country within which it is employed.

American Red Cross

When the American Red Cross (Red Cross) originally developed its model for psychological support in the context of disasters, it based the approach on the use of mental health professionals providing disaster mental health. This model has worked well in the aftermath of thousands of disasters since its implementation in November 1991.

The terrorist attacks of September 11, 2001, however, strained the Red Cross' disaster mental health model to its limits. There are many physically limiting aspects of the disaster mental health model. There are finite limits to the number of mental health professionals trained, and even more restrictions on the number free to respond at any fixed time. There are limits to the ability to transport mental health professionals to places where they are needed. It is difficult to assess the need for psychological support in events that affect an entire nation, or for that matter, a large city. In the face of a very large-scale event, disaster mental health efforts will necessarily focus on effective public health messages serving the affected masses; the needs of individuals are likely to become of secondary importance. The following portion of this chapter describes a model of PFA that may be able to complement the disaster mental health model and provide better psychological support for affected individuals.

A MODEL OF PFA FOR THE FUTURE

As noted earlier, it is the present authors' perception that psychological support in the aftermath of disasters and other traumatic events is beginning to be conceptualized internationally as consisting of two components: disaster mental health and PFA. The United States has developed some sense of the potential impact of large-scale events as a result of the terrorist attacks of September 11, 2001. The scale of those events, however, is dwarfed by the potential size of other attacks with weapons of mass destruction, and even by possible naturally occurring pandemics. The number who died in the attacks of September 11, was roughly 3,000. In contrast, the United States Centers for Disease Control and Prevention (CDC) estimated in 1999 that a pandemic flu outbreak could result in the deaths of 89,000 to 207,000 Americans (Meltzer, Cox, & Fukuda, 1999).

The Institute of Medicine (IOM), which is part of the National Academy of Sciences, received a commission in 2002 to form a committee to "highlight some of the critical issues in responding to the psychological needs that result from terrorism and to provide possible options for intervention" (Institute of Medicine, 2003, p. 3).

The first author on this chapter was one of the seven IOM committee members given this charge. The committee studied the literature and took testimony and consultation from experts in the field. It also noted the potential for numerous small-scale terrorist attacks, such as the suicide bombings that have been so prominent in Israel and Iraq in recent years, and the snipers in the metropolitan Washington area who were attacking during the committee's work, as well as the possibility of very large-scale attacks against the United States using weapons of mass destruction.

The committee determined that there was a need for a new paradigm in providing psychological support, one that would supplement disaster mental health rather than replace it. The first recommendation of the IOM committee was to "develop evidence-based techniques, training, and education in psychological first aid to address all hazards and all members of society during the pre-event, event, and immediate post-event phases of a terrorism event in order to limit the psychological consequences of terrorism" (Institute of Medicine, 2003, p. 137).

The model of PFA described by the committee is rooted in the psychological support model that has evolved within the international Red Cross movement. Nevertheless, like other programs based on the IFRC model, the concept described by the IOM committee has become a uniquely American perspective; a model that "provides individuals with skills they can use in responding to psychological consequences of terrorism in their own lives, as well as in the lives of their family, friends, and neighbors. . . . PFA can be used to deal with the daily stresses of life (e.g., family strife, job stress, the academic and interpersonal challenges faced by schoolchildren). It is in these developments that the skills are tested, practiced, refined, and generally maintained as an active part of daily life. In this way, PFA may provide daily benefit, whether there are terrorism events or not. The development and implementation of PFA as a national strategy can serve as an intervention to provide possible benefits in dealing with the psychological consequences of smaller-scale random acts of violence" (Institute of Medicine, 2003, pp. 107–108). This is a classic "all hazards" approach to psychological support. The daily utility of these skills also contributes to the sustainability of PFA.

This model of PFA intends for the general population to be educated about stress and responses to stress (including traumatic stress), active listening, resilience and coping skills, and when and how to make referrals to mental health professionals (Institute of Medicine, 2003, p. 108). Other portions of the committee's report address the need for teaching the public risk assessment and hazard analysis skills to gauge the comparative importance of the threats that they face (p. 94). It seems appropriate to add this component to the PFA curriculum, since assessing risk helps the individual determine whether he/she realistically needs to be more concerned about a terrorist attack or about having an automobile accident on the way to work that day.

This model places the focus of mental health on the individual, where realistically the responsibility has always been. Mental health professionals don't "heal" clients in therapy; they merely give them the tools to make repairs to their psyche and their coping skills. People deal with the daily stresses and hassles of life every day. Individuals develop serious health problems. Loved ones die. Relationships grow difficult or end. Children get injured or get into trouble. People respond to these life stressors by summoning their own coping skills and by turning to family, friends, spiritual leaders, and primary care providers. Even in disasters, Revel's model (Sonniks, Revel, & Jacobs, 1998) estimates that 70–90% of the individuals affected turn to those same sources for support, and they are resilient enough to work through such events. Doesn't it seem logical, then, to focus on strengthening these existing resources in enhancing psychological support, rather than to expect individuals in the face of great stress in their lives to turn to a mental health system that is not part of the individual's daily experience, and which carries with it a social stigma?

PFA can be community based. This means that it is adapted to build on the strengths of the cultural milieu within which an individual lives on a daily basis. When the first author was developing psychosocial support programs in the aftermath of the 2001 earthquake in Gujarat, India, he learned that, in the Indian view, the word *community* refers to a group of people who share common interests based on occupational, religious, and ethnic aspects of their lives. Thus, a person may be a member of several communities, while at work or school, while at home, or while participating in cultural or religious rituals and ceremonies. When PFA is taught to a group of volunteers, it can incorporate the strengths of each of these communities. And when PFA is applied, it is offered within the context of the community and can build on the resources the community offers. Moreover, because people are serving their families, friends, and neighbors, the support is provided by someone familiar with the customs, values, and needs of those being served and is likely to reflect cultural sensitivity and awareness. This is likely to reduce the chances of members of minority communities in the population being alienated from the psychological support program,

PFA is also a low-cost model of psychological support, which further contributes to the sustainability of the program. There are initial start-up costs in the training materials and initial training of trainers. But just as in the current Red Cross physical first aid program, a large portion of the PFA courses can be taught by volunteers as part of their community service, and the provision of the services themselves are performed by volunteers.

It is important to maintain a line of authority and supervision in this work, and in the model promoted by the first author this is done by having community psychological-support team leaders who would offer support for the community providers. Team leaders would receive additional training in PFA and in determining the need for referrals. Community providers could turn to these team leaders with questions or when they felt that someone had a need for a different level of care. Team leaders would, in turn, be supervised by volunteer mental health professionals, who could help determine whether there was a need to make a referral to a higher continuum of care. Each professional could supervise a number of team leaders. In this model, then, the mental health professional can focus on those genuinely in need of professional services, rather than working with a broad range of the general population and attempting to screen out those who need more professional assistance. This is a more effective use of professionals' time and expertise, and it provides the volunteer mental health professional with a more meaningful involvement in the psychological support system.

In June 2004 the Red Cross gathered a dozen technical experts at its national headquarters in Washington, DC. The first author was a member of that committee. Their charge was to shape the future of Disaster Mental Health Services within the Red Cross based on what had been learned in the first 12 years of its function. This committee noted the degree to which the September 11th relief operations strained the disaster mental health model, the success of the IFRC PFA model in countries around the world, and the recommendations of the IOM committee discussed above. They unanimously endorsed the development of an American model of community-based PFA, to be implemented in communities across the nation as part of the Red Cross psychological support preparedness program.

The authors endorse a model of PFA training that includes: what it's like to be a helper, stress and traumatic stress, active listening, risk assessment, when and how to make referrals, issues involving supervision, ethics, and self-care. This can be provided in one full-day's training, a similar commitment to that of being trained in first aid and cardiopulmonary resuscitation (CPR).

It is critically important that community PFA volunteers, and even PFA team leaders, be taught the limitations of PFA. This form of psychological support is intended to help individuals experiencing ordinary reactions to extraordinary events. In PFA training, participants learn about those ordinary reactions, and how to recognize reactions that fall outside those boundaries. The guidelines promoted by the present authors are that the PFA volunteer should consult with a team leader or mental health professional for a possible referral to the higher continuum of care when: (a) someone experiences a physical, emotional, cognitive or behavioral reaction that exceeds the limits of "ordinary reactions"; (b) when ordinary reactions last more than 4 to 6 weeks after the end of an event; (c) when an individual's reaction begins to negatively affect her or his functioning at work or school, in the family, or in the individual's private life; or (d) whenever an individual would like to receive psychological support from a mental health professional. The present authors believe that such an education of the general population will increase the public's understanding of the role of mental health professionals and reduce the stigma that may currently be associated with receiving professional psychological care.

It is important for PFA to be developed as preparedness for disasters and terrorist attacks and not as a reaction. The development of community-specific trainings can be a lengthy process, and internalizing the knowledge and coping skills taught in PFA can also take time. If a community or the nation wishes to use PFA for psychological support, the time to begin the process is now—or maybe yesterday.

EMPIRICAL EVIDENCE BASE

The evidence base for the success of PFA consists of internal qualitative reports on programs developed with the assistance of the IFRC. Beyond that, the face validity of the model is its major cornerstone. The IOM committee on the psychological consequences of terrorism recognized the importance of this issue. "It is crucial that an evidence base for PFA be developed as well as models for training. As the evidence base is developed, education regarding substance use and abuse issues should also be included. Developmentally appropriate models are needed that [can] be applied to individuals across age levels and racial/ethnic and cultural groups" (Institute of Medicine, 2003, pp. 107–108).

The present authors are currently considering models for the empirical examination of PFA. These are likely to fall into two categories. One group of studies would examine the relative merits of individual components of PFA, that is, does one technique work better than another in a given situation? The other category of studies would be to assess the psychological health of comparable communities struck by disaster in which one community has implemented PFA and the other has not. But the vagaries of disaster may realistically mean that such a comparison will not take place until a large number of communities have initiated PFA programs.

CONCLUSIONS

PFA is a form of psychological support that teaches individuals how to care for themselves and to provide basic psychological support for family, friends, and neighbors. The model of PFA promoted in the present chapter is relevant in daily life, community-based, low-cost, sustainable, culturally sensitive, appropriate for populations with special needs, and can be present wherever and whenever it is needed. It is a program that also educates the public about the role of mental health professionals and when and how to make referrals for more traditional mental health care. Mental health professionals serve as design consultants, trainers, supervisors, and bridges to the higher continuum of psychological care. Implementing such a PFA model on a national level will be challenging, and it will be a lengthy process. But the realization of such a model for psychological support will result in a nation better prepared for the next major traumatic event.

REFERENCES

Blain, D., Hoch, P., & Ryan, V. G. (1945). A course in psychological first aid and prevention. *American Journal of Psychiatry, 101*, 629–634.

Institute of Medicine. (2003). *Preparing for the psychological consequences of terrorism: A public health strategy.* Committee on Responding to the Psychological Consequences of Terrorism. A. Stith Butler, A.M. Panzer, L.R. Goldfrank (Eds.). Washington, DC: National Academies Press.

Jacobs, G.A. (1995). The development of a national plan for Disaster Mental Health. *Professional Psychology: Research and Practice, 26*(6), 543–549.

Knudsen, L., Høgsted, R., & Berliner, P. (1997). *Psychological first aid and human support*. Copenhagen, Denmark: Danish Red Cross.

Leach, J. (1995). Psychological first-aid: A practical aide-memoire. *Aviation, Space, & Environmental Medicine, 66*(7), 668–674.

Litz, B., Gray, M., Bryant, R., & Adler, A. (2002). Early intervention for trauma: Current status and future directions. *Clinical Psychology: Science & Practice, 9*(2), 112–134.

Lundin, T. (1994). The treatment of acute trauma: Post-traumatic stress disorder prevention. *Psychiatric Clinics of North America, 17*(2), 385–391.

Macy, R., Behar, L., Paulson, R., Delman, J., Schmid, L., & Smith, S. (2004). Community-based, acute posttraumatic stress management: A description and evaluation of a psychosocial-intervention continuum. *Harvard Review of Psychiatry, 12*(4), 217–228.

Meltzer, M.I., Cox, N.J., & Fukuda, K. (1999). The economic impact of pandemic influenza in the United States: Priorities for intervention. *Emerging Infectious Diseases, 5*(5), 659–671.

Mental Health Materials Center. (1955). Psychological first aid in disasters. *American Journal of Nursing, 55*, 437–438.

Mitchell, J.T., & Everly, G.S. (1994). *Human elements training for emergency services, public safety and disaster personnel: An instructional guide to teaching Debriefing, Crisis Intervention, and Stress Management Programs*. Ellicott City, MD: Chevron Publishing.

National Institute of Mental Health. 2002. *Mental health and mass violence: Evidence-based early psychological intervention for victims/survivors of mass violence. A workshop to reach consensus on best practices*. NIH Publication No. 02–5138. Washington, DC: U.S. Government Printing Office.

Raphael, B. (1986). *When disaster strikes*. New York: Basic Books.

Raphael, B. (2003). Early intervention and the debriefing debate. In R. Ursano (Ed.), *Terrorism and disaster: Individual and community mental health interventions*, (pp. 146–161). New York: Cambridge University Press.

Ritchie, E. (2003). Mass violence and early intervention: Best practice guidelines. *Primary Psychiatry, 10*(8), 43–48.

Rychlak, J.F. (1981). *Personality and Psychotherapy* (2nd ed.). Boston: Houghton-Mifflin.

Simonsen, L. F. & Reyes, G. (2003). *Psychological support with a community-based approach: A Red Cross/Red Crescent training manual*. Geneva, Switzerland: International Federation of Red Cross and Red Crescent Societies.

Singer, T. (1982). An introduction to disaster: Some considerations of a psychological nature. *Aviation, Space, & Environmental Medicine, 53*(3), 245–250.

Sonniks, M., Revel, J-P., & Jacobs, G.A. (1998). *Psychological Support. World Disaster Report: 1998*. Geneva, Switzerland: International Federation of Red Cross and Red Crescent Societies.

Streufert, B. (2004). Death on campuses: Common postvention strategies in higher education. *Death Studies, 28*(2), 151–172.

Taylor, A. J. (2002). Coping with catastrophe: Organising psychological first-aiders. *New Zealand Journal of Psychology, 31*(2), 104–109.

Von Greyerz, W. (1962). *Psychology of survival: Human reactions to the catastrophes of war.* Oxford, England: Elsevier.

Walker, G. (1990). Crisis-care in critical incident debriefing. *Death Studies, 14*(2), 121–133.

Weissberg, N. (2002). Comment on Barry Lubetkin's personal narrative regarding September 11. *Behavior Therapist, 25*(9), 172.

Wilson, J., Raphael, B., Meldrum, L., Bedosky, C., & Sigman, M. (2000). Preventing PTSD in trauma survivors. *Bulletin of the Menninger Clinic, 64*(2), 181–196.

Part II

Community Interventions

CHAPTER 4

The Mobile Member Care Team as a Means of Responding to Crises
West Africa

Karen F. Carr

AN AMERICAN PSYCHOLOGIST
WORKING IN WEST AFRICA

I woke up at about 4 a.m. the morning of September 19, 2002, in Bouaké, Côte d'Ivoire, to the sound of machine guns. Our multidisciplinary team of three, known as the Mobile Member Care Team, had just begun leading a workshop for 14 cross-cultural workers, teaching them how to facilitate Sharpening Your Interpersonal Skills workshops (Williams, 2002) across West Africa. My first thought as I lay in bed and listened to the exchange of gunfire in the distance was that the gang of robbers who had been terrorizing the city for almost a year had finally been trapped and that they were having a shoot-out with the police. But, as the gunfire became more intense and went on and on, I began to suspect that we might be having another attempted coup in the country. The radio news at 6 a.m. confirmed that rebels were attacking government troops in three strategic locations in the country, including Bouaké, the city where we were training. This was the beginning of an 8-day siege that kept us trapped in a building, caught in the crossfire between government and rebel troops until we were finally evacuated out of Bouaké by French soldiers. When we got out, we were exhausted and in need of care. This time, instead of being the ones to provide the debriefing and care, we were on the receiving end of it. And we were ready for it.

Two months before, I was in this same city responding to a large-scale crisis. Eight armed robbers had entered a boarding school campus and spent the next couple of hours holding people hostage trying to get money. As they left, they shot and killed one of the security guards and took one of the missionaries hostage, telling him that they were going to kill him, and beating him around the face and head continuously. When they pulled over the car and got out to shoot him, he managed to escape, running a zig-zag route as bullets flew around him.

Our crisis team was called within hours of the robbery. I went up along with a visiting colleague, two psychology doctoral students who were there for a student practicum, and two missionaries we had trained to be peer crisis responders. We spent the next 2 days talking with adults and children, helping them restore some sense of calm, safety, and peace of mind. I remember sitting across from the man who had been taken hostage and looking at his bruised, swollen, and severely lacerated face as he talked about his ordeal. It struck me in that moment how personal this crisis felt to me—every person that I talked with that day was someone I had previously met, either in a workshop or in some social context. These people weren't just clients to me; they were my friends and their crises had an emotional impact on me.

One couple I met with after that crisis were dorm parents for junior high boys. I had done a psychological assessment as part of their screening process and had recommended that they be accepted into that position. The man was particularly affected by the robbery of the school. He saw the robbers drive off with his friend and felt a certain level of responsibility in not being able to prevent it from happening. Some weeks before, he and some of his friends had rushed over to a mission guesthouse nearby where a single missionary woman was locked inside while robbers were trying to break in. They managed to scare them off. This man talked with me about the stress he was feeling and how he was having difficulty sleeping at night. We talked about various ways he could lower his anxiety level. Some weeks later I heard that he had gone for some medical care because he was having chest pains. He was cleared of any medical problems. The day before the war started, this man was jogging around the campus track, and he fell over and died suddenly. Understandably, the entire campus, and especially his family, friends, and the junior high boys under his care, were already in an acute state of grief and shock when the war began. I had left the workshop to spend the day with the grieving family, and as I looked in the faces of his widow and children, I thought about our conversation from several weeks before. I remembered his wife saying how relieved she was that she had not been made a widow when he had attempted to rescue his friend who was being kidnapped. "I'm just glad that I'm not a widow today." Those words haunted me as I looked at her grieving face. This woman and her children were not just clients to me. They were part of my personal life, part of the fabric of my social support system. I was in their world, they were in mine, and our worlds had been permanently changed.

The Mobile Member Care Team first came to Abidjan, Côte d'Ivoire, in 2000 to set up base and begin providing training and crisis response to missionaries across West Africa, a region about two-thirds the size of the U.S. We came with vision and passion—a vision to see missionaries and cross-cultural workers thriving in their work, not just surviving it. We came with a love for Africa and Africans and a desire to learn more about the diverse and rich cultures on the continent. We knew that by living in West Africa, we too would be exposed to crisis and trauma, and an ongoing challenge would be to maintain our own mental health while also trying to help the people around us. But, it is one thing to know the risks intellectually and another thing to live them day in and day out. That is why we were glad to receive care ourselves from mental health professionals who came from the States shortly after we were evacuated from Bouaké. They met us in Abidjan, our home base, and spent hours with us individually and as a team.

During that time, I was able to talk about the series of stressful events I had experienced over the past year and to begin to work through some of the emotional implications and personal lessons. I talked about the fears I had when we harbored 40 Liberian refugees during that 8-day siege—fear that mobs would come to kill them before our eyes. I talked about the pain of seeing people from Burkina Faso who had been burned out of their homes by Ivoirian militia, carrying all their possessions on their backs as they walked through our parking lot. I talked about the grief of seeing a country as beautiful and promising as Côte d'Ivoire begin to crumble and decay before our eyes because a few people wanted war while the majority longed for peace. I cried, I asked questions that didn't have answers, and I went back to the roots of why I was there. I found that those roots were deep and enduring and that I could finally answer the question of whether or not I was cut out to do this work. It wasn't about my strength or energy or will, really. It was about knowing that this was exactly what I was supposed to be doing and what I was made to do. As long as I could do the work with a motivation of love for the people I was helping and joy in doing that work, then I could keep going. After a period of rest and vacation, which helped to restore us to a place of renewed energy and vision, we entered into a new season of our work.

Because the war continued, we were forced to relocate to a new country. So, as a team, we moved to Ghana, next door to Côte d'Ivoire. It was still centrally located in our 14-country service area and we were able to continue our efforts. This move also opened up new doors of opportunity for us to be more deeply involved with Africans.

WHAT IS THE MOBILE MEMBER CARE TEAM?

The Mobile Member Care Team (MMCT) is a nonprofit organization designed to provide training and crisis response to missionaries and cross-cultural workers living in West Africa. We work with the more than 10,000 missionaries and cross-cultural workers living in the 14 countries of West Africa, from Senegal to Nigeria. These workers come from many areas of the world (including the U.S., Canada, Europe, Brazil, Korea, Nigeria, and Ghana) and are members of a variety of organizations that focus on different services including medical care, community development, relief work, education, literacy, Bible translation, and church planting. Our goal is to help these workers cope and function effectively and with integrity in the midst of crises and constant exposure to violence.

We do this using a Community Psychology model, aiming to improve community life by promoting psychological well-being and preventing disorder. Using a primary prevention approach, we provide psycho-education that teaches practical skills such as how to manage conflicts, how to grieve, how to handle stress, and how to help others during crisis and trauma. These workshops serve the purpose of building awareness of needed skills, increasing existing skills, building and strengthening relationships within the communities, increasing knowledge, and creating networks. The training is very interactive, utilizing various methods of adult learning including small group tasks, whole group interaction, case studies, demonstration of skills, practicing skills, and personal reflection. Believing that there are already strengths and skills within the community that can be accessed and enhanced, we provide specialized crisis response training as a way of expanding helping resources within the community (Reissman, 1990).

Secondly, we provide direct care to cross-cultural workers with psychological assessments, brief therapy, crisis intervention, and the mentoring of individuals who can provide psychological first aid to their peers of individuals (whom we call peer responders). To date, over 1000 cross-cultural workers have directly accessed these MMCT services in West Africa.

Each team member of MMCT is supported by donations from churches and individuals. There are no salaries paid to staff. Organizational costs are covered by workshop registrations and donations given by individuals and organizations who believe in the need for such a service such as this.

WHAT KINDS OF CRISES DO WESTERNERS
LIVING IN WEST AFRICA EXPERIENCE?

Initially when we came to West Africa, our primary clientele consisted of Westerners involved in mission work or humanitarian aid. These were people who came from fairly wealthy nations (U.S., Canada, England, Holland, France, Germany, etc.) who were making large personal sacrifices to work in a developing country. There are stresses and crises that are unique to someone in this situation and they can perhaps be put into several categories:

Violent crime—This is often something that missionaries directly experience, as opposed to being something they witness. The most common incidents are armed robberies, carjackings, and assaults in the course of a robbery. Typically there is not a well-developed or adequate police force to respond to these crimes. Because of corruption in some countries, the police may also be involved in or overlook the crimes.

Violence related to war—This is typically not directed against missionaries, but they are observers to it and it may involve civil unrest, mobs, riots, and evacuation. Occasionally, missionaries may be caught in the crossfire or other war-associated events.

Cultural adjustment issues—Things that are most difficult to deal with in West Africa are heat, language difficulties, dealing with poverty, not understanding or accepting cultural norms or cues, difficult traveling conditions, corruption in government officials, and infrastructure breakdown (i.e., intermittent or lack of electricity, water, trash removal, phone, and Internet).

Health and sanitation—There is the constant threat of malaria, typhoid, dysentery, parasites, meningitis, AIDS, and injury or death from traffic accidents.

Job stress—There are constant demands and pressure, not enough time off, not enough staff, etc. A person may not be in a job that suits his/her skills.

Interpersonal crises—Most commonly these stem from the unresolved conflicts and tensions that come from being on a multicultural team that one did not choose. Many team members are living and working with each other under very high-pressure situations.

Grief and loss—There are many losses including separation from family (parents, adult children, or younger children placed in boarding schools), premature death of friends and colleagues, loss of security, safety, familiarity, possessions, hopes, dreams, and constant changes of friends and living situations.

The psychological consequences of living with these types of stresses on a daily basis without adequate resources to respond to them most typically include depression, anxiety, acute stress disorder, post-traumatic stress disorder, and the exacerbation of preexisting psychological conditions (i.e., personality disorders). When people or their organizations request counseling, the most typical presenting problems are burnout (fatigue, apathy, irritability, etc.), depression, anxiety, interpersonal conflicts, or behavioral problems with children. Upon assessment, many of these symptoms are related to unresolved grief or an accumulated response to ongoing stress or trauma. It's not uncommon to hear a missionary describe multiple traumas that he/she has experienced over the years and to discover that this is the first time he/she is talking about them.

Interestingly, many missionaries have lived with these kinds of stresses and have endured numerous crises, and yet have demonstrated a level of resilience and strength that is remarkable. Few studies have been done to examine the factors that contribute most significantly to this resilience, but in conversations with many of these individuals, several core themes emerged. One is a sense of call or purpose. Those who feel that they are fulfilling their life's purpose by being in that place are more able to endure loss, hardship, and disappointments than are those who came for other motivations such as attraction to the job, a sense of adventure, or pressure from a spouse or family. The problem with these latter motivations is that one may not end up in the job one came for, the setting may not be adventurous or romantic at all, and coming because of pressure from a family member will lead to a sense of resentment later on.

A second theme that emerges as significant is having a sense of strong social/emotional support. The literature has identified two key areas of support contributing to resilience, team cohesion, and consultative leadership style (J. Fawcett, 2002, 2003). We view team cohesion as a means of promoting resilience and lowering stress level overall, and therefore much of our programming is designed to promote better communication and to develop skills related to conflict management. Secondly, many cross-cultural workers reference the presence and attitude of their leaders as being a critical factor in how they coped with various traumas and stressors. In fact, there seems to be a distinct negative correlation between expressions of bitterness or disappointment in leadership during times of crisis and ability to adapt successfully to the losses of the trauma. This may be related to the actual support given by the leadership as well as the person's perception of and trust in their leadership in general (G. Fawcett, 2003).

These observations of what contributes to resilience and successful adaptation to crisis have helped to shape our programming, which aims to promote coping and prevent those things that may lead to premature attrition or unhealthy coping responses. Those programs are described in more detail in the section titled "The Workshops of MMCT—The Training Strategy."

PSYCHOLOGICAL ISSUES TO DEAL WITH AFTER BEING IN A WAR ZONE AND EVACUATING

A unique type of stress that many expatriates living in West Africa have had to cope with is evacuating from the country they are living in during times of war and immediate danger (Carr, 2004). The experience of being evacuated from Bouaké and then subsequently from Abidjan taught me several important lessons about the psychological impact of this kind of event, which have implications for the kinds of themes that are important to address in any counseling offered post-evacuation. The key psychological issues are as follows:

Guilt—One thing in the evacuee's mind is the people who are left behind. As we drove out of Bouaké, the streets were lined with Africans who were unable to leave. The silence was damning, the expressions hopeless, our guilt acute. The evacuee wonders what will happen to the ones left behind. There is a sense of abandoning others. This feeling may be more intense after one leaves and then realizes that he or she did not leave adequate resources behind (e.g., advance pay for any employees who had to stay). Guilt may be enhanced or diminished according to what African colleagues have said to their expatriate friends before they left—whether it was a message encouraging them to leave or a plea to stay. Leaders may be particularly prone to guilt depending on how they made the decision for themselves and others to leave and how their followers or national colleagues have responded to them (e.g., with compliance or with resentment, criticism, and anger).

Anxiety—While we were under siege in Bouaké, we received frequent calls from the American embassy assuring us that they were working on getting us out of this dangerous situation. They repeatedly asked us for information about who was there and wanted to know the nationalities of each of us. We were a diverse group of 12 Americans, four Nigerians, and two Canadians. When the embassy personnel said, "Don't worry, we'll take care of our people," I reminded them that our group was not all Americans and was told that there would be no guarantee of the non-Americans being evacuated out. Our leadership team of four discussed among ourselves who would stay behind with the Nigerians if they were not allowed to come. We knew we would not leave them alone, but we did not know what the implications of that would be. There was constant uncertainty about this until the day and hour that we actually all got out. Another source of anxiety for us was related to the physical danger we faced. When the fighting was the most intense, there were bullets striking the building we were in and we all lay on the floor in a hallway corridor with mattresses against the windows to prevent being injured by shattered glass. We wondered what we would do if any of us were injured or had a medical crisis. There would be no way to get anyone safely to a medical facility. In fact, one of our participants did get malaria during these 8 days but we had medication for it with us. One of our team leaders fainted from the heat and dehydration, which gave us all a scare since our colleague from the school had died of an apparent heart attack just days before.

Another anxiety is knowing that friends and relatives who are far away are hearing the news of the war and that we may not be able to communicate with them concerning how things really are. Sometimes things are not as bad as the media is portraying it and sometimes they are worse. When we were under siege at Bouaké our phones worked the entire time we were there. I can remember at one point, when the shelling was particularly close, praying that my mother would not choose to call at that moment to find out how we were. Fortunately, she did not.

Additionally, there are anxieties and fears that come post-evacuation with the uncertainties of where one will live, what will happen to one's possessions, what will happen to those left behind, and what the future will hold in general. Ones goals and expectations all go through a process of re-evaluation and it is very helpful to have compassionate, patient leadership present during this time of questioning and uncertainty (J. Fawcett, 2002).

Grief—The evacuee feels a tremendous amount of sadness and grief during and after the evacuation. There are multiple losses. For our team, there was the loss of friends. Some of our expatriate friends and our governing board scattered to many different countries after the evacuation; others stayed behind. When we left for Ghana and said goodbye to our national friends and employees, we didn't know if we would ever see them again. There was also the loss of our home and possessions. As we left, we had to make the difficult choice of what was most important to put into a suitcase. Irreplaceable mementos such as photos and letters were the first to be packed. We were later able to have some of our things shipped over to Ghana, but others left everything behind and did not recover those things. The grief of evacuation continues after one leaves the country because many times the war is ongoing and from a distance one hears the news of atrocities such as rape, looting, mass graves, etc. This is currently the case in Côte d'Ivoire.

Anger—It's very common to feel a strong sense of anger and outrage at the injustices and senselessness of the war. This anger may be directed toward the organizational administration, particularly when evacuation decisions are made unilaterally or if the person did not agree with a team decision to evacuate. Individuals can be helped by guiding them to evaluate the intensity of their anger in relation to actual events and to find appropriate ways to express and release these feelings. One missionary child I worked with expressed strong feelings of anger toward the rebels who had started the war and said that he wanted to go fight them himself. He also manifested his anger at school and at home, getting into fights and losing his temper frequently. It helped him to be able to identify his anger as part of his grief related to the losses he had experienced because of the war. With counseling and the help of his parents, he was able to develop more adaptive ways of coping with those feelings.

Existential questions—Events such as evacuation raise questions such as "Why did this happen?"; "Why did God allow this to happen?"; "What is my purpose here?"; "Where is justice?" Many of these questions can't be answered, but just having the opportunity to ask them in the presence of a non-judging person who can sit with the ambivalence and uncertainty can be very helpful. Over time this person can gently guide evacuees to look at what they are learning from this and how they can grow as a result.

AFRICANS IN CRISIS

Shortly after we arrived in West Africa, we began to realize that even though our team consisted of all North Americans, our clientele would not just be other Westerners. There was a need and request for our services from Africans as well. At first we hesitated, feeling that what we had to offer had been developed by Westerners and might not apply to African culture. There was also the language barrier. All of our materials were in English and many of the African countries we work in are Francophone. However, Nigeria, Ghana, Sierra Leone, and Liberia are in our service area and are English speaking. We responded to a request to come to a gathering of Nigerian missionaries in 2002. This was our first test of using our workshop materials with Africans and we looked to them for input and feedback.

We spent several days speaking at the Nigerian Evangelical Missions Association (NEMA) conference. This was a spiritual renewal conference for Nigerian missionaries. The conference planners were expecting about 1,000 missionaries to come, but the overflowing main assembly hall was filled with 1,400 registered participants. We spoke twice to the whole group about managing stress, asking each of them to go through the process of identifying their stressors and their physical and emotional reactions to their stress, and then problem-solving ways that they could better manage this stress. This was done in 700 pairs! In the afternoon of each day, when the heat rose to about 102°, we did workshops for 300–400 at a time on managing conflicts. The four of us with the Mobile Member Care Team stood in the middle of a group of about 400 people who surrounded us in chairs, sitting as close together as they could. We were all outside, under a large tent covering, but the sun came through where we stood in the middle, dripping with sweat. We shouted at the top of our lungs because there was no microphone. In the back, a man stood in front of a group of about 30 people translating everything we said into Hausa, the local language, for a small group there who did not speak any English.

After a short time spent going over the handouts, we got them into pairs to talk about the areas of conflict management that they needed to work on; the sound was thunderous. I looked at the pairs and they were waving their arms, pointing to their handouts, sharing their hearts. Next we used role-play—asking two of the participants to demonstrate a scenario of handling a conflict poorly and then handling it well. Then we had them practice with made-up scenarios, handling a conflict using some general principles of healthy conflict resolution. The session addressed attitudes about conflict (e.g., a tendency to avoid it or a tendency to win at any cost to the relationship), but also addressed practical ways to resolve differences. We wondered how this seminar would translate cross-culturally. After all, in many non-Western cultures, conflicts are not resolved by face-to-face discussion, but rather through a third party or other indirect means such as storytelling. However, in many Nigerian cultures, there can be heated debate that occurs face to face and many organizations had already experienced divisions and staff attrition because of unresolved conflict. We didn't in any way discount cultural traditions of managing conflicts, but offered some alternatives, and these did not seem to present a problem for those present.

Later we met with over 100 organizational leaders who wanted to talk with us about how to improve member care in their organizations. We asked them about the kinds of stresses and challenges that their full-time volunteer staff were facing as they worked in cross-cultural settings. Many of the issues that they described overlapped with the kinds of crises experienced by Westerners living in West Africa. But there are perhaps some variations in the themes and patterns. Categories of crises for Africans working in human service careers might look like this:

Violence related to war—Rather than being mere observers, many African workers are in the midst of the war. They are direct targets because of the ethnic group or religious group to which they belong. Because of this they have experienced family members being killed before their eyes, family members being raped in front of them, torture, homes being burned down or destroyed, entire villages destroyed, disappearance of family members, separation from family members while fleeing the war (some of whom have never been reunited), and injuries caused by bombs, guns, machetes, and mines.

Economic stress/crisis—Many of the workers rely on the donations of family members, friends, or churches for their income and are under-supported, which means they are living at or below the poverty level. For many of them, this is a voluntary status—they have been educated as doctors, engineers, or teachers, but choose to volunteer their services for a para-church organization and sacrifice the security of a set income.

Children's education—Whereas Westerners tend to have schooling options for their kids such as boarding school, international schools, or home schooling, Africans do not have as many options and face serious challenges with getting a proper education for their children.

Job expectations and lack of margin (an insufficient reserve of time, energy, or finances)—Many African pastors and church workers are expected to be available to those in need 24 hours a day and do not feel that they have the right or permission to turn people away or to set office hours that would allow them to have rest and margin. This leads to neglect of families and self-care.

Although the types of crises or sources of stress may differ between Africans and Westerners, many of the internal stresses are the same. Cultural norms may affect patterns of response such as unwritten rules about how grief or anger is expressed, but often the cognitive, behavioral, and emotional responses to trauma, grief, and loss are remarkably similar. It is the human reaction to loss to deny, be angry, fearful, and sad, to withdraw, and gradually to re-enter and rebuild with new strengths, hopes, and the ability to help others (Greeson, Hollingsworth, & Washburn, 1990). This pattern is commonly manifested regardless of culture, age, religion, or gender.

In Rwanda there is a proverb that says a man should swallow his tears. Many African men that I have talked to have told me that in fact it is very unusual for an African man to cry (although it really does depend on the ethnic group he comes from). Of course, we often hear this from North American men as well. Recently, we conducted a workshop with 24 participants, half of whom were men from Nigeria and Ghana. One of the facilitators was a man and as he shared one story, he became tearful. Rather than being ashamed of this behavior or rejecting it, several of the Africans stood up at the end of the workshop and thanked this man for being a role model and for communicating that it was okay to cry.

In general, we seek to understand and respect cultural differences and norms as we work with people who are not from our own culture. But, we have learned that certain aspects of any culture (including and maybe especially North American culture) are not necessarily right or healthy just because they are the norm. We feel that we have gained the credibility and permission, by staying in a position of learners, sometimes to challenge cultural norms to the extent that they do not contribute to effective interpersonal relationships or to adaptive responses to trauma. A specific example would be a cultural norm that says that a woman who is raped should be ashamed of herself and should never talk about what happened. We are not value-free in our profession. We are not neutral. We have a mission and it is about promotion of mental health and the prevention of mental illness. Sometimes that means challenging cultural values and norms.

There are aspects of certain African cultures that seem to enhance one's ability to endure hardship. Some of the themes I have observed in many Africans that seem to promote resilience and community are:

- A lack of entitlement. Not always expecting to get what you want or what you think you have a right to helps one to endure disappointments and the failure of others.
- A tendency to apply grace when mistakes are made.
- An expectation that life will be difficult—not being taken by surprise when bad things happen.
- A strong sense of family and community—loyalty to one's relatives, clan, and tribe are extremely important.
- A high value placed on generosity and hospitality—this means giving freely to and welcoming others who are in need or who have less than you.

THE TRAUMA HEALING WORKSHOP—
A WORKSHOP FOR AFRICAN CHRISTIAN LEADERS

In 2004, our team was asked to help facilitate a trauma workshop that had been developed by staff from a mission that focuses on Bible translation into African languages and the application of scriptural principles to everyday life in Africa. The workshop was particularly designed for Christian community leaders from African countries that were currently experiencing or had recently experienced the trauma of war or ethnic conflict. Participants in this workshop came from Burundi, Uganda, Democratic Republic of Congo, Chad, Nigeria, Ghana, Côte d'Ivoire, Liberia, and Sierra Leone.

They all had personal stories of trauma, experienced in their hometowns, because of war and ethnic conflicts. Some of the violence was related to rebels seeking to destabilize the country and overthrow the ruling party. Some of it was related to two ethnic groups at odds with each other. Other violence related to tensions between Muslims and Christians.

One man described being in a bus that was ambushed. When the perpetrators left, 20 people had been killed. Another man talked about working with children who had been kidnapped and forced to be soldiers. He worked with a boy who had been forced to club his mother and then watch as other children were forced to club her to death. Another man described his personal trauma of losing his father, sister-in-law, and 6-year-old nephew during a raid on his village by Muslim fundamentalists. His father was a retired pastor and was shot and killed in front of his own house.

Still others talked about the kinds of atrocities that they had witnessed themselves or heard about from friends and family during the wars in their countries. They spoke openly about women being raped, sometimes with inanimate objects, people's arms and hands being chopped off, brothers selling their sisters for sex with soldiers, pregnant women being disemboweled, people being made to clap and dance as their houses burned down, and people being buried alive.

These were the images, sounds, and memories that people brought to the workshop. For many, the way to deal with these experiences had been just to try to forget them and to concentrate on moving on and helping others. Some were restricted by misconceptions of how Christians should deal with grief (e.g., that they should not show any grief or sadness, but should immediately move into a joyful or triumphant state). These misconceptions had blocked genuine healing from trauma.

We started each morning in a classroom setting using a textbook that was specifically developed for Africans (Hill, Hill, Bagge, & Miersma, 2004). Each chapter opens with an illustration from an African village setting. Half the group received their lessons in French and the other half in English depending on their country of origin. Topics included how emotional wounds can be healed, the process of grief and how to help people who are grieving, how to help children who are traumatized, how to help women who have been raped, helping people with AIDS, caring for the caregivers, a process for releasing emotional pain, forgiveness, dealing with ethnic conflicts, and crisis contingency planning. We looked closely at the kinds of spiritual questions that people ask during these types of events, such as, "Why does God allow suffering?" During these teaching sessions, our process included lecture, large and small group discussion, role-plays and demonstrations, stories, and case studies.

All but one of the 28 participants were men and for most of them this was the first time they had publicly discussed the topic of rape, which has typically been a taboo subject. We talked about the physical and emotional impact of rape on a woman and the kinds of things that make it worse for her (e.g., being blamed or ignored). We discussed ways that women who are raped can be helped medically as well as psychologically. Many of the men indicated that they never knew how women were affected by rape, and they committed to hold rape awareness seminars in their home towns as a way of more supportively responding to rape victims.

After the teaching sessions, the group went into their separate language groups and began to translate the written lessons into their own mother tongue so that these things could be taught in their home villages when they returned. Their translations were later checked by the staff to ensure true understanding of the meaning of the material, leading to accuracy of translation.

The group also had the opportunity to ask questions of the professional counselors present or to meet with them individually if they wanted. Some of the questions included things like wondering how to help a brother who had been forced to drink blood and was now having nightmares, or wondering how to help a friend who had been very angry and violent since the war. I had individual counseling sessions with several men from Côte d'Ivoire with the assistance of a translator. Many of them came asking for help with their children who were manifesting post-trauma behavioral problems such as regressive behavior, acting out, and difficulties in school.

Another strategy that we used to facilitate the expression of emotional pain was to give them the exercise of writing a song of lament in their own language. The elements of this song would include the wrongs that had been done to them, how they felt about it, and some kind of affirmation of their trust in God as their helper and provider. Each person wrote his or her own song and put it to traditional music and then shared it with the whole group.

Each evening, a few would come before the whole group and share their personal stories of trauma and pain. Even though most African men do not cry in public, some of those in our workshop did weep openly as they shared their stories. For some, it was the first time they had ever talked publicly about what they had experienced. For many, it was the first time they had shared their pain without having someone give them a pat answer or a sermon or tell them to stop thinking about it. The group responded to each person by quietly listening and then gathering around them with expressions of support and praying for them.

During the second week of the seminar, each person was given an opportunity to write down on a piece of paper the experiences and feelings they had were bringing them the most pain. They had a time of personal reflection and then shared these things in pairs. Afterwards the group came together and, in a special ceremony, each person walked to the front of the room where there was a large wooden cross and laid his or her paper at the foot of the cross, symbolizing the act of giving their pain over to Christ, who according to Christian beliefs is the pain-bearer. Then the papers were gathered up, taken outside, and burned as we all stood watching and quietly singing.

After this ceremony, one man shared that ever since his house had been destroyed, he had been obsessed with drawing up new house plans. He would draw plans over and over again and then destroy them. His wife tried to get him to stop but he felt that it was out of his control. After taking his wounds to the cross, this man testified that the destruction of his house was one of the things he had written on his paper and he genuinely felt that he had been released from his compulsion to draw house plans. The way he said it was, "My sickness of 'house' has been healed."

Two nights later, after the "taking our wounds to the cross" ceremony, we had a session where we identified where we ourselves were culpable. Many people in the midst of trauma had also done things that they were ashamed of or engaged in actions they knew were wrong. And many began to realize that they were still holding onto hatred and bitterness towards the people who had harmed them, killed their family members, burned their homes, and committed many atrocities. It was very hard to let go of this. Yet it seemed clear that this hatred and bitterness was the fuel for ongoing pain, deepening wounds, and a desire for revenge that seems to feed the continuing cycle of violence in so many countries. Forgiveness is a central aspect of the Christian faith. Jesus forgave His persecutors as He died on the cross and He commanded His followers likewise to forgive their enemies. However, it's a command that many Christians struggle with and are loathe to follow, especially when their persecutors have not asked for forgiveness and even continue to harm them and seem glad for their pain. Nonetheless, that evening, we all wrote down areas where we needed forgiveness and once again took those things to the cross. In the testimonies afterwards, many shared that they felt they had now forgiven the ones who had hurt them the most deeply. And for some, we could see a transformation in their facial expressions—from anger and pensiveness to genuine joy.

The seminar ended with a time of planning for the future. Specific goals were set for workshops like this to be held in the local areas in the coming months and for us as a group to meet again in early 2006 to assess progress and continue to do translation work together.

One always wonders about the long-term impact or effectiveness of a particular seminar. Time will tell, but immediately after the workshop, we gathered written evaluations from the participants to try to determine what the significance of the training had been for them. Many spoke of now having more hope and a decreased sense of anger and sadness. Quite a few referenced the significance of being able to let go of bitterness and to forgive the ones who had wronged them. Some referred to the value of better understanding the grief process and their plan to encourage others to mourn more genuinely rather than trying to cover over their feelings and deny their pain.

Overall, it seems that the aspect of the workshop that most impressed each person and resulted in life change was the process of identifying wounds, symbolically taking them to the cross (surrendering them to a trusted source), and choosing to forgive those who had caused their wounds. In a world filled with violence that has been perpetuated through the generations, perhaps workshops like these are a start to trying to end the cycle of retaliation and revenge.

THE WORKSHOPS OF MMCT—THE TRAINING STRATEGY

Three workshops currently form the core of our training strategy: Sharpening Your Interpersonal Skills (SYIS), Peer Response Training (PRT), and Member Care While Managing Crises (MCMC).

Sharpening Your Interpersonal Skills (SYIS)

The SYIS is a four-and-a-half day workshop developed over a period of nearly 30 years by Dr. Ken Williams of International Training Partners. MMCT has conducted 29 of these workshops over the past 4 years with 645 participants. This workshop provides training in key knowledge, attitudes and skills needed for developing and maintaining healthy relationships. Some of the topics are: listening, building trust, living in community, helping others manage grief, confrontation, conflict resolution, and managing stress. We facilitate six to eight of these a year in the region with about 24 participants from various mission organizations and countries of service in each workshop.

Aside from the personal growth that many experience through this workshop, we see other benefits too: We as an MMCT team are coming to know many missionaries in the region and are identifying the natural "people helpers" who are potential peer responders for the future. In addition, we are able to begin working relationships with mission leaders who take the workshop, which later makes a difference when we are called in as consultants during crisis situations. Also, missionaries from several organizations who have worked in the same area for decades are sometimes for the first time in a setting where they can build community and informal support networks across organizational lines. This is crucial on the front lines of mission work and far too often not the case. Additionally, for many of these cross-cultural workers, it may be the first time they have interacted with a psychologist. This gives them an opportunity in a non-threatening environment to develop a relationship with a mental health professional and break down negative stereotypical views about them.

Peer Response Training (PRT)

Building on the basic interpersonal skills covered in the SYIS, the PRT is a 6-day workshop designed for those already coming alongside their peers as helpers. The PRT workshop requires an application process that includes recommendations from their SYIS facilitators affirming their basic interpersonal skills; from their mission leader confirming their confidence in them, their availability to serve and the mission's intention to use them once trained; and from a mission peer who expresses confidence in their interpersonal skills in crisis situations.

MMCT has offered this workshop three times and has trained 51 cross-cultural workers to be peer responders. Participants learn about the typical impact and effects of crisis, the potential pathological effects, how to make initial contact, and how to provide one-on-one psychological first aid. The workshop also includes personal assessment of attitudes toward suffering. Other topics include when and how to make referrals and ethical issues such as confidentiality and boundaries. The last session of each day is a coaching group time when a group of four participants meets with the same staff person to share with one another what they have been learning and experiencing. These coaching relationships lend themselves to ongoing post-workshop mentoring through email, phone, and occasional visits as we travel through the region.

Recently there was a renewed eruption of fighting in Côte d'Ivoire and about 200 missionaries were evacuated from the country (some of them for the third time). They were scattered to at least four surrounding West African countries. In each of these locations, peer responders who had been trained by MMCT were involved in providing practical help in housing, food, and child care, as well as emotional and social support and the opportunity to talk about the crisis they had just experienced. At the time, all of the MMCT staff were off the continent and so were only able to provide coaching and mentoring from a distance. The feedback we received from the recipients of the peer debriefing care was very positive. One organizational administrator wrote the following to us after the crisis:

The Peer Responders met together a couple of times in Dakar to determine how best to handle all the different missions and needs. It was GREAT to see! Our group not only had a group debriefing, we also had Peer Responders come to talk with the children, youth and one on one individual debriefings. I was so thankful for how well our group accepted the whole concept and heard over and over how helpful it was for them. You all have done a great job of training people.

Though we still need objective measures to determine the efficacy of our programs, it was good to see that during a major crisis situation, those who had been trained to respond were available, worked cooperatively across organizational lines, and were very appreciated by the community they served.

Member Care While Managing Crises (MCMC)

By participating in the 5-day MCMC workshop, a mission leader will learn about normal responses to crisis and how to support others through the necessary stages of grief after loss or trauma. We address the strategic role a mission administrator plays in member care while managing crisis situations. Given the evidence that team cohesion and trust in leadership are two key factors in the mitigation of acute stress reactions in traumatic situations, this training is a particularly important strategy in trying to enhance the strength and skills of organizational leaders and to increase their leadership competence in crisis situations (J. Fawcett, 2002). Specific topics include: the impact of crisis; developing policies, procedures, and protocols; the dynamic of trust for leaders in crisis situations; confidentiality and communication; information management; assessment of vulnerable members; unique needs in cases of suicide, sexual assault, or evacuation; leadership styles in crisis; and the when, why and hows of debriefings and crisis committees. From 2000–2004, MMCT conducted four MCMC workshops with 86 organizational leaders and managers.

After the evacuation of about 200 missionaries from Côte d'Ivoire, a regional administrator who had been through this training and has also been involved on our Governing Board wrote the following related to the efficacy of the MMCT crisis training:

Congratulations, if you were to die tonight I think you could rest in peace because MMCT-WA is a total success in that an evacuation of a large country is taking place with no members of MMCT-WA on the continent and yet every mission group seems to be well cared for through the joint efforts of an army of trained peer debriefers. So yea, the hours registering people, writing materials, hauling suitcases from airport to airport, workshop training, coaching and sleeping in less than adequate conditions has paid off.

Six years ago that wouldn't have happened, or at best it would have been a fumbling attempt. Now because of MMCT there is a sort of missions without borders happening where the various mission communities are no longer in their own little boxes, but they know and are friends with others through common workshops and training and now they are helping each other and working for each other's well being.

Other Services of MMCT

Other programs of MMCT include providing assessment, short-term counseling, crisis intervention, and making referrals. The team has one psychologist who works with other mental health professionals who come for short-term visits. She is also able to work with a consulting psychiatrist who lives in Côte d'Ivoire when medical evaluations are warranted. MMCT has been involved in 164 clinical cases and has served 384 cross-cultural workers through psychological intervention over the past 4 years. Written requests for feedback regarding the effectiveness of this treatment have yielded positive self-reports related to recovery time, ability to remain in overseas service, self-acceptance as opposed to self-criticism, and depth of understanding of normal responses to trauma, which has decreased a sense of confusion and inadequacy.

MMCT also has a resource library in Ghana with over 900 volumes related to issues such as cross-cultural relationships, leadership, stress, grief, and trauma. These books are lent to any missionary working in West Africa. Smaller libraries have been established in several other countries.

PERSONAL CHALLENGES FOR A PSYCHOLOGIST WORKING IN WEST AFRICA

Multiple Relationships: Over these 4 years, I have worked closely with missionaries and cross-cultural workers who have been shot at, beaten, robbed, taken hostage, carjacked, had their babies kidnapped, or lost their children or spouses to malaria. At first, the people I worked with were strangers to me, but as I interacted with workers through our workshops and other events, I became part of the community and formed friendships. At times I have wondered if every missionary I ever met or socialized with would one day need some kind of crisis intervention. At first I tried to set apart certain missionaries who would be my friends and for whom I would never provide crisis intervention. However, this is not practical when there are few other mental health professionals available to help. In the 14-country area we serve, there are only three mental health professionals (including one) available to serve missionaries and cross-cultural workers. So multiple relationships cannot be avoided. In fact, I think that they can enhance the quality of service as long as a certain degree of objectivity is maintained and as long as the mental health professional maintains healthy boundaries and knows when to disqualify himself or herself from service (e.g., when I was evacuated from Bouaké we did not agree to provide counseling for the kids who had been evacuated from the missionary school in the same town. Instead we helped to arrange for counselors to come from the U.S. who could help them as well as us).

Chronic exposure to stress and trauma: We came to care for those working on the front lines and to try to prevent unnecessary psychological/emotional damage resulting from trauma. The fact that we live here and are also experiencing our own trauma of war, evacuation, robberies, and cross-cultural stresses does increase our credibility with those we came to serve. However, we also realize that we have a daily challenge of making sure that we also do not fall prey to burnout or trauma-related illnesses.

Several things have helped in the prevention of burnout for our team members—a governing board, the nurturance of healthy team relationships, and a balance of work, rest, and fun.

The MMCT Governing Board consists of nine mission leaders who live and work in West Africa. They embrace the vision of the Mobile Member Care Team and meet with us regularly to discuss our goals, strategies, progress, failures, hopes, and frustrations. One of their foremost goals is to ensure that we are taking the vacation and rest that we need in order to be renewed and refreshed. They take this role very seriously and hold us accountable to good self-care.

When much of our focus is on helping others manage conflicts and build healthy team relationships, our credibility hinges on having a well-functioning team. This is a daily goal and is assisted by having a team covenant that focuses on our commitment to accountability, encouragement, open and honest communication, conflict resolution, trust, and consensus decision-making.

Finding the balance of work, rest, and play is not easy in this setting but seems crucial to our longevity. There's a value among missionaries that promotes working to the point of exhaustion or illness. Our work can be intense and often involves long hours and a rigorous travel schedule. One principle we try to honor is to maintain Sundays as days of rest and reflection, as a way of rejuvenating and regaining perspective. Vacations can be a challenge in this part of the world—even a nice hotel on the beach may have disruptions and hassles that increase rather than decrease stress (e.g., there's no running water, or the electricity goes off, or rodents are sharing the room with you). As a team, we are committed to sometimes taking a few weeks off the continent on a regular basis for retreat and focused reading.

Few mental health professionals: It's a challenge to be in a place where there are so few mental health professionals. Oftentimes when I am working on a case or in a difficult situation, I use the phone or e-mail to consult with fellow mental health professionals in North America. But this is costly and time-consuming and I can't get immediate feedback. This is a luxury that we take for granted in North America. Before I came to West Africa, I worked in a community mental health setting where consultations, supervision, and case staffings were daily events. Staying up to date with clinical knowledge and getting consultation in areas where I do not have as much expertise is a continual challenge.

The overwhelming need: Simply put, when someone is in an environment where he or she is surrounded by genuine need and suffering, it is a challenge not to become overwhelmed and not to feel hopeless or weary. I am constantly aware of my limitations and weaknesses. I have to continually go back to the priorities we have set and the vision we have, and try to resolve each day to do my part to contribute to them. To try to do more is to burn out. To do less is to forsake compassion.

FUTURE GOALS

The Mobile Member Care Team—West Africa was started in 2000 with a goal of providing crisis response and training to missionaries in West Africa. It is the first team of its kind, but we and our Global Advisory Board envision other teams like this being set up in other parts of the world. Although the types of stresses and trauma may be different, many of the principles of intervention would remain the same. Our strategy is to identify staff who can help to implement the MMCT model in other parts of the world and to train them through an apprenticeship with MMCT in West Africa. We hope to begin doing this within the next couple of years.

Another goal is to conduct outcome research to assess more objectively the effectiveness of the MMCT model in enhancing coping skills and preventing maladaptive responses to trauma in this setting. A research project is currently under way in a collaborative effort between MMCT and Dr. Frauke Schaefer of the Duke University Health System, titled "Coping with Stress and Trauma in Cross-Cultural Mission Assignments." The purpose of this study is to provide a more accurate estimate of the prevalence of PTSD symptoms, depression, and anxiety symptoms among missionaries in West Africa as well as to identify resilience factors that help them cope. This will help us to do a better job of evaluating the needs in the field and to customize our services to respond to those needs.

CONCLUSION

Why do I do this kind of work? The living conditions are difficult, the income is negligible, and the risk for secondary trauma is high. But I wouldn't trade this work for anything. When I'm sitting across from a missionary family and experiencing the thrill of being a part of their personal growth and recovery, or when I'm in the midst of a workshop and looking at relationships forming and conflicts being resolved, or when I'm enjoying the closeness and companionship of my teammates knowing that we've been through some of the most incredible experiences together (e.g., lying in a hallway while shells went off close by), then I know that I'm exactly where I'm supposed to be. By God's grace, I'll endure the hardships and continue to walk the road that I encourage others to walk.

WEBSITES FOR FURTHER INFORMATION

http://www.mmct.org (The MMCT)

http://www.itpartners.org (The International Training Partners)

REFERENCES

Carr, K.F. (1997, October). Crisis intervention for missionaries. *Evangelical Missions Quarterly, 33.* Wheaton, IL: Evangelical Missions Information Service.

Carr, K.F. (2004). Who are the better missionaries: Those who leave or those who stay? *World Pulse, Vol. 39*(7). Wheaton, IL: Evangelical Missions Information Service.

Fawcett, G. (2003). Preventing trauma in traumatic environments. In J. Fawcett (Ed.), *Stress and trauma handbook* (pp. 40–67). Monrovia, CA: World Vision International.

Fawcett, J. (2002). Preventing broken hearts, healing broken minds. In Y. Danieli (Ed.), *Sharing the front line and the back hills* (pp. 223–232). Amityville, NY: Baywood.

Fawcett, J. (Ed.). (2003). *Stress and trauma handbook.* Monrovia, CA: World Vision International.

Greeson, C., Hollingsworth, M., & Washburn, M. (1990). *The grief adjustment guide.* Sisters, OR: Questar.

Hill, M., Hill, H., Bagge, D., & Miersma, P. (2004). *Healing the wounds of trauma.* Nairobi, Kenya: Paulines Publications Africa.

Jerome, D. (2001). Mobile Member Care Team—West Africa: Our journey, and direction. In K. O'Donnell (Ed.), *Doing member care well: Perspectives and practices from around the world* (pp. 117–126). Pasadena, CA: William Carey Library.

Jerome, D. & Carr, K. (2002). Mobile Member Care Teams. In J. Powell & J. Bowers (Eds.), *Enhancing missionary vitality* (pp. 399–407). Palmer Lake, CO: Mission Training International.

Reissman, F. (1990). Restructuring help: A human services paradigm for the 1990's. *American Journal of Community Psychology, 18*(2), 221–230.

Williams, K. (2002). *Sharpening your interpersonal skills.* Colorado Springs, CO: International Training Partners.

CHAPTER 5

Telecommuting to Support Workers in Disasters

B. Hudnall Stamm and Amy C. Hudnall

INTRODUCTION

The technology that has become available in the past quarter century has profoundly changed the way the world operates. Typically, we think of a global economy with bank transfers of money, corporations shifting information, and governments working together to address both legal and governmental issues. In addition, we often think of telehealth linking hospitals together. What is not often considered is that this same technology emerged from battlefield applications and is still used to support wars (both fighting and recovery) and disasters. The level and types of technology used vary from location to location around the globe, reflecting both the local culture and the sophistication of the warring parties, or of the governments that respond to a disaster.

In this chapter, we will discuss how we literally stumbled onto using relatively simple technology to support rescue and recovery efforts in conflict zones and disaster sites. Two of us have joined forces to write this chapter. B. Hudnall Stamm (BHS) brings to the chapter a pre-psychology career in search and rescue and a psychology career with interests in clinical and community research and service. Amy C. Hudnall (ACH) is a historian who shares an interest in using psychological knowledge to respond to and even prevent disasters and wars.

Combined, we have over 25 years' experience responding to disasters (BHS, 15 years; ACH, 10 years). Over the past 15 years, we have provided disaster planning and intervention support via telehealth technology. Using the Internet, telephone, and teleconferencing, we have worked with people in cities, remote villages, and in the field in Alaska, Africa, the Middle East, Indonesia, and scores of other locations. We support people "on the ground" by means of telecommunication using a methodology that is a simple extension of one of our work environments (BHS), staffing the command-and-control activities for mountain search and rescue organizations from 1979–1988. Although overall technology has changed profoundly in the past 25 years, the principles we use remain constant—*use whatever technology is available to provide reliable communications between the parties needing to communicate.* In the low-infrastructure environments of developing nations or disaster locations, the older, simpler technologies shine. For example, in the early hours and days following the December 26, 2004, tsunami in Southeast Asia, ham radios were the only means of telecommunication (National Association for Amateur Radio, 2005). In another example taken from a project with which we worked peripherally, a remote village recovering from profound civil violence was able to obtain a single laptop that they ran off of a solar power generator. After everyone in the village had completed their e-mail chores, a runner would take a single floppy disk and run 2 days to a nearby city where they would send the e-mail, wait overnight for the replies, download them onto a disk, and run back to the village. This simple but effective method sped up communications from weeks to days.

Natural and human-made disasters are common and occur in scales large and small. They may receive a great deal of attention, such as the 2004 tsunami in Southeast Asia, or they may occur with little or no publicity, such as the Teton Dam Disaster in 1976. This human-made disaster began in Freemont County, Idaho, and ultimately affected homes and communities for more than 75 miles downriver. It resulted in the total destruction of more than a dozen communities, the deaths of 14 people, and the dislocation of thousands of people throughout this sparsely populated area. The disaster barely made the news yet caused over $1 billion (1976 value) in damage (Johnson, 2004; Sylvester, no date).

Although the triggers, interpretations, and expressions of extreme fear are likely culturally driven, it seems that as humans we share the capability to experience extreme fear (Stamm & Friedman, 2000). This fear, and its concomitant physical and psychological outcomes, can disrupt our individual and communal ability to attend to the normal activities of our lives. Because disasters and civil conflicts disrupt communities, not just the individuals who live in them, the response must consider the community. Moreover, community disruptions can lead to fluid and often chaotic environments that provide a breeding ground for civil violence and even war (Stamm, Stamm, Hudnall, & Higson-Smith, 2004). If the disaster is of human origin—either directly, such as a terrorist attack, or indirectly, such as a corporation violating rules of good conduct and causing an environmental disaster—the long-term consequences are typically more negative than would be seen with a natural disaster (cf. Solomon & Green, 1992; Stern, 1976).

Through our work, we have learned two key lessons. First, regardless of the location of the disaster, it is important to understand how the community's culture and historical events combine to create the world in which the people live and in which one will be working. When there has been a history of colonialism or other cultural disruption, we call that *cultural trauma* (Stamm, Stamm, et al., 2004). We have also learned that the workers, be they local or expatriates who have come to assist in the disaster, are profoundly affected by the work they do (Stamm, Higson-Smith, & Hudnall, 2005). In this chapter we will discuss both of these areas, using illustrations from various interventions in which we have worked. In some cases, the stories we share will be as they happened; in other cases, to protect the identities of those with whom we worked, we will blend stories to illustrate our points.

The chapter will proceed in three broad sections. First, we discuss some of the fundamental human and technical aspects of telecommuting to disaster sites. Second, we discuss cultural trauma, something that we believe must be considered whenever working with a community. Third, we finish with a lengthy discussion on protecting workers who respond to disasters, specifically from traumatic stress. Throughout this chapter, we draw these thoughts together using case studies that we hope will illustrate the potential benefits of others using our methodology, or recognizing that their phone calls and e-mails to disaster sites may already be providing the same type of support that we have learned is so valuable to those with whom we work.

TELECOMMUTING TO DISRUPTED COMMUNITIES: THE ROLE OF TECHNOLOGY IN DISASTER RESPONDING

Telecommuting to a disaster site provides particular challenges that do not exits in face-to-face encounters. For example, one may not be privy to visual cues, particularly with the use of e-mail over the Internet or a voice over the telephone. At times, one has to listen to the sounds of destruction without being able to see what happened to the people to whom one is talking or knowing if those people are still alive to continue the conversation. The qualitative and quantitative results of our work suggest that, although these technology-mediated encounters are very different than face-to-face encounters, having expert decision support assistance via telehealth can be very beneficial to those who are on the ground at the disaster site.

Although telecommuting to a disaster site clearly will not meet all the needs of those at the disaster, there are multiple advantages to using this method as part of the overall disaster response. The most obvious of these is not placing still more people in harm's way. Additionally, it reduces the management burden for those working in command and control by reducing the number of people at the site. Finally, there are less obvious advantages having to do with dissipation of the terror and distress that can exist. As one colleague put it, having decision support resources from those not under fire reminds those at ground zero that there are safe places in the world, giving them hope that their place will soon be safe again.

Establishing a Virtual Field Presence with Telehealth

Today the application of telecommunication in the field has greatly enhanced aid workers' reach and increased their contact with the "home team." In particular, the use of telehealth and telemedicine is viewed as one of the most important, yet untapped, advancements for health care during crises. There are two broad classes of telehealth applications: (a) store-and-forward technologies (asynchronous) and (b) real-time interactions (synchronous). Store-and-forward technologies are similar to e-mail in that they are sent by one party at a time convenient to them and reviewed at a future time convenient to the recipient. Telehealth applications can be as simple as a brief e-mail or they may contain multi-media attachments or links providing a vast array of information. Synchronous interactions typically occur over telephone or videoconferencing and take place in "real time" with two (or more) sites interacting at the same time. The majority of telehealth activities takes place using store-and-forward, even though most people imagine a videoconference when they think of telehealth.

Telecommunication is often compared to the invention of the printing press, taking knowledge that had been available to a very few and sharing it with the world. However, the expense of establishing telecommunication and the knowledge it provides to the world pose the second and more serious problem. The term "digital divide" describes the separation of those with information and telecommunication technology (ITC) access from those without. Forty percent of the world's population—2.5 billion people—live in rural areas in emerging nations. Only a fraction of these people have access to telecommunications, which is usually voice telephony with little capacity for even modest Internet or videoconference access. Population, income, culture, geographic location, and race are all predictors of access. Higher density areas, wealthier people, more Westernized countries, and whites are more likely to have higher quality access than are others.

All countries have experienced dramatic increases in their access to ITC over the last decade; but the increase has been unevenly distributed. Based on analysis of data gathered by the U.S. Central Intelligence Agency's *World Fact Book* and the *CyberAtlas* (http://cyberatlas.internet.com), Iceland is the most "connected" country in the world with 60% of its citizens online. There are five countries with more than 50% of their citizens online, although just barely: Sweden (50.56%), the United States (53.60%), Hong Kong (54.17%), the United Kingdom (55.37%), and Iceland (60.07%). Data from 72 of the world's 227 countries account for 72.8% of the world's population (4,566,053,061 people out of 6,262,471,109 people). Of these 4.5 billion people, an estimated 9.4%—or 429,422,100—are online; only an estimated 7% of the world's population have Internet access, whereas the countries providing documented census reports on Internet access averaged individual connections to be about 10–20%. Africa is the least connected continent, with only four countries included in the global Internet census (Stamm, 2004a, 2004b).

ITC itself does not discriminate across culture lines, but the availability and the applications of ITC are culturally linked. For example, consider a micro-view of the distribution of Internet access. In the United States, access to ITC is concentrated in the largest cities. In fact, according to the 1998 report, 'Net Equity (Moss & Mitra, 1998), 86% of the world's Internet capacity was found in the 20 largest cities in the United States. Is it any surprise that within each of these cities the access is further concentrated in the financial and scientific districts? Although by 2002 ITC access within these cities was becoming a little more evenly distributed, it is very clear that the differences between those with access and those without, in those cities were defined by race, gender, income, and population density (Stamm, 2004c). The divide becomes even more profound when one takes into consideration the form of access: the more expensive and faster broadband access or dial-up access. In other words, it was first thought that ITC would be the world's "great equalizer," and to some extent this is happening. Many people are finding that their "voices" are being heard as never before. However, as is often the case, ITC continues to be concentrated in the hands of those in power and serves to further marginalize those already disempowered.

A final area of concern in regard to ITC is the interaction of culture and technology. Although many proponents of ITC continue to believe it will be the great equalizer, dissenting voices offer the concern that ITC is merely another form of Western imperialism. In this regard a number of potential, culturally specific problems arise. For example, cultures that are based on an oral tradition may find it difficult to adapt to a written culture such as that common to the Web. Language may also be a barrier. The majority of Internet users are English-speaking and thus most Internet content is in English. Built-in translators are sometimes available, but they do not provide the richness of translation necessary to understand many complex ideas. In some cases they are actually inaccurate. At best, relaying Western language and ideas to non-Western communities via the Internet provides opportunities for positive cultural transmission, but at worst it places less powerful cultures at risk of losing their heritage to a sort of Western cultural homogeneity.

All of the problems and potential concerns aside, telehealth may be one of the best resources for providing workers the tools to support the health of communities in crisis. This is perhaps most poignant when working with communities that experience severe deprivation and civil conflict. Collier and colleagues (2003), at the World Bank built models based on economic data from 1960–1999 and concluded that marginalized countries are more susceptible to civil violence. Their figures indicate that a low-income country has a 17.1% chance of falling into civil war in a given 5-year period. Improving the economic status of that country by only 2% reduces the risk to 12.3 %. Health is linked to productivity and ability to be proactive. The health sector, often supported by telehealth, provides more and higher-paying jobs. Thus, telehealth may well be irrevocably linked to the future viability of an emerging nation itself.

Technology-Mediated Interventions

Typically, our team (BHS, ACH, and colleagues) is somehow linked to the disaster responders. The linkage may come through word of mouth, or it may result from an Internet search and an e-mail to us with a request for support. Below are three case examples, one in the United States following the events of September 11, 2001, and one following the Southeast Asia earthquake and tsunami disaster of December 26, 2004.

Global Nomads Group and September 11th

Following the September 11, 2001, Trade Center bombings in New York City, we were linked to an organization, the Global Nomads Group (GNG) (http://www.gng.org), through an e-mail that traversed multiple steps from a for-profit telecommunications company, through a specialist in end-of-life care, to a medical school with a telehealth program known for disaster and war telehealth applications, to us (BHS). The request was for assistance with making a decision about proceeding with a classroom-to-classroom video-conference 12 days after the bombing, when one of the classrooms was from a school essentially located at ground zero.

The concern that was raised, appropriately, was how to handle the student dialogue should it digress to the bombings. The planners wanted to proceed, as the students had spent a great deal of time preparing for the videoconference; they believed it was important to show by action to the students that their world was not totally unpredictable (a cardinal concern in post-traumatic stress disorder). They also wanted to make sure to protect the students from further harm. I was contacted on September 18, 2001. By September 24, 2001, we had completed a curriculum for the teachers and students that had been reviewed by a major traumatic stress treatment program as well as several psychologists with school experience, some of whom lived in the New York City area and were responding to the disaster. We had also identified and vetted three licensed clinical psychologists with grief and trauma expertise who volunteered to be at the three videoconference sites available to assist the students and teachers should they be needed. In those short 7 days, my e-mail logs show 73 e-mails involving 25 people, four large agencies, and three countries. There is also evidence of five conference calls. Clearly, this was rapidly done and the materials were in place prior to the critical moment of need. It is difficult to estimate the number of hours that were used to accomplish this effort, but it seems to be more than 200 in those 7 days. The videoconference proceeded as scheduled, without incident, and was later highlighted on the *Today Show*.

Although no formal evaluation was done, the students and teachers informally reported positive reactions at the time of the videoconference, and some students reported continued positive responses up to a year later. We still work on occasion with GNG on other projects, and the curriculum has been revised to include more trauma-informed information through a grant from the National Child Traumatic Stress Network (Grant No. #1 UD1 SM56114–01 from the U.S. Department of Health and Human Services, Substance Abuse and Mental Health Services Administration)

Pulih Centre for Trauma Recovery and Psychosocial Intervention and the Southeast Asian Earthquake and Tsunami, December 26, 2004.
Our connections with Pulih predate the founding of the organization and originated from an e-mail request from one of the founders, Livia Iskandar-

Dharmawan. She had written in 2000 with a request for technical assistance in using our (BHS) secondary traumatic stress scale (see section below) in her work with internally displaced people in West Timor. In 2000, I linked her with a colleague in South Africa (Craig Higson-Smith [CHS]) who did similar work. Over the years, we (BHS, LID, ACH, & CHS) shared data, met in person, and presented at international conferences (Iskandar-Dharmawan, Stamm, Hudnall, & Higson-Smith, 2001), submitted grant proposals together, and maintained an ongoing dialogue about protecting workers dealing with difficult humanitarian disasters. In addition, Iskandar-Dharmawan traveled to South Africa to work with Higson-Smith.

When the news of the earthquake and tsunami disaster came, we contacted Iskandar-Dharmawan with our condolences and offers of support, should that be appropriate. Because she was headed to Aceh Province, she linked us with some of her staff at Pulih. One of the initial things that we did was some reconnaissance work for the staff about how to locate funding in the swirl of international money that was pouring into the region. After several days of e-mail dialogues, two needs emerged. First, there was a need for well-sorted, brief, educational, and training documents for the people at Pulih. Second, there was a need to link to journalism organizations to find ways to support reporters in reporting about the disaster successfully, that is, without causing further harm and in reporting accurate information.

In response to the need for training and public education materials, we moved very quickly (in one day) to provide initial information. Over the next several days, guided by their e-mails and our knowledge of their system, we put together a website that contained the necessary well-sorted and organized materials as well as created an "Aid Worker Pocket Card" (http://telida. isu.edu). All pocket cards need locations for users to find further, more detailed information. Thus, after obtaining their permission, we linked the user to Psychosocial.org as the referral site. Psychosocial.org is a branch of *Actions Without Borders* (http://www.psychosocial.org). Our relationship with them reached back to the first international conference devoted specifically to preventing aid worker trauma (http://www.idealist.org/conferences/psychosocial/) (Stamm & Hudnall, 2004). Like most of our projects, the path is composed of a dizzying array of linkages that could really only be accomplished using the Internet. In all, within a few weeks, we had conducted about 200 e-mails to about 50 people in five countries.

The website was posted January 7, 2005, just over a week after we began the dialogue and about 2 weeks after the disaster. As it turned out, this website was used by multiple NGOs as well as the National Child Traumatic Stress

Network Terrorism and Disaster Branch and several U.S. federal agencies. Although there is really no way to tell for sure, we estimate that the pocket card e-mail went out to about 10,000 people. Unfortunately, we did not get a hit counter on the Web site until a week after it opened, but since January 15, 2005, the site has received 1747 hits.

The second activity was linked to an ongoing Pulih effort to care for journalists. In the year before the tsunami disaster, one of Pulih's programs in response to the Jakarta JW Marriott hotel bombing, was to publish a small handbook for journalists on traumatic events. The book had two aims. First, it aimed to assist journalists in knowing how powerful their medium could be for survivors of disasters and to assist them in providing sensitive coverage and reporting so as to minimize secondary trauma and retraumatization, and ideally even to facilitate the healing process. The second aim of the publication was to help journalists understand their own risks of secondary trauma as a result of their work covering disasters. The publication had sections on understanding the phenomenon, how journalists could take care of themselves in this regard, and how the media companies can take care of their journalists after working in difficult situations. Given the scope of the tsunami disaster, the people at Pulih were interested in linking with international organizations that shared similar concerns. We were able, through several e-mails to other colleagues, to link Pulih with press colleagues and with the Dart Center for Journalism and Trauma (http://www.dartcenter.org). As it turned out, the Australian branch of the Dart Center was doing the direct responding and one of the contacts there was someone with whom I (BHS) had corresponded some years before when he was completing his graduate work and using my secondary trauma scale. It is this very type of linkage that makes our work so amazing, both to us and to those who seek our assistance. In so many cases, we have contacts around the globe from years of e-mail dialogues.

H-Net and Interdisciplinary ITC Collaborations

Spinning out from the dialogue around journalism was an idea by one of us (ACH) to use the history and social science fields to provide important cultural and historical background information that could be used by journalists, planners, or expatriate workers headed to the field. The result was an effort by H-Net (http://www.hnet.org). H-Net is an international consortium of scholars and teachers that creates and coordinates Internet networks with the common objective of advancing teaching and research in the arts, humanities, and social sciences. The central purpose of the initiative is to recruit well-qualified field experts in selected topics related to the language, history, culture, mores, religions, and political practices of areas where relief operations are active. These experts create fact sheets, provide press interviews, and otherwise offer background information for reporters, journalists, relief workers, and other individuals entering the disaster area. This material will help make the relief effort more sensitive to local cultural conditions and relevant historical events, thereby improving the efficiency of these operations. It may also help to reduce the potential for secondary trauma among relief workers exposed to an extremely stressful and culturally unfamiliar environment of death, suffering, and destruction. The briefing and background material will be available from a website offered by H-NET.

These three case histories provide information about how the Internet, in particular, can serve as a vehicle for linking people in need with those who have resources. In the following sections, we will discuss the two key issues that we keep in the forefront of our work, cultural trauma and protecting workers responding to disasters.

CULTURAL TRAUMA

Many of the areas in which ethnic conflict and/or disasters occur are already struggling with the affects of human-driven cultural trauma (Stamm, Stamm, Higson-Smith, & Hudnall, 2004). The theory of cultural trauma is a framework for understanding disruptions that can affect an "original" culture can affect through the arrival of a hegemonic, "more progressive" culture. The model suggests that when this occurs, as in earlier periods of colonization, the original group becomes unable to sustain its vitality and uniqueness, ultimately risking the health of individual group members and the group as a whole. The Cultural Clash Model (See Fig. 5–1) posits that before outside contact, original cultures have identifiable and sustainable economic, social, political, and spiritual systems. When the original culture is exposed to dramatically new cultures and ideas without a reasonable evolution toward those new ideas, then the exposure can radically alter the character and sustainability of the original culture. At worst this exposure can directly lead to the disappearance of the culture; at best we suggest that there is an opportunity for the revitalization and reorganization of the "injured" culture.

Aid workers need to be particularly sensitive to the pre-event community dynamics. To a community that has had its cultural underpinnings disrupted, even small exposures like the inclusion of international/outside aid workers in a disaster can be frightfully confusing. Moreover, when a community accepts the well-intentioned outpouring of international aid to reconstruct their physical infrastructure, they further change their local culture as the international aid

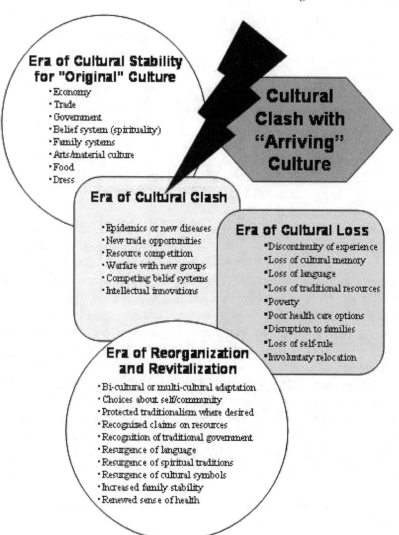

FIGURE 5.1 Cultural Clash Model

often comes with workers and plans of how the community should be re-built. For example, post-disaster housing may be nothing like the traditional housing with which the community is familiar. Similarly, the food imported to feed disaster victims may be dramatically different than the native foods, causing changes in both eating habits and food preparation and consumption rituals. Although it is easy to dismiss the importance of a community's traditions in the face of life threat following a disaster, it is important to remember that the community itself is the basis of the reconstruction and survival. Consequently, we believe that every effort should be made to accommodate people's naturally occurring patterns of helping, working through the local systems when they are healthy, and helping respectfully to reestablish or establish local systems when they have become too disrupted to be functional.

PROTECTING WORKERS WHO ARE RESPONDING TO DISASTERS

Aid Workers and Their Agencies

The humanitarian crises that follow natural or human-made disasters often separate individuals and communities—whether they have experienced cultural trauma or are thriving and healthy—from familiar resources and surroundings, creating even further vulnerabilities to stressful events. Population dislocations and disruptions to food, water, and medical supplies also occur. There may be gruesome tasks such as burying mounds of bodies or attending to people suffering from starvation, injuries, or interpersonal violence. Aid workers thus are often placed in situations where they have the dual roles of protecting and helping victims, as well as protecting themselves as they do their work.

As we noted in "The Terror Part of Terrorism" (Stamm, Tuma, et al., 2004), disaster responding is a growth industry at international, federal, and local levels. In the 1990s, international nongovernmental organizations (NGOs) doubled from 23,600 in 1991 to 44,000 in 1999, and the number continues to expand (United Nations, 2000). What has become apparent with the increase in the number of agencies, with their different interests, funding, and agendas, is that coordinating the NGOs alone has become a Herculean task. Sadly, the desire to help has resulted in well-intentioned NGOs rushing to the scene to be the first to respond, to procure the best contacts, or even to get the best physical location from which to work. Collectively, the NGOs represent an enormous global enterprise, spending an estimated US$ 12–13 billion annually (Skavdal, 2003). Yet the resource competition and lack of collaboration and coordination that can exist among many NGOs is resulting in wasted money and resources intended to assist the target population.

As well as struggling to succeed within the chaos that can result from competing NGOs, individual workers within these organizations are at risk of suffering from the negative effects of working in disaster settings. The settings are sometimes dangerous or macabre. Workers are often expected to work with unanticipated cross-cultural difficulties that strain their ability to provide care.

Although traumatic loss may have universal components, responses to events are likely expressed within specific cultural contexts (Stamm & Friedman, 2000; Stamm, Tuma et al., 2004). Expatriate workers may struggle to understand the culture and customs of the places where they are deployed. Local workers may struggle with providing care and simultaneously grieving their own personal losses. Across cultures, differences in the organization of infrastructures—such as where one obtains help or even if trained professionals are available—may affect the service delivery (Stamm, Higson-Smith, & Hudnall, 2004). This, coupled with issues of group identity, mediated by ethnicity, language, religion, and privilege, make it difficult for helpers to provide care (Higson-Smith, 2003).

Worker Exposure to Primary and Secondary Traumatic Stress

Every disaster-response field team either has, or should have, a support management team that works with them. Frequently, those working on support management do not enter the field setting. Supporting and working with staff responding to an event—whether they arrived for disaster responding or are local staff responding to an event in their home community—presents multiple risks, including exposure to trauma indirectly and directly, exhaustion, exposure to disease, hunger. They may also be at risk of attack from people taking advantage of the chaotic disaster situation or from those they seek to assist should the rescuees believe that they are not helping as much as they should/could. Addressing the impact of trauma on the staff can be incredibly complex (Stamm, Higson-Smith, & Hudnall, 2004).

Direct exposure to trauma has been studied at length. As a field, we are becoming better and better prepared at handling people's responses to direct exposure. Secondary trauma, however, in a post 9/11 world, is being recognized by the larger public as posing serious risks to helpers. Work-related trauma is insidious and can catch a person unaware, as it is intricately tied to the act of helping itself. To reduce the risk of secondary trauma, compassion fatigue, and/or burnout, we believe organizations should establish structures that provide ongoing support for their workers, both in terms of global environments and specific forms of intervention. We are not advocating mandatory counseling or mass mandatory debriefing or other simplistic "fixes" that are more "tacked on" in their nature. Although immediate trauma counseling and debriefing can be very useful for some people, they may cause problems for others (Everly & Boyle, 1999; Everly & Mitchell, 2000; Gist & Devilly, 2002; Van Emmerik, Kamphuis, Hulsbosch, & Emmelkamp, 2002). The real key seems to be thoughtful administration that considers the professional quality of life and mental health of workers long before an event occurs. For communities, the best predictor of post-event function is pre-event function (Sundet & Mermelstein, 1996). Although there is no clear research on organizations, we can hypothesize that this pre-event prediction of post-event function could apply to organizations in similar ways that it does to communities. Psychologically healthy workplaces typically have lower turnover, fewer sick days, better loyalty, lower health care usage, and better employee longevity than do organizations with a less positive focus on preserving human capital.

Human capital is a term borrowed from economics that originally referred to investments in the things that support the health of the human workforce: investments in education, public health infrastructure, and health care services. These variables link directly to personal and national income; the health status of a population drives a nation's economy and subsequently the nation's growth potential (Becker, 1964; Grossman, 1972; Mushkin, 1962). We (Stamm, Stamm, et al., 2004) and others (Rudolph & Stamm 1999; Rupp & Sorel, 2001) have used human capital as one method to understand the larger impact of traumatic stress, suggesting that traumatic stress may inhibit communities or nations from reaching their optimum levels of productivity and individuals from reaching their potential levels of either health status or income.

Because responding to disasters is so strongly reliant on human capital, this resource is central to the organization of how relief organizations are structured. Comprehensively, we believe an organization should strive to establish an environment of caring, one in which relief workers know that their mental health is important. The articulation occurs both through employee materials and daily modeling by supervisors. The importance of the difference between local workers, who are living in the disaster area and will stay there when the recovery effort is completed, and expatriate workers, who have their homes in other locations, cannot be overestimated. Regardless, some key factors can provide a more secure organization. These include: relevant training; a place for relaxation and informal interaction when "off duty"; regular staff meetings that foster support and collaboration and provide continuity and routine; ways that staff can have regular and meaningful interaction with their personal social support system, including services and supports for local workers' families; time alone to rest and regenerate; visible support from supervisors, including listening to and responding to workers' concerns and suggestions; and organizational policy that facilitates or even demands that workers take time off.

At times, we help support workers returning from the field. We encourage agencies and organizations to view their organization as having a "caring environment." We remind them that their expatriate workers are returning to a world without violence or crisis, without chronic emergencies. This sudden change can be confusing, even for those workers who have successfully re-entered many times before. Local workers may wish to return to work to rebuild their own family's resources and in doing so can be perceived by the community as being selfish. As with working, the transition back to routine life can be smoothed by following some basic principles in designing program-specific re-entry plans. These include some form of re-entry debriefing or discussion; creating an opportunity (both physical and psychological) to talk about the worker's experiences; encouraging workers to take time off and get some extra rest, if at all possible; helping the person catalog some positive experiences; and teaching them basic coping strategies for dealing with the negative memories that may come. Both colleagues and family/friends can be helpful.

Measuring the Positive and Negative Effects of Helping

As psychologists, we use science to inform our practice. The Professional Quality of Life Scale (Stamm, 2002; Stamm, 2005) was developed with a dual purpose of researching and monitoring the negative and positive effects of caregiving. Many consultations have arisen from people using our website (http://www.isu.edu/~bhstamm) and writing for consultation about implementing monitoring programs using the measure. In addition to providing specific information about an individual, either for self-care or institutional support, group data has been used to suggest potential management changes. Because the measure includes positive outcomes as well as negative ones, it can provide a starting point for "meaning making" that seems to add to resilience. We, and the organizations with which we work, believe that the long-term success of their team is linked to the professional quality of life their staff enjoys. It is important to note that our research has shown that workers who can report positive effects of caregiving can often continue their work even in the face of negative outcomes such as traumatic stress symptoms (Stamm, 2002).

The Professional Quality of Life Scale has a long and steadily refined history. The first version of this test was the Compassion Fatigue Self Test, introduced in 1995 by Figley. It has since been added to and modified (Figley, 1995; Figley & Stamm, 1996; Stamm, 2002), in part because, as more data from the test were collected, psychometric difficulties were noted by more than one author (Figley & Stamm; Good, 1996; Jenkins & Baird, 2002; Larsen, Stamm, & Davis, 2002; Stamm, 2002). Specifically, the subscales, although theoretically separate, tended to show serious co-linearity between the scales, particularly between burnout and compassion fatigue. As the test grew in length it became unwieldy, raising the potential for user fatigue. After a great deal of evaluation, a final revised version was formulated by retaining the strongest items and strengthening the subscales with necessary new items. To reflect the changing nature of the construct, which includes positive as well as negative items. The measure was given a new name, the Professional Quality of Life Scale, or the ProQoL (Stamm, 2002, Stamm, 2005).

To affect this change, the authors created three subscales that were clearly shown through factor analyses as representing positive work-related items (compassion satisfaction), and two negative scales, one characterized by fear (compassion fatigue/secondary trauma) and the other by lack of efficacy (burnout). Compassion satisfaction represents the degree of pleasure you feel in doing your job as a helper. There are multiple terms for the negative affects of caring. Compassion Fatigue (CF), also called secondary traumatic stress (STS), is related to Vicarious Trauma (VT). Often, the terms are used interchangeably and the differences between them can be elusive and perhaps even nonsensical. Compassion fatigue is about work-related, secondary exposure to extremely stressful events. An example of secondary trauma or compassion fatigue is when the caregiver of people involved in a train wreck begins to exhibit symptoms similar to the victims, which mirror many of the symptoms of PTSD. The symptoms of CF/STS are usually rapid in onset and associated with a particular event. They may include being afraid, having difficulty sleeping, having images of the upsetting event pop into your mind, or avoiding things that remind you of the event. The final subset is burnout. Most people have an intuitive idea of what burnout is; it generally comes on slowly and is manifested in feelings of hopelessness, difficulties in doing your job well, etc. Burnout can be the reflection of a very high workload and/or a non-supportive work environment.

The revised instrument resolves many of the problems the authors identified in the earlier test by formulating these three subsets. In addition, the overall length of the measure dropped from 66 to 30 items, reducing the potential for user fatigue. To date, three broad classes of workers have been tested, general health workers, including clinicians through administrators; child/family workers, which include residential and child protective care workers; and school personnel, which includes teachers, counselors, and administrators.[1] An instrument of this nature provides a ready tool for monitoring the positive and negative effects of helping.

---

[1]To assist in giving feedback, a test feedback sheet is available at http://www.isu.edu/~bhstamm. The measure, psychometric information, and scoring key are located at the same site.

CONCLUSION

When we consult with helpers who are trying to manage staff in the field, we encourage them to make worker mental health issues routine. We also encourage them to treat all people equally so that no one person feels singled out, weaker, or guilty; there is no question about whether one staff member requires unique or different help. In the past, many organizations have seen and still see secondary trauma as a sign of weakness instead of a reasonable reaction to traumatic events. Unfortunately, this kind of attitude weakens staff support networks and may stigmatize the worker, thereby increasing the chance of negative responses to the trauma (Stamm & Hudnall, 2004). It is essential that the organization provide a climate in which secondary trauma is viewed as an understandable response to traumatic events and not an aberration. It is also essential that those looking after staff have their own professional support systems. This is a role that we have enjoyed playing for some years and anticipate enjoying for many years to come. Our collaborations with people around the globe provide us with ongoing opportunities to be encouraged that, in the face of disaster and civil conflict, there are many who find deep satisfaction in providing support for the recovery of individuals and their communities. As our contacts grow, so does our ability to link organizations with resources. The more communities and organizations with which we work, the more resources we have to draw on in the future. We provide linkages. It is a simple thing, labor intensive, yes, but simple in the end. Yet that simplicity seems to have great meaning for those who are on the front lines. In the words of one of our e-colleagues writing from the field in response to materials we sent, "THANK YOU. I am (for lack of better expression at this moment) touched by its simplicity. It will be a great tool for us in the field."

REFERENCES

Becker, G. (1964). *Human capital*. New York: National Bureau of Economic Research and Columbia University Press.

Central Intelligence Agency. (n.d.) World Factbook. Retrieved August 21, 2005, from http://www.cia.gov/cia/publications/factbook/

Collier, P., Elliott, L., Hegre, H., Hoeffler, A., Reynal-Querol, M., & Sambanis, N. (2003). *Breaking the conflict trap*. New York: Oxford University Press.

CyberAtlas. (n.d.) Retrieved August 21, 2005, from http://cyberatlas.guggenheim.org/home/index.html

Everly, G.S., & Boyle, S.H. (1999). Critical Incident Stress Debriefing (CISD): A meta-analysis. *International Journal of Emergency Mental Health, 1*, 165–168.

Everly, G.S., & Mitchell, J.T. (2000). The debriefing "controversy" and crisis intervention: A review of lexical and substantive issues. *International Journal of Emergency Mental Health, 2*, 211–225.

Figley, C.R. (1995). *Compassion fatigue: Coping with secondary traumatic stress disorder in those who treat the traumatized.* New York: Brunner Mazel.

Figley, C.R., & Stamm, B.H. (1996). Psychometric review of compassion fatigue self test. In B.H. Stamm (Ed.), *Measurement of stress, trauma and adaptation* (pp. 127–130). Lutherville, MD: Sidran Press.

Gist, R., & Devilly, G.J. (2002). Post-trauma debriefing: The road too frequently travelled? *Lancet, 360*, 741–742.

Good, D.A. (1996). Secondary traumatic stress in art therapists and related mental health professionals. (Doctoral dissertation, University of New Mexico, 1996). *Dissertation Abstracts International, 57/06-A*, 2370.

Grossman, M. (1972). *The demand for health: A theoretical and empirical investigation.* New York: National Bureau of Economic Research.

Higson-Smith, C. (2003). *Supporting communities affected by violence: A casebook from South Africa.* Oxford, UK: Oxfam.

Iskandar-Dharmawan, L., Stamm, B.H., Hudnall, A.C., & Higson-Smith, C. (2001, December). Workers in conflict-disrupted communities in South Africa & Indonesia. 17th Annual Meeting of the International Society for Traumatic Stress Studies. New Orleans, LA.

Jenkins, S.R., & Baird, S. (2002). Secondary traumatic stress and vicarious trauma: A validational study. *Journal of Traumatic Stress, 15*, 423–432.

Johnson, E. (2004). Teton Dam flood. Retrieved January 23, 2005, from http://www.ida.net/users/elaine/idgenweb/flood.htm

Larsen, D., Stamm, B.H., & Davis, K. (2002). Telehealth for prevention and intervention of the negative effects of caregiving. *Traumatic StressPoints, 16*, 4.

Moss, M.L., & Mitra, S. (1998). 'Net equity. New York: School of Public Service, New York University.

Mushkin, S. (1962). Health as an investment. *Journal of Political Economy, 70*(5, Part 2), 129–157.

National Association for Amateur Radio. (2005). *"Angel of the Seas"*: Post-Tsunami news coverage raises ham radio's global retrieved visibility. Retrieved January 23, 2005, from http://www.arrl.org/news/stories/2005/01/04/2/?nc=1

Rudolph, J.M., & Stamm, B.H. (1999). Maximizing human capital: Moderating secondary traumatic stress through administrative and policy action. In B.H. Stamm (Ed.), *Secondary traumatic stress: Self-care issues for clinicians, researchers and educators* (2nd ed.). Baltimore: Sidran Press.

Rupp, A., & Sorel, E. (2001). Economic models. In E. Gerrity, T.M. Keane, & F. Tuma (Eds.), *The mental health consequences of torture* (pp. 89–107). New York: Kluwer Academic/Plenum.

Skavdal, T. (2003). NGO networking and cooperation towards total disaster risk management in Asia. *Proceedings of the International Conference on Total Disaster*

Risk Management, Kobe, Japan (pp. 191–193). Retrieved January 23, 2004, from http://www.adrc.or.jp/publications/TDRM2003Dec/top.htm

Solomon, S.D., & Green, B.L. (1992). Mental health effects of natural and human-made disasters. *PTSD Research Quarterly, 3*(1), 1–7. Retrieved January 23, 2004, from http://www.ncptsd.org/PDF/RQ/V3N1.PDF

Stamm, B.H. (2002). Measuring compassion satisfaction as well as fatigue: Developmental history of the compassion fatigue and satisfaction test. In C.R. Figley (Ed.), *Treating compassion fatigue* (pp. 107–119). New York: Brunner Mazel.

Stamm, B.H. (2004a). *Modeling telehealth and telemedicine: A global geosociopolitical perspective.* Proceedings of the 26th annual conference of IEEE Engineering in Medicine and Biology Society.

Stamm, B.H. (2004b). Telehealth and telemedicine. *The encyclopedia of distributed learning.* Thousand Oaks, CA: Sage Press.

Stamm, B.H. (2004c). Cultural access and the Digital Divide. *The encyclopedia of distributed learning.* Thousand Oaks, CA: Sage Press.

Stamm, B.H. (2005). /The ProQOL Manual: The Professional Quality of Life Scale: Compassion Satisfaction, Burnout & Compassion Fatigue/Secondary Trauma Scales/. Baltimore, MD: Sidran Press.

Stamm, B.H., & Friedman, M.J. (2000). Cultural diversity in the appraisal and expression of traumatic exposure. In A. Shalev, R. Yehuda, & A. McFarlane (Eds.), *International handbook of human response to trauma* (pp. 69–85). New York: Plenum Press.

Stamm, B.H., Higson-Smith, C., & Hudnall, A.C. (2004). The complexities of working with terror. In D. Knafo (Ed.), *Living with terror, working with terror: A clinician's handbook* (pp. 369–395). Northvale, NJ: Jason Aronson.

Stamm, B.H., & Hudnall, A.C. (Facilitators). (2004, April). Chronic stress and secondary trauma working group notes. Proceedings: Tending the Helper's Fire, 12–13. Retrieved January 23, 2005, from http://www.idealist.org/psychosocial/conferences/docs/conferenceReport.pdf

Stamm, B.H., Stamm, H.E., Hudnall, A.C., & Higson-Smith, C. (2004). Considering a theory of cultural trauma and loss. *Journal of Loss and Trauma, 9*, 89–111.

Stamm, B.H., Tuma, F., Norris, F.H., Piland, N.F., van der Hart, O., Fairbank, J.A., et al. (2004). The terror part of terrorism. Invited article for *Engineering in Medicine and Biology, 23*, 149–161.

Stern, G.M. (1976). From chaos to responsibility. *American Journal of Psychiatry, 133*, 300–301.

Sundet, P., & Mermelstein, J. (1996). Predictors of rural community survival after natural disaster: Implications for social work practice. *Journal of Social Service Research, 22*, 57–70.

Sylvester, A.G. (n.d.). Teton Dam failure. Retrieved from http://www.geol.ucsb.edu/faculty/sylvester/ Teton%20Dam/welcome_dam.html

United Nations. (2000). *Human development report 2000*. New York: Oxford University Press.

Van Emmerik, A.A.P., Kamphuis, J.H., Hulsbosch, A.M., & Emmelkamp, P.M.G. (2002). Single session debriefing after psychological trauma: A meta-analysis. *Lancet, 360*, 766–771.

CHAPTER 6

New York University and 9/11

Viewing Terrorism Through a Dormitory Window

Kathryn A. Dale and Judith L. Alpert

> The NYU community lived through the attack of the World Trade Center in a manner that no other major university did. We did not need to watch it from the television; we could look south from our windows through the crystal clear September air to see the entire tragedy unfold.
>
> – New York University President John Sexton

The terrorist attacks of September 11th, unprecedented on American soil, affected millions of people both in New York City and throughout the fifty states. Because of the extraordinary number of people who lived, worked, and attended school near ground zero, mental health professionals in the New York City area faced a daunting task.

People were at increased risk for post-traumatic stress symptoms and disorder based on their geographic proximity to the World Trade Center (WTC) disaster (Galea et al., 2002, Blanchard et al., 2004, & Schlenger et al., 2002), and, as some studies have shown, on their level of exposure to the disaster (North et al., 1999 & Smith et al., 1999). The literature indicates that the effects of a disaster are most acute when two of the following factors exist: severe and prevalent property damage; financial repercussions to the community; human-made disaster; and injury, threat to, or loss of life (Norris, Byrne, Diaz, & Kaniasty, 2001). The events of September 11th were unquestionably traumatic and will most likely affect the people of New York City and the surrounding areas now and in the future.

On September 11, 2001, as people throughout the world viewed the World Trade Center attacks on their television screens and through other media, the students, faculty, and staff of New York University viewed it first hand, through their dormitory windows, from the rooftops of their office buildings, and from their urban campus sidewalks. New York University (NYU), one of the largest private universities in the nation, houses 14 schools and colleges and has approximately 14,000 undergraduate and 14,000 graduate students. The university, located less than one mile from the World Trade Center, does not have a traditional, centralized, self-contained campus for dormitories and other college buildings. Rather, it weaves into the fabric of New York City. Historically, members of the NYU community looked to the Twin Towers amid the city's spiky skyline as a way of orienting themselves in the city. When students exited their dorms or classrooms they often looked to the Towers to get their bearings. On September 11th, they looked to the towers and witnessed tragedy firsthand.

Tuesday, September 11th, dawned a clear and brilliant late summer day. In the five boroughs, many New Yorkers got an earlier start than usual to vote in the city's primary elections. At New York University, faculty, staff, and students prepared for their second week of the fall semester. Some at NYU witnessed a plane flying overhead moments before it struck the first Tower. Others were awakened by the impact of the plane hitting the first Tower or alarmed by the sight of smoke and fire in the southern sky. Members of the NYU community and local residents lined the streets wondering what had happened. When they saw a second plane, many realized that this was not a coincidence. They later learned from the news media that, at 8:46 a.m. a Boeing 767 airplane crashed into the North Tower and 18 minutes later a second Boeing 767 replicated the act of the first, crashing into the South Tower. Many NYU students lived in dormitories located less than a mile from the World Trade Center complex. These students were close enough to witness the Towers burning, people jumping and falling from the Towers, and the Towers collapsing to the ground. Some watched and witnessed the tragedy unfold for over an hour. By 10:28 a.m. both Towers had collapsed. Smoke and debris billowed into the air and sifted into some of the NYU dormitories, making it difficult for dormitory residents to breathe and leading city police and NYU authorities to order six dormitories, housing an estimated 3,000 students, to be evacuated. Resident Assistants led students north to NYU's Coles Sports Complex. Once the students made their way to the street level, they witnessed people running down the street, covered in gray ash and soot. At Coles Sports Complex, the students and various community members were met by student volunteers, faculty, and staff who offered news updates, first aid, counseling, food, and free phone banks for students to contact their families and friends.

One NYU mental health professional commented that on September 11, 2001, NYU psychologists and administrators looked to Maslow's hierarchy of needs for guidance (C. Fleming, personal interview, March 9, 2004). Their initial focus was on meeting the physiological, safety, and belongingness needs of the NYU students and community members. As students evacuated their dormitories and arrived at the Coles Sports Complex, NYU psychologists and other mental health professionals verified the students' physical well-being and offered them food and water. They also gave the NYU community up-to-date information. Research indicates that such information calms as well as facilitates the expression of emotions (Williams, Zinner, & Ellis, 1999). In addition, they reassured the students that NYU planned to provide them with shelter, facilities for bathing, and a stipend for clothing and necessities. Once these basic needs were met, they offered crisis counseling. At the same time, the mental health professionals were informally screening students and NYU community members who might require more in-depth treatment.

Numerous topics related to trauma and terrorism in the university setting have been addressed in the literature, including: the impact of natural disasters on a university (Miller, 1995; McCarthy & Butler, 2003); trauma and the development of post-traumatic stress symptoms in college-age students (Rothman, 2004; Purves & Erwin, 2002); emergency preparedness in a university setting (Stone, 1993); crisis intervention in elementary and high schools (Kerr, 2003; Underwood & Kalafat, 2002; Motomura, Iwakiri, Takino, Shimomura, & Ishibashi, 2003; Luna, 2002; Eaves, 2001); crisis intervention with children after terrorist attacks (Vogel, 2004; Coates, Schechter, First, Anzieu-Premmereur, & Steinberg, 2002; Pferrerbaum, 2003); social work interventions, disaster recovery, and traumatic stress services (Soliman & Silver, 2003); the psychological consequences of mass terrorism (Lowry & Lating, 2002); and the role of the workplace in responding to a disaster (Schouten, Callahan, & Bryant, 2004). To date, however, university mental health professionals' response to terrorism both on campus and in the larger community is absent from the literature. Given the lack of attention to this topic and the possibility of future terrorist attacks in locales that are home to universities and colleges, an academic autopsy of a university's reaction to terrorism is indicated.

Specifically, this chapter considers how mental health professionals at New York University responded to the terrorism events of September 11, 2001. Immediate, secondary, and long-term responses to the terrorist attacks of September 11th are described for five populations: students, parents, teachers, administrators, and surrounding community members. In addition, brief vignettes are presented to exemplify immediate, secondary, and long-term responses. We posit lessons that may serve as a framework for future practice and research.

For purposes of this chapter, the term "mental health professionals" refers to faculty and doctoral students from the Department of Applied Psychology at NYU, as well as NYU administrators who are also psychologists. Many of the NYU psychology doctoral students consulted in the New York City (NYC) public schools during the 2001–2002 academic year; thus, their response to some of these schools is considered. Here we operationally define "immediate responses" as responses that took place on September 11th and in the 2 weeks that followed. "Secondary responses" are defined as responses that took place more than 2 weeks after September 11th and in the 3 months that followed. "Long-term responses" are defined as responses that occurred after 3 months had passed and in the two and a half years (at the time of this writing) that have followed the events of September 11th. The information presented here is derived from written material prepared by the university, the authors' personal experiences, and interviews with NYU administrators, faculty, and graduate students. As both authors are housed in the Department of Applied Psychology in the Steinhardt School of Education at NYU, most of the interviews were conducted with people in that department and school. Only some highlights are presented here. The chapter is organized as follows: Under each main section (immediate response, secondary response, and long-term response) there is an exemplifying vignette and then a consideration of work with (a) students, (b) parents, (c) community members, (d) faculty, and (e) administrators. As some responses were the same under each of these sections, there is some repetition. Readers can refer to the sections most relevant to their needs.

IMMEDIATE RESPONSES

Vignette

News of the World Trade Center disaster reached one New York University professor at her home on the morning of September 11th. Her thoughts quickly shifted from early semester classroom preparation to focusing exclusively on responding to the terrorist attack. She considered volunteering at a local hospital and donating blood; however, thanks to a number of listservs, information on trauma, disaster response, post-traumatic stress disorder, coping strategies, and resources for children, adolescents, teachers, and parents poured into her e-mail inbox. She recognized the importance of disseminating this information to several New York University listservs whose members include clinical, counseling, and school psychologists, professors of psychology, and School Psychology alumni and current graduate students. During the weeks and months following 9/11, the professor continued to send online information about trauma and coping, and continued to consult, both formally and informally, with members of the NYU community.

This professor, as others, made their classrooms a forum for discussing and processing events related to 9/11. Within a trauma course, for example, students were encouraged to write about and process their personal experiences. They discussed the effects of traumatic events, strategies to minimize the negative effects, and strategies to increase the chances of a positive outcome. The focus of a School Consultation practicum course shifted to cover the ways the Psychology doctoral students could support children, teachers, and other school staff during the aftermath of 9/11.

Working with Students

On the day of September 11th and in the 2 weeks after, NYU mental health professionals talked to NYU students. Their primary goal was to informally assess students' psychological needs. In addition, they helped students locate other students and relatives and they provided students with food, cots, and free phone banks to enable students to call home. Support for NYU students, both inside and outside of the classroom, involved both individual and group discussions. One professor, who taught one of the few classes held the morning of 9/11, devoted class time to discussing the events and comforting students. Other professors encouraged their students to write and talk about the traumatic events.

During the first 2 weeks after 9/11, administrators, faculty, and students reported that communication was vital. NYU administrators and mental health professionals utilized computer resources. They addressed the school community and posted emergency and resource information. These postings were followed by invitations to join Steinhardt School of Education faculty, staff, and other students for "companionship, conversation, and refreshment." Similarly, in the New York City Public schools, NYU psychology doctoral students led group discussions and participated in school assemblies.

Professors also disseminated information about coping with trauma to NYU students. Various listserves, such as the Trauma List Serve, and websites, such as those supported by the American Psychological Association

(APA) and the National Association of School Psychologists (NASP), were particularly helpful in obtaining this information. NYU psychology doctoral students, in turn, utilized listserves and web-sites in their consultation work with school personnel and parents.

In addition to informal support provided by university professionals, counselors were available for walk-in appointments at the main university clinic and at various sites throughout the campus. Counseling services were extended to include evening and weekend hours and arrangements were made to have counselors meet with pre-arranged groups of students in both classrooms and dormitories.

Working with Parents

Parents of college-age students, as well as of those in the New York schools, sought contact with their children on 9/11. In the New York City schools, NYU psychology doctoral students responded to parents' telephone calls. In addition, they greeted parents at the entrance to the school and retrieved children from their classrooms. Similarly, at the university, phone banks were established and NYU students were encouraged to call home. Also, NYU established a web-site for parents to obtain updated information on conditions in New York City and at New York University. Three days following the WTC disaster, the dean of the School of Education sent a letter to parents indicating the actions the school had taken and reassuring them of their children's safety.

NYU psychology doctoral students, who were doing fieldwork in the New York schools, provided a structure for parents to talk about their concerns related to the WTC disaster. They also distributed information and literature on children and trauma. Likewise, for members of the NYU community who were also parents, faculty-led discussions were offered. These discussions focused on the reactions and needs of children and ways to talk to children about the recent tragedy.

Working with Community Members

New York University mental health professionals serviced community members both directly and indirectly. The direct services they provided included volunteering for the WTC counseling services at a triage center, staffing phone banks at rescue and other agencies as well as at the university, and helping people at local hospitals who were searching for missing persons. On an indirect level, mental health professionals reached a broader audience through the media, as NYU psychologists were interviewed by journalists and broad-casters. In at least one case, an NYU psychologist was on national television discussing ways of talking to children about the tragedy.

Working with Faculty

Faculty were assisted in the initial time period following the WTC disaster. They were provided with opportunities to process their own reactions to the WTC disaster and to learn how to help their students. NYU faculty members led discussions on post-traumatic stress interventions and provided informa-tion about referral services for students. The university also established open counseling sessions to help faculty members' cope.

Likewise in the NYC schools, NYU psychology doctoral students led discus-sion groups for faculty members and consulted with public and private school teachers. Furthermore, workshops and presentations were held both in the New York schools and at NYU for faculty members to address their concerns about how to help others as well as how to help themselves while helping others.

The Faculty and Staff Assistance program at NYU assembled a crisis debriefing team, which provided services to NYU staff and faculty. These services were available twice daily during lunch hour. They also distributed a contact number for those faculty and staff members who were seeking in-dividual counseling, as well as a 24-hour phone counseling service for all university employees. In addition, they posted a list of references on their web-site to help children and families cope with tragedy. Furthermore, the Faculty and Staff Assistance program ran debriefing groups for faculty, staff, and their families for 2 weeks after 9/11 (on a walk-in basis) from 10 a.m. to 4 p.m. After the initial 2 weeks following the WTC disaster, NYU counselors offered to debrief groups or individuals who wanted additional services.

Working with Administrators

Services similar to those described above were offered to administrators in the NYC public and private schools by NYU psychology doctoral students.

SECONDARY RESPONSES

Vignette

(These workshops were videotaped; they document how drama can help chil-dren transform a terrifying experience into a more hopeful one [Stern, n.d.]).

For first-year graduate students in the school of psychology program at NYU, the World Trade Center attacks effectively set the tone for the academic year. Their first field-based practicum class, which had been scheduled for September 11th, was canceled. It was clear that the needs of the schools that the NYU Psychology doctoral students would be working with had changed. As a result, their field-based coursework had to be altered. In the month following September 11th NYU Psychology doctoral students began to collect data on how school personnel responded to the terrorist attack. Together, the students with their professor analyzed the data and wrote an article for *Communiqué*, the National Association of School Psychologists (NASP) newspaper (March, Hooker, Arnold, Dale, Deteso, Godder, Grossman, Gullesserian, Marrom, Sattin & Shrem, 2001). The students believed that many lessons could be learned from the various responses to the attacks, and that those lessons could be shared with other school psychologists, teachers, and administrators. The students presented their findings and conclusions about the role of the school psychologist in times of tragedy at the annual NASP conference.

These graduate students channeled their personal and professional experience into providing a service to the profession. Their documentation of how and why schools responded to the disaster of September 11th enabled them to indirectly help the victims. They learned and helped.

Working with NYU and NYC Students

During the weeks and months that followed September 11th, NYU continued to develop and offer mental health services to their students. For example, in October the university offered a seminar on coping strategies for traumatic events.

Similarly, in the New York Public Schools services continued. Interventions focused on anxiety, grief, and bereavement (Hooker & Fodor, 2003). NYU Psychology doctoral students offered individual counseling to those students who were experiencing the loss of a family member or had a family member who survived the attack. In addition, the NYU Psychology doctoral students led group discussions which facilitated the processing of the horrific events.

Working with Parents

Many members of the NYU community are themselves parents. Therefore, in the months that followed the World Trade Center disaster, New York University continued to respond to the needs of parents within the NYU community. The university recognized the importance of understanding the needs of children, particularly learning how to talk to them about the tragedy, and, therefore, it added additional faculty-led discussions for all parents in the NYU community. Likewise, in the New York City Public Schools, mental health professionals and NYU psychology doctoral students provided parent workshops on topics such as trauma, grief, and post-traumatic stress disorder, as well as information about how to talk to children about disasters.

Working with Community Members
Community members in the NYC area continued to receive support from New York University mental health professionals. One example involves the International Trauma Studies Program at NYU. This group helped to create "community recovery forums" (Saul, 2002), which provided opportunities for parent associations across schools to meet and exchange information. It was designed to "affirm the competency of the parents and teachers" around issues related to talking to NYC students who had been affected by 9/11 (Saul, 2002).

Working with Faculty
NYU psychologists and psychology doctoral students provided consultation to faculty members. Many New York City school teachers and NYU professors had questions about how to serve the needs of both individuals and groups. NYU psychology doctoral students supported New York City teachers by consulting with them and, in some cases, co-leading discussions with the teachers. Furthermore, they provided workshops on trauma, grief, post traumatic stress disorder, and helping children cope with the events of 9/11. Likewise, at New York University, faculty members were invited to participate in seminars on coping strategies during times of trauma. Support groups for faculty members dealing with grief and loss were also offered.

Working with Administrators
During this time mental health professionals at NYU and in the New York City schools continued to meet with and advise administrators on how to meet the needs of the students and faculty.

LONG-TERM RESPONSES
Vignette
As local schools struggled to determine how to help their students cope in the aftermath of the WTC disaster, some NYU faculty members who are psychologists consulted with schools. One psychologist, for example, conducted trauma workshops with a class of 4th and 5th grade students who had viewed the WTC

disaster from their classroom window. These workshops were videotaped; they document how drama can help children transform a terrifying experience into a more hopeful one. This film should be helpful to other professionals.

Working with Students

New York University continued to respond to the needs of its students. One way the University accomplished this was through one-credit seminars focusing on 9/11. These seminars considered topics such as the role of educators after 9/11 (including how to best serve the needs of students and their families) and the gathering of oral history testimony pertaining to the disaster. Furthermore, at the first year anniversary of September 11th, space was provided for reflection, meditation, and interaction with other NYU community members. In addition, walk-in hours were extended at the University Counseling Center, and group discussions and seminars also were held at the University Counseling Services.

Working with Parents

The mental health professionals who work at the New York University Child Study Center have developed many ways to continue to support parents who are members of the NYU community. For example, the Child Study Center has developed an online resource called About Our Kids (1999). This website contains articles and resources for helping children cope with traumatic events. One resource, for example, is a "parent letter" entitled "Talking to Kids About Terrorism or Acts of War" (Goodman & Gurian, 2004).

Working with Community Members

As a result of September 11th, many psychologists at NYU have engaged in research that will further our knowledge and understanding of trauma. Mental health professionals at NYU are conducting research on drug use and risky sex post 9/11, terrorism and school consultation, self-care of NYC school psychologists, and the promotion of resilience in response to terrorism. In addition, a fact sheet for psychologists working with children has been developed (American Psychological Association, n.d.). Further, the NYU Institute for Trauma and Stress was established in September 2002. The mission of the Institute "is to assess psychological, social and biological impact of traumatic events on childhood across developmental stages from toddler years to young adulthood, to develop effective treatments and interventions which ameliorate these effects and to understand the role of individual resilience and community support in the process of recovery, to advance the field of trauma studies by educating and training future clinicians and researchers, to enhance the awareness and understanding of trauma and its effects through education and outreach to the community" (New York University Child Study Center: The Institute of Trauma and Stress, 2002).

Working with Faculty
Since December 2001, NYU mental health professionals have continued to offer services to NYU students and faculty members. For example, during the anniversaries of September 11th, the counseling services are open for walk-in hours all day.

Working with Administrators
During the months and years following September 11th, NYU mental health professionals continue to meet with NYU administrators in order to modify and improve their Disaster Response Plan, as well as to develop a team of mental health professionals that will be available to provide services to NYU community members in the event of another traumatic event.

CONCLUSION
Mental health professionals and administrators at New York University took action both during and prior to 9/11. Because of the "Y2K" scare in January of 2000, NYU developed a "command center" for the university. From this center the administration could contact NYU security and health services and was able to monitor all university systems. This center also served as a central meeting place for administrators to coordinate services and outreach. The administration had a Disaster Plan in place that they were able to utilize. The Y2K command center facilitated timely response and clear communication by bringing people together to work collaboratively and efficiently.

Challenges that confronted New York University include how to prevent burnout and vicarious traumatization in mental health professionals following a disaster, when the need for their services and time is the most demanding. In addition, it is important not to assume that all "psychologists" at the university setting are clinicians who know how to deal with trauma. A team of professionals should be trained and all faculty and staff, including adjunct professors and graduate assistants, should receive routine training on how to help students cope with trauma, as well as how to identify possible warning signs for post traumatic stress disorder. Finally, although many professors at NYU have conducted research on the impact of 9/11, some did not feel able to conduct research. They were too traumatized. Therefore, it seems important to develop research teams across universities for purposes of collaboration.

Since September 11, 2001, life in America has been transformed. There is a loss of innocence in the United States. Life in New York City and at New York University has changed too. In New York City and the surrounding areas, there are many reminders of 9/11: the landmark World Trade Center buildings no longer loom overhead; many community members look to the sky when planes fly overhead; there is the presence of the military (especially in the months following 9/11) and the constant security updates, modifications, and practice drills. There are countless examples serve as constant reminders of the trauma that NY residents experienced on 9/11. Nonetheless, our community and our school have moved forward. During this time, New York University has responded to the largest scale attack on our nation, on our soil, in our country's history. New York University managed to assist faculty, staff, students, parents, and community members in the aftermath of September 11th. It is our hope that this chapter will serve to help other universities further develop their Disaster Response Plans in the case of a traumatic event in their community.

REFERENCES

About Our Kids. Retrieved February 8, 2004, from New York University (NYU) Child Study Center website http://www.aboutourkids.org

American Psychological Association. (n.d.). *Fostering resilience in response to terrorism: For psychologists working with children* [Fact Sheet]. Washington, DC: Author.

Blanchard, E. B., Kuhn, E., Rowell, D. L., Hickling, E. J., Wittrock, D., Rogers, R. L., et al. (2004). Studies of the vicarious traumatization of college students by the September 11th attacks: Effects of proximity, exposure and connectedness. *Behaviour Research & Therapy, 42*(2), 191–205.

Coates, S. W., Schechter, D. S., First, E., Anzieu-Premmereur, C., & Steinberg, Z. (2002). Thoughts on crisis intervention with New York City children after the world trade center bombing. *Psychotherapies, 22*(3), 143–152.

Eaves, C. (2001). The development and implementation of a crisis response team in a school setting. *International Journal of Emergency Mental Health, 3*(1), 35–46.

Galea, S., Ahern, J., Resnick, H., Kilpatrick, D., Bucuvalas, M., Gold, J., et al. (2002). Psychological sequelae of the September 11 terrorist attacks in New York City. *New England Journal of Medicine, 346*(13), 982–987.

Goodman, R., & Gurian, A. (2003). Talking to kids about terrorism and war in Iraq. The NYU Child Study Center Parent Letter. Retrieved April 3, 2004, from http://www.aboutourkids.org/aboutour/parent_letter/war_E.pdf

Hooker, K. E., & Fodor, I. E. (2003). Helping others while caring for themselves: A New York school psychology community responds to September 11. *New York University Psychoeducational Center*, 1–34.

Kerr, M. M. (2003). Preventing and addressing crises and violence-related problems in schools. In M. D. Weist, (Ed.),U Maryland School of Medicine (Ed.), *Handbook of school mental health: Advancing practice and research issues in clinical child psychology; handbook of school mental health: Advancing practice and research* (pp. 321–334). New York: Kluwer Academic/Plenum Publishers.

Lowry, J. L., & Lating, J. M. (2002). Reflections on the response to mass terrorist attacks: An elaboration on Everly and Mitchell's 10 commandments. *Brief Treatment & Crisis Intervention,* 2(1), 95–104.

Luna, J. T. (2002). Collaborative assessment and healing in schools after large-scale terrorist attacks. *International Journal of Emergency Mental Health,* 4(3), 201–208.

March, R., Hooker, K., Arnold, J., Dale, K., Deteso, J., Godder, G., Grossman, S., Gullesserian, J., Marron, E., Sattin, J., & Shrem, M. (2001, December). September 11th: Perspectives from New York City School Psychologists. *Communique, 16.*

McCarthy, M. A., & Butler, L. (2003). Responding to traumatic events on college campuses: A case study and assessment of student postdisaster anxiety. *Journal of College Counseling,* 6(1), 90–96.

Miller, R. S. (1995). Largest earthquake at an American University, January 1994: University counseling perspective. *Crisis Intervention & Time-Limited Treatment,* 1(3), 215–223.

Motomura, N., Iwakiri, M., Takino, Y., Shimomura, Y., & Ishibashi, M. (2003). School crisis intervention in the Ikeda incident: Organization and activity of the mental support team. *Psychiatry & Clinical Neurosciences,* 57(2), 239–240.

New York University Child Study Center: The Institute for Trauma and Stress (2002). Mission, Vision and Values. Retrieved February 8, 2004, from http://www.aboutourkids.org/aboutus/programs/trauma_stress.html.

Norris, F. H., Byrne, G. M., Diaz, E., & Kaniasty, K. (2001). The range, magnitude, and duration of effects of natural and human-caused disasters: A review of the empirical literature. Retrieved March 1, 2004, from http://www.ncptsd.org/facts/disasters

North, C. S., Nixon, S. J., Shariat, S., Mallonee, S., McMillen, J. C., Spitznagel, E. L., et al. (1999). Psychiatric disorders among survivors of the Oklahoma City bombing. *Journal of the American Medical Association, 282*(8), 755–762.

Pfefferbaum, B. (2003). The children of Oklahoma City. In R.J. Ursano (Ed.), *Terrorism and disaster: Individual and community mental health interventions* (pp. 58–70). New York: Cambridge University Press.

Purves, D. G., & Erwin, P. G. (2002). A study of posttraumatic stress in a student population. *Journal of Genetic Psychology, 163*(1), 89–96.

Rothman, P. D. (2004). The influence of the quality of adult attachment and degree of exposure to the World Trade Center disaster on post-traumatic stress symptoms in a college population. *Dissertation Abstracts International, B64*(8), 4060.

Saul, J. (2002, September 11). 2 pillars are crucial to helping children adjust. *New York Times,* p. A17.

Schlenger, W. E., Caddell, J. M., Ebert, L., Jordan, B. K., Rourke, K. M., Wilson, D., et al. (2002). Psychological reactions to terrorist attacks: Findings from the national study of Americans' reactions to September 11. *Journal of the American Medical Association, 288*(5), 581–588.

Schouten, R., Callahan, M. V., & Bryant, S. (2004). Community response to disaster: The role of the workplace. *Harvard Review of Psychiatry, 12*(4), 229–237.

Smith, D.W., Christianson, E. H., Vincent R., & Hann, N. E. (1999). Population effects of the bombing of Oklahoma City. *Journal of the Oklahoma State Medical Association, 92,* 193–198.

Soliman, H. H., & Silver, P. T. (2003). Social work intervention in disasters and traumatic stress events: An emerging practice arena. *Journal of Social Service Research, 30*(2), xiii–xv.

Stern, P. (n.d.) *Standing Tall.* Retrieved February 6, 2004, from http://www.fanlight. com/catalog/films/393_st.shtml

Stone, G. L. (1993). Psychological challenges and responses to a campus tragedy: The Iowa experience. *Journal of College Student Psychotherapy, 8*(3), 259–271.

Underwood, M. M., & Kalafat, J. (2002). Crisis intervention in a new context: New Jersey post-September 11, 2001. *Brief Treatment & Crisis Intervention, 2*(1), 75–83.

Vogel, J. M. (2004). After disasters, what about the children? *PsycCRITIQUES.* Retrieved December 15, 2004, from PsycINFO (1840-Current) database.

Williams, M. B., Zinner, E. S., & Ellis, R. R. (1999). The connection between grief and trauma: An overview. In E.S. Zinner & M.B. Williams (Eds.), *When a community weeps: Case studies in group survivorship* (pp.3–17). Philadelphia, PA: Brunner/Mazel.

CHAPTER 7

Psychosocial Assistance to Civilians in War

The Bosnian Experience

Ragnhild Dybdahl

BACKGROUND

The war in Bosnia-Herzegovina broke out in the spring of 1992 and ended with the Dayton peace agreement, which was signed in November 1995. The war caused vast suffering to the whole population, and continues to do so for many. It is estimated to have caused 250,000 deaths and rendered 2 million people homeless. About 4 million people were refugees or internally displaced (Petevi, 1996). It has been reported that 90% of the wounded and dead in the war in Bosnia were civilians.

Geographical, historical, and cultural closeness made the war in Bosnia and the suffering feel nearer to many people in Western Europe, and also in the U.S., than did many other wars. The media focus was enormous, not least regarding the issue of war rape (see Agger, 2001, for a discussion), and the international community wanted to help.

In 1994, I was given the opportunity to work in Bosnia for Norwegian People's Aid, a nongovernmental organization, coordinating a project providing psychosocial assistance to women traumatized by war. Later, I was involved in research projects focusing on children. My work was carried out in and near Tuzla, a multiethnic industrial town in the northeast with a pre-war population of about 100,000.

The consequences of the war were numerous shooting and shelling; sexual violence and torture; lack of food, security and shelter; the loss of loved ones, health, and homes. The war damaged the society's infrastructure and there was widespread lack of food, transport, housing, and medical services. The impact on the family was severe, with family separations and the toll of living with distressed family members. Children suffered loss of parental support and protection. Children's education was disrupted, and many lost educational opportunities in spite of large-scale programs implemented by UNICEF and other agencies to support schools in a variety of ways. Thus, there were many direct and indirect consequences of the war (see also Cairns, 1996).

Exposure to extremely traumatic events involving the destruction of economic, political, social, and healthcare infrastructure have immediate and long-term negative consequences for many aspects of the lives of individuals, families, and communities. Survivors of extremely stressful events have been found to be at high risk for developing psychiatric disorders and psychosocial problems (e.g., de Jong, Scholte, Koeter, & Hart, 2000; Mollica, 2000), also in the long term (Bramsen & van der Ploeg, 1999). These include depression, complicated grief, suicide, generalized anxiety disorder, substance abuse, and post-traumatic stress disorder (PTSD). PTSD consists of symptoms of arousal, avoidance, and intrusion, and has received particular attention in the last decade. Following war trauma, there is also likely to be an increase in violence (criminal and domestic), and the problems can affect at least the next two generations (Agger, 1995). People who have been continually exposed to violence, especially where the attacks and abuse were carried out by people who were previously trusted, will nearly always experience a significant change in their lives and attitudes (Machel, 1996).

Until recently, aid programs for civilians affected by armed conflicts have primarily targeted physical health. However, the last decade has seen a significant increase in psychosocial aid efforts to populations in armed conflicts and refugee crises (e.g., Agger, 1995; Barat, 2003; deMartino & von Buchwald, 1996; Dyregrov, 1997; Husain, 2001; Smith & Surgan, 1996). Psychosocial emergency assistance aims at promoting "mental health and human rights by strategies that enhance the existing psycho-social protective factors and decrease the psycho-social stressor factors at different levels of intervention" (Agger, p. 13).

In response to these needs, psychosocial assistance was offered by international and local organizations in Bosnia. Although 185 projects implemented in Bosnia-Herzegovina and Croatia were described and the effort was "unprecedented in other war contexts" (Agger, 1995, p. 12), Agger's report indicated that the number of local professionals in Bosnia-Herzegovina and Croatia was sufficient to cover less than 1% of the estimated needs for psychosocial assistance of the traumatized.

With the increased awareness of traumatization of women in war, programs aimed at providing support and recovery for women in the former Yugoslavia became numerous (e.g., Mulders, 1997; Pecnik, 1997; Smith & Surgan, 1996). Many of these programs aimed at tackling women's problems including "shattered self-esteem, lack of control over their own lives and powerlessness" (Pecnik, p. 363) and were group based. Although the primary objective of many such support programs was related to sexual violence, a wider approach was usually chosen, rather than an isolated focus on sexual trauma (e.g., Mulders, 1997).

Recently, it has been suggested that the most common psychosocial approaches during this crisis were too dominated by the concept of posttraumatic stress disorder, and perhaps greater emphasis should have been placed on sociopolitical aspects of psychosocial projects (Agger, 2001). Increasing attention is being paid to targeting the public mental health aspects of complex humanitarian and political emergencies in a political, community, and social context (de Jong, 2002).

THE PROJECT

A number of studies have demonstrated high prevalence of psychological problems, including PTSD, depression, and anxiety, in children who are victims of emergencies (e.g., Garbarino & Kostelny, 1996; Smith, Perrin, Yule, Hacam, & Stuvland, 2002; Thabet & Vostanis, 2000) such as wars. While working with women in Bosnia, the need to provide support for children became clear. Many children appeared to be suffering from anxiety and depression, and mothers expressed concern about their ability to care for their children under such difficult circumstances. Based on experiences from weekly groups for women led by local professional or paraprofessional therapists (Dybdahl, 2000; Dybdahl & Pasagic, 2000), I developed a program aimed at helping mothers help their children, and wanted to investigate possible effects of this program.

The Intervention

The intervention consisted of weekly group meetings for mothers during a period of 5 months. Each group was led by a paraprofessional group leader and consisted of about five mothers. In addition to experiences from the support groups for women, the content of the program was based on trauma psychology and developmental psychology, and focused on coping with problems and promoting good mother–child interaction (Dybdahl, 2001a). The program aimed at promoting children's healing and healthy development through parental education, support, and involvement, and focused on the importance of mother–child interaction for children's well-being. The content and strategies of the support program were a combination of elements from trauma recovery programs (e.g., UNICEF projects such as Dyregrov, 1997) and early childhood development programs (in particular, International Child Development Program, ICDP, Hundeide, 1996). The topics of education and discussion in the groups (see Dybdahl, 2001a) were:

- Child development and children's needs
- Increased awareness about children's needs and the important role of the mother
- Interaction between the child and the caregiver (mother)
- Trauma and loss

Social interaction between mother and child focused on both social and cognitive communication, such as the importance of affection, shared focus, and dialogue. The topics of trauma and loss included information about common reactions as well as suggestions for ways to help mothers cope, and ways mothers could help their children. The mothers were encouraged to share their experiences and discuss strategies that had been helpful in the past.

All the families in the study were provided with monthly free basic health care during the intervention period. This service was provided by local physicians and made easily accessible. Vitamins or iron was given to children who needed it; two children were referred to specialist treatment for serious health problems that were discovered and are not included in the study.

Method

Internally displaced mothers and children (N = 87 mother–child dyads, children's mean age = 5.5 years) were recruited. They were mainly from rural areas and had experienced many potentially traumatizing events, such as death of relatives, witnessing their house being burnt, being shot at, experiencing grenade attacks (shelling), or family members being injured. The participants were randomly assigned to an intervention group (n = 42), where they took part in the psychosocial intervention program and received monthly basic medical care, or a control group that received medical care only (n = 45). The children and their mothers were monitored before and after the intervention period to assess psychological and physical health and cognitive development, using several indicators, such as mothers' and children's self reported symptoms and functioning, observations by physicians and psychologists, and the use of Raven's Color Matrices to measure cognitive development (for more details, see Dybdahl, 2001b).

Results

Positive effects of the intervention program were found in the reduction of children's problems as judged by the interviewer, in children's weight gain, mothers' reduction of trauma symptoms, and their increased life satisfaction. The same tendency was found in the relatively greater improvement in children's cognitive performance, perceived social support, mothers' overall description of their children, and reduction in children's problems. Specifically, the children in the intervention group were rated as more intelligent and active by their mothers than the controls and as happier, less restless, less distractible, less clingy, and with less drastic mood changes by the interviewers than were controls.

Improvement in the expected direction, although not statistically significant, included children's self-reported well-being today and reduction in children's concentration problems and other problems as judged by their mothers. For the depression scores and well-being today, as judged by the children themselves, as well as changes in hemoglobin levels, the results were in the opposite direction, although not statistically significant. Of all the variables (scales and subscales), seven showed significantly ($p < .05$) greater improvement for the intervention group than for the control group, and another six showed a statistical tendency ($p < .10$) in the same direction. The results of 13 variables were not statistically significant. Of these, nine were in the expected direction, whereas four were in the opposite direction (see Dybdahl, 2001b).

CHALLENGES AND LESSONS LEARNED
Working in War Conditions

This study combined assessment of trauma exposure and mental and physical health problems with an intervention project. Although many of the experiences on which the project was based originated in an emergency phase of the war, it was also important that experiences from the recovery phases were integrated. Activities and experiences from both the emergency and recovery phases of the war seemed valid and strengthened the program.

One of the first lessons learned was related to the significance of identifying and establishing collaborating partners, professionals, institutions, and organizations. In addition to thorough assessment of trauma exposure, problems, and needs, the importance of assessing available resources and acceptable forms of interventions was a major lesson learned.

The study used available local resources to a large degree. Although the main emphasis was on a psychosocial approach aimed at strengthening resiliency and coping, there was also a link to specialized medical and psychiatric services. From a coordinating perspective, this network of personnel, institutions, and services was experienced as a major strength of the project because it provided a chain of supervision and back-up (Dybdahl, 2001a).

A number of people of different backgrounds and professions took part in the project over a period of several months. Lack of transport and electricity, for example, posed challenges for the implementation of the project, and practical solutions had to be found. The security and material situation was also difficult, requiring logistical and practical support. Coordinating the project therefore involved many challenges. Having worked in Bosnia for several months before starting the research intervention project, and therefore having established a professional network and become accustomed to local needs and ways, a least to some degree, was a major advantage in planning and executing this project. Both for motivational and ethical reasons, emphasis was placed on supervision, training, education, and self-care for those who took part in implementing the project.

Working Factors and Long-term Effect

The working factors of the program are not known. Possible mechanisms were mothers' improved mental health and social networks, and increased allocation of social and physical resources to the target child, that is, that the child became more salient because of the program.

In an attempt to look at possible long-term effects, we tried to trace the families in 2001. However, only about half the children were found and there was little evidence that the intervention had had statistically significant long-term effects, although the small number made it difficult to draw such conclusions. The mothers in the intervention group said that the group participation had been very positive and that they themselves believed it had had a lasting effect.

Program Content

Studies of families and children affected by war should be informed by general developmental psychology. Similarly, the interventions to assist war-traumatized populations are closely linked to our general knowledge of ways to promote health and well-being.

The needs of children are remarkably universal. All children need nutritious food, health care, education, shelter, and a safe and loving family (Machel, 1996, p. 5). Early child development has now captured the attention of the international community. In particular, the years 0–3 are seen as critical for the development of intelligence, personality, and social behavior (Young, 1997). Children who are exposed to unhealthy, unstimulating environments may develop poorly and suffer lifetime consequences of impeded development. Young argues that after this critical age it "may be too late to counteract negative physical, neurological, psychological, and social factors associated with early deprivation and inadequate stimulation" (p. 1).

One of the most immediate effects of war is the disruption of food supplies. This study demonstrated that physical health and nutrition were of a major concern to the participants. This is also illustrated by findings in Bosnia by Husain and his colleagues (1998, p. 1719): "deprivation of food, water and shelter had a severe adverse impact on the children . . . [and] was associated with significantly increased symptoms of avoidance and hypervigilance." Both poverty and war increase people's, especially children's, risk of exposure to environmental hazards and health problems. Poor waste disposal, poor hygiene, and inadequate or contaminated water add to the vicious circle of malnutrition and infection. The effects interact with each other, for example with respect to malnutrition, cognitive development, and mental health.

There is a general need for more attention to be paid to the impact of traumatic stress on physical health. For young children many health problems are linked to malnutrition (Machel, 1996). Long-term malnutrition and protein-energy undernutrition "result in cognitive and social–emotional impairment, with little improvement upon nutritional recovery" (Sternberg & Grigorenko, 1997, p. 27). Malnutrition weakens children's resistance to common childhood diseases and has negative impact on children's cognitive development. The need for a holistic view of health is also illustrated in Article 39 of the Convention of the Rights of the Child, where it is stated that State Parties are required to take measures to promote children's physical and psychological recovery and reintegration.

Early child development programs (ECDP) often target children's basic physical needs of health care, nutrition, and protection from harm, as well as basic psychosocial and educational needs such as interaction, stimulation, affection, and learning. ECDPs provide services that promote young children's development and there is evidence that such programs are successful (Young, 1997). There now are a number of well-documented child development and education programs. These include the Home Intervention Project for Preschool Youngsters (HIPPY) (Eldering & Vedder, 1999), the Turkish Early Enrichment Project (TEEP) (Kagitcibasi, 1999), the Integrated Child Development Services (ICDS) (Muralidharan & Kaul, 1999), the Perry preschool Project (see Myers, 1995), and the International Child Development Program (Hundeide, 1991, 1996). These programs have all integrated experiences that were made in earlier intervention programs such as Project Head Start, for example that the program must be sensitive to the culture and ecological context of childhood (Bronfenbrenner, 1975). Also, the intensity and duration of the programs have been increased since the earliest projects, and the focus has expanded from children only to also include parents, family, and the community (Eldering & Leseman, 1999).

Based on some of the findings from early child development programs, it is possible that the intervention program should have targeted younger children and that the intervention period could have been longer. The program was only integrated with other programs to a very limited extent, for example, the basic health care program. In the period before implementing the project, there were attempts at integrating the program with a mine awareness program, but this did not take place in the actual implementation of the program. In the future, psychological help is likely to profit from being combined with other types of assistance, such as more extensive physical health care programs, sports, and music activities for children, and with income-generating programs, to avoid the development of separate mental health programs (Machel, 1996), but it is also important to consider this integration carefully to avoid people feeling coerced into using mental health services (Dybdahl & Pasagic, 2000).

Group-based work has both advantages and disadvantages. One aspect to consider in this respect is what topics can be targeted in a group. Child rearing practices, mother–child interaction, and a psychoeducative approach seem to be suited for group work, as was the involvement of paraprofessionals, that is, group leaders who have relatively little training as therapists or counselors. Using encouragement, praise, recognition, and understanding as methods in the group work also seemed fruitful. This is in line with the recommendation that emphasis should be placed on "constructive programming" compared to "compensatory programming" (Myers, 1995). This implies that much knowledge is *discovered*, and points to the significant role of active and participatory learning. "Therefore the discoveries of traditional knowledge (constructed over time and through experience) must be recognized, with attention given to building on positive elements in a given setting rather than simply identifying and correcting errors" (Myers, p. 455). Myers also emphasizes the importance of integrating different intervention programs.

Culture

The degree to which PTSD is a valid construct in non-Western societies, and whether Western interventions are appropriate in these settings, has been much debated (Summerfield, 1999). Machel (1996) states: "Western diagnostic approaches can be ill-suited to a context in which people are more likely to turn for assistance to family, friends and traditional healers than to seek medical help for their problems" (p. 34). However, recent studies of folk diagnoses and emotional distress among traumatized populations provide support for the usefulness of combining very different world views (Bolton, 2003; Mollica, 2001).

The cultural and social context in this study was more similar to the Western European/North American context than it would have been in many other parts of the world, which is likely to have played a role and facilitated the use of the selected tests and tasks and also to have allowed the close cooperation with local professionals and paraprofessionals. However, common psychotherapy traditions and child-rearing practices in rural Bosnia differ in many ways from those of Western Europe and the U.S. Close cooperation with Bosnian colleagues over an extended period in preparing the intervention, as well as in implementing it, was perceived as extremely important in order to provide a culturally appropriate program.

Ethics

Relief workers and researchers face many ethical challenges when working in conflict situations in a foreign country, as was the case in this project. My work confronted me with questions that were specific for the situation in which I worked, but also with many that are common to aid work and research in many other war and post-war settings. These constituted challenges throughout the study, and they continue to do so.

In a situation where people's basic survival was not guaranteed and the need for food and safety was urgent, should scarce resources be allocated to psychosocial efforts and research? The international community now provides substantial psychosocial assistance also in times of war and crises, through the work of UN organizations and governmental and nongovernmental organizations. With this expansion, evaluations and strategies to improve services have become increasingly important. For ethical reasons, there is a need to describe interventions so that others (e.g., the scientific community and local authorities) can evaluate them. There is also an ethical obligation to evaluate aid efforts so that scarce resources can be used to maximum benefit.

One guiding principle is that research must be of benefit to the affected populations. Research priorities in field settings are integrated with the interests of non-research institutions, community leaders, and participants (Eyde, 2000). The research must not inflict harm on people, nor put people in situations or positions that could endanger or retraumatize them. At the same time, many participants in this study said that it was important to them that others knew what they were going through.

Researchers should maximize participants' well-being and benefit from the study. It is also important to consider the quality of the research, as "bad science makes for bad ethics" (Rosenthal, 1999, p. 408). Therefore, difficult working conditions caused by war should not excuse bad research.

The topics that were either targets of investigation or were otherwise brought up in this project were sensitive issues, such as atrocities, political activism, religious beliefs, rape, mental health, and evaluation of support programs. These pose particular challenges, both regarding data collection and presentation of results. Moreover, the participants in this type of research are often vulnerable, such as children, refugees, the poor, and people with mental health problems, which raises special concern. In war conditions, both individuals and the society as a whole at a national and community level are affected and this adds to the vulnerability. Well-functioning local institutions are important as they can play a role in the protection, cooperation, and control of ongoing research; when these are lacking, even more responsibility is placed on the researcher.

Informed consent and voluntary participation must be considered carefully because of the challenges related to war, poverty, illiteracy, and cultural differences. For example, people may feel coerced to participate because of cultural or situational factors, such as power relationships and the need for money or food. Also, researchers' autonomy and professional and personal integrity must be considered. In this project there was a close collaboration with local organizations and governmental institutions, which made this an issue that had to be considered regularly.

Design, methodologies, and interpretations should be open to scrutiny by the international scientific and health care communities. The communities and participants that take part in the research and whom the findings concern need to have access to the findings and an opportunity to express their views. This often means that the findings also should be made available in the local language. If the illiteracy rate is high, in addition to written reports, other means of communicating should be used, such as radio presentations or presentations at a community meeting. Providing feedback to the people who took part in the study often presents a challenge, but is critically important. One woman in a Bosnian refugee settlement told me of her feeling of disappointment after she had taken part in a survey some time ago: "A foreign woman came and did a questionnaire and we never saw her again." I therefore went back to Bosnia to inform about the findings of the study. I reached collaborators (who had taken part in the data collection or the interventions or were liaisons in the refugee settlement and the school where participants were recruited) with reasonable success, although at that time only very few participants (women and children) were reached, at least directly. Sharing the experiences and results of research, under conditions of war and crises, can be very rewarding.

This research was carried out in a field setting. Sieber (2000) has outlined several of the ethical risks that may arise in such settings, for example how group members may get information that the participant intended only for the researcher. Private information may be revealed about persons who did not agree to take part in the research. The safety of the researchers and research assistants may be at risk. Research in war often involves witnessing human rights violations and massive human suffering. Also, other personnel involved in the work carried out, such as research assistants and interpreters, are likely to be exposed to human pain, which can be difficult to cope with. Researchers must consider ways to address this issue and provide support to their personnel.

Facing massive suffering is likely to make neutrality difficult, and at times this work may give the feeling that one accepts inhumanity. In war conditions, propaganda will be used and the researcher must therefore be a critical receiver and mediator of information.

Although there are many practical and ethical obstacles, there are also a number of arguments supporting the idea of carrying out research under such conditions. From a human rights' perspective, information is important for the international community's awareness and ability to act. Such information needs to be more than haphazard, sensational, and anecdotal stories or snapshots. Instead, systematic, valid, and reliable knowledge is needed about individuals, groups, and communities in conflict situations; for example, their experiences, reactions, and factors that promote vulnerability, resiliency, and healing. Sound research can contribute to the understanding of human beings, which in turn can be used for purposes of intervention and preventive measures to influence policy and promote peace. By cooperating with indigenous researchers and other local people, some of the difficulties can be overcome. In addition, the expatriate researchers will hopefully leave behind knowledge and skills that continue to be useful after they have gone home. Equally important, the expatriate researchers will take home knowledge and experiences that they will continue to use—whether at home or in another war zone.

Implications: "Going to Scale?"

This small-scale project showed positive effects of a relatively inexpensive and simple intervention for children. As there were several benefits, including weight gain, the implications are that psychosocial intervention can have measurable effects and lend support to studies that show that this is good way of supporting people who have been victims of war. An additional implication is that the program possibly should continue, and even expand. However, if so, under what conditions should this take place?

There are humanitarian, economic, and political reasons for wishing to scale up a pilot project to reach many people with services or programs that have demonstrated success. In fact, more than a decade ago UNICEF stated that there is less need for small-scale pilot projects than before, but instead that the challenge lies in disseminating our knowledge "to a scale that can lead to universal coverage of most of the basic services for human development" (UNICEF, May, 1989, quoted by Myers, 1995, p. 369).

Myers (1995) discusses the "growing frustration within organizations arising from the fact that many small-scale research, pilot, or demonstration projects have failed to get out of the 'hothouse' to have the desired large-scale influence on policies, programs, and people" (pp. 369–370). "How many times during the last three decades of intensive development efforts has a demonstration or pilot project provided "the answers" to a development problem? Everyone is flushed with enthusiasm and optimism. The model that proved so useful on a small scale is expanded with the hopes of benefiting a larger population. All too often, however, impact decreases or disappears completely" (Pyle, 1984, cited in Myers, p. 369).

As discussed by Myers (1995), scaling involves a host of challenges and processes. The differences between a project such as the one I implemented in Bosnia and a large-scale program tend to be numerous. Myers provides a useful comparison of the two based on Pyle's (1984, cited in Myers) manuscript "Life after Project," and many of these elements are likely to be relevant for this project, if it were to be implemented on a large scale. These include: (a) the project had specific time-bounded objectives, whereas most large-scale programs have vague, ambitious objectives without time boundaries; (b) the project targeted a specific population, whereas large programs tend to lack targeting; (c) there was a result orientation, whereas larger programs are concerned with inputs; (d) teamwork was crucial compared with larger programs' typically hierarchical relations; (e) training was an ongoing process during the whole project period; (f) selection of collaborators and participants was based on motivation, values, and non-monetary incentives versus large scales programs' selection by objective criteria; (g) supervision had a training focus, not a control focus, and was basic to the project; (h) administrative control was largely local, flexible, and autonomous compared with large programs' administration, which tends to be centralized, rigid, and bureaucratic; and (i) information was collected to make changes, whereas in large-scale programs information collection is often haphazard and there is little feedback. Thus, all of these elements should be considered if an expansion were planned.

Moreover, Myers (1995) points out that the transition from small-scale project to large-scale program must be associated with a learning process where the program is created based on the experiences and resources of all involved. The management and administrators of the program should continue to spend time in the field and keep in contact with the operators and participants. There is unlikely to be a blueprint for going to scale; rather Myers recommends looking to traditional wisdom and practice in programming and working with custodians of traditional knowledge and with those who are recognized as successful in rearing their children.

In Bosnia, a variety of projects and programs for women and children were carried out during and in the aftermath of the war, and some have continued their work. One way of going to scale would be to seek scale through association, that is, by combining results of several of these actions, which work for a common goal but have approached the problem differently and worked independently. This approach would favor local initiative, decentralization, and working with a wide range of bodies and nongovernmental organizations whose activities could be facilitated through training, materials, travel, communication, resources, and supervision. Thus, building on Myers' (1995) recommendations, scale could be sought by incorporating trauma and child development (i.e., the elements of the current project) into existing large-scale programs, such as health programs, mine awareness, breastfeeding promotion, food supplementation, income-generating programs, or programs supporting cultural activities, where these elements are missing. Involving the local and national government would be important with regard to the objectives of the program as well as for providing continuity and commitment for resources and in the implementation of the program.

ACKNOWLEDGMENTS

The author wishes to thank the University of Tromsø, UNICEF, and Norwegian People's Aid for financial and logistic support. She also wishes to thank the participants in the study and her colleagues in Bosnia, with whom this work was carried out.

This chapter is based on Ragnhild Dybdahl's Ph.D. thesis: Dybdahl (2002). Bosnian women and children in war: Experiences, psychological consequences and psychosocial intervention. Dissertation for the Doctor Psychologiae degree, Department of Psychology, Faculty of Social Science, University of Tromsø.

REFERENCES

Agger, I. (1995). *Theory and practice of psychosocial projects under war conditions in Bosnia-Herzegovina and Croatia.* Zagreb, Croatia: European Community Humanitarian Office.

Agger, I. (2001). Psychosocial assistance during ethnopolitical warfare in the Former Yugoslavia. In D. Chirot & M. E. P. Seligman. (Eds.), *Ethnopolitical warfare. Causes, consequences, and possible solutions* (pp. 305–342). Washington, DC: American Psychological Association.

Barat, A. (2003). Cultural art therapy in the treatment of war trauma in children and youth: Projects in the Former Yugoslavia. In S. Krippner & T. M. McIntyre (Eds.), *The psychological impact of war trauma on civilians. An international perspective* (pp. 155–170). Westport, CT: Praeger.

Bolton, P. (2003). Assessing depression among survivors of the Rwanda genocide. In S. Krippner & T. M. McIntyre (Eds.), *The psychological impact of war trauma on civilians. An international perspective* (pp. 67–78). Westport, CT: Praeger.

Bramsen, I., & van der Ploeg, H. M. (1999). Fifty years later: The long-term psychological adjustment of ageing World War II survivors. *Acta Psychiatrica Scandinavica, 100,* 350–358.

Bronfenbrenner, U. (1975). Is early intervention effective? A report on longitudinal evaluation of preschool programs. In M. Guttentag & E. L. Struening (Eds.), *Handbook of evaluation research* (pp. 519–603). London: Sage.

Cairns, E. (1996). *Children and political violence.* Oxford, U.K.: Blackwell.

de Jong, J. (2002). Public mental health, traumatic stress and human rights violations in low-income countries. A culturally appropriate model in times of conflict, disaster and peace. In J. de Jong (Ed.), *Trauma, war and violence. Public mental health in socio-political context* (pp. 1–92). New York: Plenum.

de Jong, J., Scholte, W. F., Koeter, M. W. J. & Hart, A. A. M. (2000). The prevalence of mental health problems in Rwandan and Burundese refugee camps. *Acta Psychiatrica Scandinavica, 102*(3), 171–177.

deMartino, R., & von Buchwald, U. (1996). Forced displacement. Non-governmental efforts in the psychosocial care of traumatized peoples. In B. A. van der Kolk, A. C. McFarlane, & L. Weisaeth (Eds.), *Traumatic stress. The effects of overwhelming experience on mind, body, and society* (pp. 193–217). New York: Guildford Press.

Dybdahl, R. (2000). Sexualised violence against women in war. In H. Valestrand (Ed.), *Nord og nedenfra. Papers by Tromsø scholars for Women's Worlds 99, Kvinnforsk skriftserie, 3*. University of Tromsø, 84–105.

Dybdahl, R. (2001a). A psychosocial support programme for children and mothers in war. *Clinical Child Psychology and Psychiatry, 6*(3), 425–436.

Dybdahl, R. (2001b). Children and mothers in war: An outcome study of a psychosocial intervention programme. *Child Development, 72*, 1214–1230.

Dybdahl, R. (2002). Bosnian women and children in war: Experiences, psychological consequences and psychosocial intervention. Ph.D. Dissertation. Department of Psychology, University of TromasÁ,.

Dybdahl, R., & Pasagic, I. (2000). Traumatic experiences and psychological reactions among women in Bosnia during the war. *Medicine, Conflict and Survival, 16*(3), 281–290.

Dyregrov, A. (1997). Teaching trauma intervention—Lessons learned. In D. Ajdukovic (Ed.), *Trauma recovery training. Lessons learned* (pp. 49–72). Zagreb, Croatia: Society for Psychological Assistance.

Eldering, L., & Leseman, P. P. M. (1999). Enhancing educational opportunities for young children. In L. Eldering & P. P. M. Leseman (Eds.), *Effective early education. Cross-cultural perspectives* (pp. 3–16). London: Falmer Press.

Eldering, L., & Vedder, P. (1999). The Dutch experience with the Home Intervention Program for Preschool Youngsters (HIPPY). In L. Eldering & P. P. M. Leseman (Eds.), *Effective early education. Cross-cultural perspectives* (pp. 259–286). London: Falmer Press.

Eyde, L. D. (2000). Other responsibilities to participants. In B. D. Sales & S. Folkman (Eds.), *Ethics in research with human participants* (pp. 61–73). Washington, DC: American Psychological Association.

Garbarino, J., & Kostelny, K. (1996). The effects of violence on Palestinian children's behavior problems: A risk accumulation model. *Child Development, 67*, 33–45.

Hundeide, K. (1991). *Helping disadvantaged children. Psychosocial intervention and aid to disadvantaged children in third world countries*. London: Jessica Kingsley Publishers.

Hundeide, K. (1996). *Ledet samspill* [Guided interaction]. Oslo, Norway: Vett og viten.

Husain, S. A. (2001). *Hope for the children: Lessons from Bosnia*. Tuzla, Bosnia: Behram-Begova Medrsa.

Husain, S.A., Nair, J., Holcomb, W., Reid, J.C.; Vargas, V. & Nair, S.S. (1988). Stress reactions in children and adolescents in war and siege conditions. *American Journal of Psychiatry*, 155, 1718–1719.

Kagitcibasi, C. (1999). Empowering parents and children: The case of the Turkish Early Enrichment Project. In L. Eldering & P. P. M. Leseman (Eds.), *Effective early education. Cross-cultural perspectives* (pp. 235–258). London: Falmer Press.

Machel, G. (1996). *Impact of armed conflict on children.* New York: UNICEF.

Mollica, R. F. (2000). Invisible wounds. *Scientific American, 282*(6), 54–57.

Mollica, R. F. (2001). The special psychiatric problems of refugees. In M. Gelder (Ed.), *Oxford textbook of psychiatry* (pp. 1591–1601). Oxford, U.K.: Oxford University Press.

Mulders, M. (1997). Psychosocial health care for women war victims in Former Yugoslavia. In D. Ajdukovic (Ed.), *Trauma recovery training. Lessons learned* (pp. 351–360). Zagreb, Croatia: Society for Psychological Assistance.

Muralidharan, R., & Kaul, V. (1999). Integrated Child Development Services (ICDS): The Indian experience. In L. Eldering & P. P. M. Leseman (Eds.), *Effective early education. Cross-cultural perspectives* (pp. 287–303). London: Falmer Press.

Myers, R. (1995). *The twelve who survive. Strengthening programs of early childhood development in the third world* (2nd ed.). Ypsilanti, MI: High/Scope Press.

Pecnik, N. (1997). Training for psychosocial work with refugee and displaced women. In D. Ajdukovic (Ed.), *Trauma recovery training. Lessons learned* (pp 361–372). Zagreb, Croatia: Society for Psychological Assistance.

Petevi, M. (1996). Forced displacement. Refugee trauma, protection and assistance. The contribution of the United Nations High Commissioner for Refugees. In Y. Danieli, N.S. Rodley, & L. Weisaeth (Eds.), *International responses to traumatic stress* (pp. 161–192). Amityville, NY: Baywood Publishing.

Rosenthal, R. (1999). Science and ethics in conducting, analyzing, and reporting psychological research. In D. N. Bersoff (Ed.), *Ethical conflicts in psychology* (pp. 407–413). Washington, DC: American Psychological Association.

Sieber, J. E. (2000). Planning research: Basic ethical decision-making. In B. D. Sales & S. Folkman (Eds.), *Ethics in research with human participants* (pp. 13–26). Washington, DC: American Psychological Association.

Smith, B., & Surgan, B. (1996). Model mental health program serves war-weary Sarajevo. *Psychology International (APA Office of International Affairs), 7,* 1–4.

Smith, P., Perrin, S., Yule, W., Hacam, B., & Stuvland, R. (2002). War exposure among children from Bosnia-Herzegovina: Psychological adjustment in a community sample. *Journal of Traumatic Stress, 14,* 147–156.

Sternberg, R. J., & Grigorenko, E. L. (1997, Fall). The cognitive costs of physical and mental ill health. Applying the psychology of the developed world to the problems of the developing world. *Eye on Psi Chi,* 20–27.

Summerfield, D. (1999). A critique of seven assumptions behind psychological trauma programs in war-affected areas. *Social Science and Medicine, 48,* 1448–1462.

Thabet, A., & Vostanis, P. (2000). Post-traumatic stress disorder reactions in children of war: A longitudinal study. *Child Abuse and Neglect, 24,* 291–298.

Young, M. E. (Ed.). (1997). *Early child development: Investing in our children's future. Proceedings of a world conference on Early Child Development: Investigating the future, Atlanta, GA, April 8–9, 1996.* Amsterdam: Elsevier.

CHAPTER 8

Play and Adaptation in Traumatized Young Children and Their Caregivers in Israel[1]

Esther Cohen

> Playing ... is the activity through which the human subject most freely and intensively constitutes himself or herself. To play is to affirm an "I", an autonomous subjectivity that exercises control over a world of possibilities; at the same time, and contrarily, it is in playing that the I can experience itself in its most fluid and boundaryless state ... (Rubin, 1994, p. 280)

[1] I am grateful to Dr. Saralea Chazen, who inspired this work by introducing me to the the Children's Play Therapy Instrument, took part in the scoring process, and provided creative suggestions and insights throughout the project. I also wish to thank my two graduate assistants, Moran Lerner and Efrat Maimon, for their devotion, resilience, and partnership in the emotionally taxing process of data collection and analysis. In addition, I am indebted to the parents, teachers, and children who participated in our project and allowed us to share their experiences. Special thanks go to the following psychologists for their help in recruiting families: Yochi Kalmanzon, Mazal Menachem, Liora Barak; Naomi Eini, Danielle Amram, Ruth Pat-Horenczyk, and Hana Oppenheim. Finally, financial support was obtained through a grant from the Levi Eshkol Institute for Economic, Social and Political Research at the Hebrew University of Jerusalem.

THE CONTEXT OF THE PROJECT

This chapter presents a project that I initiated in the context of the escalating number of terrorist incidents in Israel, during the second Palestinian "Intifada." This violent "uprising," which began in September 2000 and is still rampant, resulted in many casualties on both sides of the Israeli–Palestinian conflict. The project focuses on the psychological effects of these events on young Israeli children who were exposed to the violence of terrorism. One must recognize, however, that similar, and even worse, ill effects have been experienced by Palestinian children and families (Lavi, 2003; Hazboun, 2003; Thabet, Abed, & Vostanis, 2004). My concern for the future psychological development and mental health of young children caught in violent political conflicts around the globe is the driving force behind the project.

The Scope of Terrorism, Trauma, and Repeated Traumatization

The unique characteristics of acts of terror make them potentially more traumatic than other life-threatening events. Terror is a man-made threat, targeting innocent civilians and seeking to spread fear and panic among the targeted population to achieve political or ideological goals. It is cruel, unpredictable, indiscriminate, and difficult to prevent (Klingman & Cohen, 2004). In the case of suicide bombers, the gruesomeness and inherent negation of the sanctity of human lives implied in the act are particularly bewildering. During the current Intifada the frequent terrorist incidents in Israeli cities and villages have included devastation caused by explosions and suicide bombings in busy public places. Residents of the settlements in the West Bank (Judea and Samaria) have additionally become victims of frequent ambushes of vehicles, involving stoning and shootings, as well as of infiltrations into homes by terrorists and consequent shootings of their inhabitants. Some outlying settlements and city neighborhoods (e.g., Gush Katif nearing the Gaza district and Gilo in Jerusalem) have suffered extended periods of mortar and rocket attacks.

According to the December, 2004, data of Israel's Social Security Administration, since September 2000, Israeli civilians have been exposed to 7,622 terrorist incidents, resulting in 725 deaths and 6,897 injuries. Children under the age of 17 comprise about 15% of all casualties. Other sources report that about 50% of adults and about 45% of children were exposed to a terror event through personal involvement (Manenti, 2003).

The impact of these direct traumatic exposures is multifold, as they often entail subsequent life-changes and continuing stresses, such as coping with a serious injury, living with a recently disabled parent, dealing with loss of attachment figures, and moving. The psychological effects of direct exposures may further be aggravated through indirect exposures to additional terrorist events via the media, which often serve as "reminders" of the original trauma and may complicate the recovery process. Moreover, living in a community with a high level of exposure to terrorism may involve mechanisms of "secondary traumatization," that is, being exposed to the reactions of others who have been traumatized by a terrorist event (Klingman & Cohen, 2004; Galovski & Lyons, 2004). This combination of stressors may present a high risk to the development, adaptation, and mental health of the children involved (Allwood, Bell-Dolan, & Husain, 2002; Joshi & O'Donnell, 2003).

The Risk

In the last 2 decades we have witnessed a major change in the understanding of the relationship between trauma and child psychopathology. Growing evidence (Pine & Cohen, 2002; Perrin, Smith, & Yule, 2000; Silverman & La Greca, 2002) shows that children are not immune to the effects of trauma, as was previously assumed, and are in fact at risk for developing post traumatic stress disorder (PTSD) (American Psychiatric Association, 1994, 2000), or PTSD-related symptomatology. Additionally, children who are victims of trauma are found to be prone to various behavioral problems and emotional difficulties (including anxiety and depression), and they may suffer from more general mal-effects to their brains, interpersonal relationships, and developmental course (Wright, Masten, Northwood, & Hubbard, 1997; Smith, Perrin, & Yule, 1999; Joshi & O'Donnell, 2003). Furthermore, although studies on the incidence of PTSD in children vary greatly (depending on the nature of the trauma and on the measurement tools and procedures), most of the evidence (including meta-analytical data) suggests that children may even be at a greater risk than adults to develop the disorder.

A close examination reveals that the majority of the epidemiological studies do not include young children in their samples (Hoven et al., 2002). Moreover, the majority of intervention programs that have been developed in recent years to prevent and treat post-traumatic difficulties have focused on adolescents and on latency children (Goenjian et al., 1997; March, Amaya-Jackson, Murray, & Schulte, 1998; Perrin et al., 2000; Chemtob, Nakashima, & Hamada, 2002; Saltzman, Steinberg, Layne, Aisenberg, & Pynoos, 2002). In a recent review of studies evaluating treatment of children suffering from traumatic stress, only one out of the eight studies reviewed targeted young children below the age of 8 years (Taylor & Chemtob, 2004). This paucity of information relating to young children has been repeatedly pointed out in the literature (Scheeringa, Zeanah, Drell, & Larrieu, 1995; Almqvist & Brandell-Forsberg, 1997; Yule, Perrin, & Smith, 1999; Salmon & Bryant, 2002; Joshi & O'Donnell, 2003) and some of its sources have been attributed to the inadequacy of currently available criteria, tools, and procedures for diagnosing young children's post-traumatic disorders.

It is, however, this state of affairs that poses a risk for neglecting the identification of the needs of young children. This neglect is particularly worrisome since many clinical reports document the severity of post-traumatic reactions in young children (Terr, 1990; Gil, 1998). Existing research on young traumatized children, albeit limited, supported by extrapolations from related developmental research, suggests that the immaturity of young children in emotion regulation, social cognition, information processing, as well as language and memory, may result in diminished means of coping with trauma (Salmon & Bryant, 2002; Almqvist & Brandell-Forsberg, 1997; Scheeringa, Peebles, Cook, & Zeanah, 2001). It may especially affect the ability to create a coherent and clear trauma narrative, which helps in the integration of the traumatic memory into the self-schema of the victim (Wirgen, 1994). Magical thinking, typical at this age, may increase guilt, and the inability to comprehend the concept of death may lead to anxiety and confusion. Multiple exposures may place youngsters at higher risk for developing post-traumatic symptoms because children may merge similar incidents into a single representative memory (Howe, 1997).

The Challenges and Obstacles to Intervention

Given the above-mentioned risks to the mental health of young children exposed to terror, the relatively limited use of outpatient mental health services by children and their caretakers in Israel is striking: All treated children above age 4 years constitute only 12% of the outpatient population, although they make up 25% of the general population (Lerner, 2003). Young children in particular are very rarely referred to therapy, although free mental health services are available for victims of terror. What we have observed, prior to and throughout our project, were the workings of massive denial mechanisms in relation to young children's post-traumatic difficulties, in parents, school personnel, community leaders, and mental health professionals. This impression is supported by a number of studies, both in Israel and elsewhere, that have demonstrated that parents tend to underestimate PTSD-related distress of their children (Osofsky, 1995; Perrin et al., 2000). As Terr (1990) described based on her experiences in following up on the kidnapped children from the Chowchilla incident, it seems that defenses go up very fast after trauma strikes. The affected youngsters, their families, and the community erect walls of suppression, since people do not want to think of themselves as abnormal, hurt, or changed.

This suppression or denial may also be seen as a defense against the general anxiety invoked in adults when exposing young, vulnerable, and "innocent" children to the grim realities of life and the ensuing guilt experienced by adults for their inability to protect them. Such feelings may need to be denied more intensely by Israeli parents whose ideologically based decisions (such as living in the settlements) may put their own children at an increased risk for physical and mental health hazards. Osofsky (1995) has commented, in a similar vein, on the public tendency to believe erroneously that young children who are exposed to violence are too young to know or remember what has happened, in spite of clear findings on the post-traumatic effects of exposure to violence among very young children.

In addition to denial due to guilt, we have observed a neglect of children's psychological needs and emotional difficulties in families and schools in Israel. These systems appear overburdened by growing needs, mounting stresses, and psychological burnout. Many families are large and are struggling with economic, physical, and functional survival needs while coping with repeated losses and insecurities related to their future. Although everyday life for most people continues in a seemingly usual manner—unlike in war times—it still requires major daily adaptation to enhance safety and constitutes a vigilant way of coping, referred to in the local culture as "emergency routine." This routine allows very little energies for reflecting upon children's mental health or for taking action related to it.

Given the mentioned parental dynamics and the ongoing stresses, families, as well as social and educational systems, seem to activate processes of habituation and normalization as an adaptation to the helplessness experienced in facing repeated traumatic exposures and their impact. These adaptations, including an increase in tolerance for behavior problems, risk-taking behaviors, lack of concentration in schools, and regressive behaviors in the families, appear necessary and useful in the short run. However, they create some new risks. We know from the literature (Perrin et al., 2000; Joshi & O'Donnell, 2003) that the difficulties of young children in processing trauma are often expressed in a range of behaviors that are vague and that may mask the magnitude of the distress and its origin. These include somatic complaints, sleep difficulties and nightmares, clingy and regressive behaviors, fears, inability to concentrate, avoidance of talking about the event, irritability, hypervigilance, acting-out behaviors, and repetitive play. Under these circumstances parents and teachers often appear more concerned with daily coping and attempt to either ignore or shape the disturbing behaviors, rather than being concerned with their origins or long-term developmental consequences.

These tendencies to ignore, deny, belittle, or tolerate the post-traumatic difficulties of young children are supported by a wider context related to community defensiveness and political ideology. In light of the continuous political conflicts and mounting pressures in regard to dismantling the settlements, the population in these areas, driven by a strong ideological commitment to prevent this move, is extremely sensitive to their public image. Their struggle involves the projection of a strong coping stance, both internally and externally, to the media and to Israeli and international public opinion. They are therefore very suspicious of research projects or mental-health services, which may tarnish their coping image. The communities therefore support internal natural support systems and the use of faith and religion as resources rather than professional interventions.

In spite of the mentioned obstacles to the possible identification and treatment of traumatized young children, a major consideration driving the careful introduction of this project is a recognition of the central importance of the significant adults in a child's life in mediating the effects of the traumatic experience on children (Klingman & Cohen, 2004). Available knowledge demonstrates that parental suppression of awareness of their children's suffering, conflicts, and symptoms has deleterious effects on children's adjustment (Laor, Wolmer, Mayes, & Gershon, 1997; Scheeringa & Zeanah, 2001). Keeping in mind the dynamics of parental avoidance behavior, it became clear that a respectful, nonthreatening, and nonburdening way to reach out to caretakers was needed. In practical terms it meant that we had to travel to their areas of residence, rather than expect them to come to us. A major goal of the project was to invoke interest in caregivers in their children's inner experiences, and to help them realize their important role in their children's processing of trauma.

THE PROJECT: RATIONALE, PROCEDURE, AND TOOLS

The project was designed as a study and pilot intervention focusing on the inner experiences of young children (4–7 years old) identified as having been directly exposed to terrorism. After securing parental permission, a videotaped individual play-therapy session was conducted with each child. The session (45 minutes in duration) was child-centered and nondirective, and was carried out in a private, quiet room, close to the child's classroom, by a skilled adult (the project director and her two graduate students, or the involved school psychologist in a small number of cases), using a set of toys and materials traditionally used in play therapy.

Given the shortage of adequate assessment tools for the identification of post-traumatic problems in young children, we adopted the current recommendation, embraced by trauma specialists (American Association of Child and Adolescent Psychiatry, 1998; Yule, 2001; Salmon & Bryant, 2002), to use multi-modal multi-source information in assessing the clinical status of the children. Therefore, in addition to a videotape of each child's play, independent ratings of the children's adaptation by their parents and when possible also by their teachers were obtained. Background information on family stresses and resources (including exposure history and parental PTSD, previous life events, and loss of psychosocial resources) was also collected to help identify children at risk.

We adopted the recommendation of the American Association of Child and Adolescent Psychiatry (AACAP, 1998) to identify and offer treatment to children exposed to traumatic events, even if they do not meet the criteria of PTSD, based on the limitations of the DSM-IV (American Psychiatric Association, 1994) criteria for diagnosing PTSD in young children. We therefore focused on the general adaptation of the traumatized children, using a wide perspective, and targeting post-traumatic distress or functional difficulties, and developmental changes.

With the parents we used an innovative PTSD questionnaire and diagnostic criteria especially adapted to young children and sensitive to developmental changes (Scheeringa, Peebles, et al., 2001; Scheeringa, Zeanah, Myers, & Putnam, 2003), but we were interested in the presence of symptoms and not only in a PTSD diagnosis. In addition we used the Child Behavior Checklist (CBCL) to assess general behavior problems (Achenbach & Edelbrock, 1983). However, we considered play observation as the most important tool, as it allowed more direct access to the child's subjective experience. Because of the limited ability of young children to use self-reports, play becomes a major modality for learning from the children themselves, in their language, about their experience.

Much clinical work shows that play is a central tool for understanding children's inner experience (Winnicott, 1971; Gil, 1998; Ryan & Needham, 2001; Chazan, 2002). The various therapeutic functions of play in helping the child rework unpleasant experiences have been emphasized, including: emotional release; gaining self-efficacy by changing the passive victim role into an active one; making negative experiences more predictable through repetition; reconstructing experiences in order to increase comprehension and create meaning; and figuring out solutions for unresolved conflicts and for improved coping (Marans, Mayes, & Colonna, 1993). The use of play observation and its analysis does not involve any direct reality-oriented questioning or re-exposure of the child, which may be an important consideration in planning interventions with children subjected to repeated exposures and reminders of trauma, in a context that encourages denial and ongoing coping. As a potential therapeutic intervention it creates a space for caregivers to listen to an individual child's narrative and for symbolically and experientially processing the trauma, without necessarily directly interpreting it.

The parents were offered the opportunity to view the child's videotape and to discuss it with us. Alternatively they could request that we discuss our clinical impressions regarding the child with the responsible school psychologist. These observations, based on the child's play, were considered a relatively nonthreatening, potential basis for invoking parents' interest in the child's inner world, and for reflecting on his or her coping processes and current needs. Both sources of information, the child's play and the parent's reports (on the familial situation, the child's exposure, and the child's symptoms and behaviors), were used together to learn about risk and resilience factors in the processing of trauma, and to clarify children's needs. Pre-arranged contacts with several trauma treatment centers ensured that children who might be referred from the project for therapy would receive immediate access to services.

Trauma has been demonstrated to affect a child's play activity in various distinct ways, which reduce its inherent psychological usefulness to the child. Terr (1983) and, following her work, a number of other clinicians (Wershba-Gershon, 1996; Varkas, 1998; Gil, 1998; Nader & Pynoos, 2000; Drewes, 2001) have attempted to clarify the pathological aspects of traumatic play, indicating its serious, somber, driven quality; repetitive re-enactments with unresolved themes; increased aggressiveness; fantasies linked with rescue or revenge; increased withdrawal; and reduced symbolization and concretization. It is worth noting that the DSM IV-TR (American Psychiatric Association, 2000) considers as one of its criteria for PTSD in children, the appearance of repetitive play and trauma reenactments in play as evidence for intrusive recollections of the trauma.

Building on this work, we undertook the challenge of systematically observing, documenting, and reliably analyzing the play patterns of children, by using the Children Play Therapy Instrument (CPTI) (Kernberg, Chazan, & Normandin, 1998; Chazan, 2000, 2001, 2002), which we have adapted for post-trauma reactions together with Chazan (2003). The CPTI rating system for traumatic play offers many measures of the affective, narrative, dynamic, developmental, and social aspects of the child's play. Additionally it enables rating the child's quality of coping with the demands and stresses of the trauma, as revealed through play, along a spectrum of coping strategies ranging from adaptive to increasingly maladaptive and defensive. This focus, which goes beyond Terr's (1990) more categorical classification of traumatic play, allows the identification of resilient as well as pathological mechanisms for coping with trauma, rendering a fuller and more specific description of the child's play activity response to trauma. These mechanisms were organized in the revised version of the CPTI in three clusters (for a more detailed account see Chazan, 2003):

Cluster One: Re-Enactment with Soothing
Children using this cluster appear to re-enact aspects of the trauma and use mechanisms that allow them to gain relief and to achieve some closure. Examples of such coping strategies are: problem-solving, sublimation, affiliation, humor, and altruism

Cluster Two: Re-Enactment Without Soothing
Children using this cluster appear to repeatedly re-enact disturbing aspects of the trauma and use mechanisms that fail to bring relief or satiation. Examples of such strategies are: identification with the aggressor, splitting, omnipotent control, devaluation, doing and undoing, regression, turning aggression against the self.

Cluster Three: Overwhelming Re-experiencing
Children using this cluster appear overwhelmed by their feelings and are either paralyzed to the point of being unable to play or to significantly interact with others, or alternatively, they re-experience such overwhelming feelings while encountering in play reminders of their traumatic experience that they seem to lose control of the play and of their actions, until the play is interrupted. Examples of strategies employed are: constriction, freezing, de-differentiation, dispersal, and dismantling.

Clinical impressions from the Play Project
In conducting the play sessions with the children we learned not only of the feasibility of this procedure, but also of the interest and eagerness with which most children responded to it. Almost all the children in the study were able to develop some kind of relationship with the unfamiliar attentive adult, and

only two children requested to go back to the classroom prior to the planned termination of the session. Most children, however, seemed hungry for the adult's interest and validation, and none seemed completely dissociated. The majority of the exposed children were able to use fantasy play and seemed invested in re-enacting painful aspects of their experience. Some children showed unusual resilience and coping abilities and managed to sooth themselves successfully, while re-enacting aspects of their traumatic experience. Many children, however, appeared to lack sufficient soothing mechanisms and had difficulty in breaking away from repeated stressful re-enactments. A number of children appeared overwhelmed by their anxiety and pain; they resorted to either intense chaotic play that included sadistic acting-out or risk-taking elements, or conversely, appeared extremely constricted, avoidant, distracted, and unable to play.

MAJOR FINDINGS FROM THE STUDY

Although a detailed and full account of the data analyses and findings of the research part of this project are beyond the scope of this chapter and will be published separately, some major findings are briefly presented as they are pertinent to our approach to risk, identification, and intervention. The data are based on comparisons between a group of 29 children directly exposed to terrorism, and a group of 25 children, of comparable age and socioeconomic background, who were not exposed (except through the media) to a terror event. The research findings confirmed our concern in relation to the heightened mental health risk for young children exposed to terrorism. Children in the exposed group were diagnosed more frequently with PTSD (almost one third as compared to none in the non-exposed group) based on parental reports, and using the criteria for young children. The exposed children also manifested significantly more post-traumatic symptoms, including developmental regressions, and exhibited more behavioral problems (about 25% exhibited behavior problems at a clinical level as compared to none in the non-exposed group). As suspected, we found that these directly exposed young children may also be exposed to secondary traumatization risks including through the effect of their caregivers. Parents of the exposed children were diagnosed more frequently as suffering from PTSD and demonstrated more post-traumatic symptoms than did parents of the non-exposed children. Parents' levels of post-traumatic symptomatology together with their level of loss of psychosocial resources were strongly associated with child maladaptation.

We found that the play videotapes could be analyzed in a satisfactorily reliable fashion by trained observers, using the revised CPTI (Chazan, 2003).

Moreover, the validity of these ratings was demonstrated by the significant differences in the play patterns of exposed children in comparison with their non-exposed peers. The exposed children exhibited in their play activity more intense and frequent negative affective responses, displayed more "acting-out" or externalizing themes, and also exhibited less "awareness of themselves as players" than did the non-exposed group of children.

In a further examination of the group of exposed children for within-group differences, specific indices of play correlated significantly with the level of post-traumatic adaptation. Negative emotional responses in play were associated with the number of PTSD symptoms. In addition, the use of coping and defensive strategies in play typical of the "overwhelming re-experiencing" cluster correlated highly and positively with frequency of post-traumatic symptoms. However, a number of attributes of play activity were found to be negatively correlated with post-traumatic symptomatology, including the use of the "re-enactment with soothing" strategies cluster, the use in play narratives of "care-taking and protection" themes, as well as a warm and cooperative relationship with the adult (therapist).

CLINICAL IMPLICATIONS OF THE FINDINGS
Play Activity as a Measure of Adaptation

The results of the study strengthen our initial assumption that play observation can be used to identify children who are highly distressed or malfunctioning following a traumatic terror event. Although further research may be needed to support our findings, they seem to enrich the available clinical literature on post-traumatic play, and offer a more specific list of measures of play activity based on analyses according to the trauma-adapted CPTI (Chazan, 2003) to be used as signs of risk for posttraumatic maladaptation. These include:

Affective components. Expressions of an overall negative or distressed affect, a narrow range of affects, or affects incongruent with the content of play or the situation (e.g., sadistic laughter); direct and symbolic manifestations of fear and anxiety; anger and aggressiveness; sadness and worry.

Themes. A preponderance of "acting out" and externalization themes, such as: body damage, breaking rules, death, destruction, devouring, falling, messing, revenge, and sadism.

Coping and defensive strategies. An "overwhelmed re-experiencing" pattern of coping, expressed in one of two extremes: either intensely driven, repetitious re-enactments, which rapidly deteriorate into chaotic play, or severe constriction and freezing, involving the loss of the ability to play or interact (due to anxiety, depression, or hypervigilance).

Awareness of oneself as a player. Signs of loss of boundary between fantasy and reality, feeling victimized by the play, and losing the sense of being the player or the director of the play.

Identification of Post-Traumatic Distress Through Play

The following example from the project demonstrates the utility of conducting a play session with a child as a means of identifying post-traumatic distress, when the parents and even a therapist are insensitive to its presence.

A case-vignette: "Trying to digest the indigestible"

The traumatic incident. The C. family, including father, mother, 5-year-old Saul, and 4-year-old Miriam, were traveling in their car when it was fired upon from behind by a single terrorist, gravely injuring Saul. The boy spent 5 days in intensive care, and a few weeks later recovered amazingly well. The parents came to a trauma center about 5 months after the event seeking treatment for the father, who had stopped functioning both at work and at home. He was diagnosed as suffering from PTSD and depression. Both children were reported to be doing well. The parents' only concern regarding the children was the persistence of Saul's alopecia (sudden hair loss), which developed subsequent to the traumatic incident.

Contact. The father's therapist at the center, who had been working with the couple, obtained permission for me to videotape both children in a play session, as a pretest to the project. Having a play session with both children in a separate room during the parents' session was agreeable to all, as the children would otherwise be playing by themselves while waiting for their parents' therapy to end.

Play sessions. I first conducted a play session with Saul, who exhibited invariable sad affect and traumatic play involving repeated relentless re-enactments of danger, destruction, death, and resurrection, with some soothing abilities.

I then saw Miriam, who waited eagerly for her turn. Miriam showed some adaptive capabilities in her non-verbal affiliation and cooperativeness with the therapist and her adaptation to the demands of the situation. She seemed to be able to use the therapist as a secure base, enabling her to begin to explore and process intense feelings, thus showing some re-enactment with soothing coping mechanisms. However, her mood was somber throughout the play session and her play was by and large surprisingly regressive and worrisome, showing a predominance of coping/defensive mechanisms of re-enactment without soothing, which at times deteriorated into overwhelming re-experiencing. Miriam exhibited silent and repeated engagement in two dominant themes. The first theme involved intentional repeated dropping and dispersal of falling figures and objects, while mimicking nonverbally (with her face and hands) "what happened." The therapist's attempts to find out what happened, and her repeated reflections of the fall of the doll figures, were met with a shoulder shrug, communicating: "I don't care; I don't know." The second theme involved successive indiscriminate mouthing and dismantling of objects including dangerously small ones, human figures, sharp painful utensils (a plastic knife), and extremely large objects (a slinky) that she inappropriately tried to push into her mouth. In response to the therapist's continuous wondering about "what is this mouth that wants to bite on everything?", she finally responded verbally (for the first time) toward the end of the session, announcing "I am the witch and I'm going to eat the children for dinner." She then moved on to throwing the play figures and objects into a dark garage, repeatedly locking the door. She was unable to bring the play activity to a conclusion when the time was up, and needed to be interrupted.

Further intervention. Miriam's play included many indicators of risk: her negative affect, regressive mode, her externalization themes and the use of defensive mechanisms from Cluster Two (turning aggression against the self, omnipotent control, identification with the aggressor) and Cluster Three (de-differentiation and dispersal). This, however, appeared in contradiction to the reports given to the father's therapist by the parents. I shared my concerns with the therapist while also acknowledging the child's strengths, and I asked him to inquire more about the girl's experience and functioning.

Following the next session the therapist contacted me excitedly to inform me that he was surprised to learn from the parents that during the traumatic incident Miriam "was forgotten in the family car." They reported that, when her injured brother was taken out of the car and laid down by the roadside, she was left buckled up in her seat. While they were busy calling for help and tending to Saul, she remained in the car immobile, covered with his blood, for about 15 minutes. Some passers-by, who had stopped to help, noticed her in the car. These strangers volunteered to drive her to her grandmother's home. She saw little of her parents and brother in the ensuing weeks of her brother's hospitalization and recovery. Soon after her brother's return home, her father's situation started to deteriorate.

It became apparent that Miriam never got a chance to figure out and validate her story of the trauma, and to process the many feelings aroused by it. Only in the session did she begin to "digest the indigestible." A follow-up conversation with her preschool teacher revealed that the teacher too was concerned about changes in her behavior, but she was hesitant to inform the parents as she did not want to burden them. It became clear that therapy needed to accommodate the needs of both children, and to open up a space in this overburdened family to help Miriam process her experience.

This single play session with Miriam can be viewed not only as an assessment but also as a meaningful intervention. Chazan (personal communication, January 2, 2005) remarked in response to viewing the videotape that by identifying with the aggressor within a safe, humanized arena, sensing the strong human holding capacity of the therapist, the child could begin to process the symbolic meaning of the traumatic event. The child gradually allowed herself to approach the evil by playfully becoming the evil.

Play as a Realm for Healing and for Engaging Caretakers

The mental health risk demonstrated in this study subsequent to exposure to acts of terror validates the need to find ways of reaching out to caregivers of exposed young children. Only 1 out of the 29 exposed children or families who participated in our study was receiving therapy—a few were followed upon sporadically by the school psychologist—in spite of the children's apparent distress, regressions, and behavior problems. It is interesting to note that the parents recognized these difficulties in their reports, although we do not know if they under-reported these difficulties. However, this recognition was not translated into help seeking. The finding that the children most at risk are those whose parents have been more impaired psychologically by the exposure to terrorism presents a challenge to intervention strategies. It seems that intervention may need to take into account the parents' impoverished psychological resources by involving additional significant adults to work with the children, while at the same time offering help, in a nonstigmatizing way, to the parents themselves. A nondemanding stance of the availability of a mental health professional for periodical consultations, even by phone, may be a feasible starting point for building a therapeutic helping relationship with these parents. Offering periodic educational and experiential workshops to parents through schools and community centers, which does not constitute a crisis intervention following a terrorist event, as commonly practiced, may be another way of reaching out to parents. These would focus on resiliency and risk factors related to living under "emergency routine" and their impact on parent–child relations and on children's developmental needs. Establishing contact with the parents to discuss their children's play has proven in our project to be a potential nonthreatening strategy to engage the parents in reflecting upon their children's experiences and becoming more attuned to their needs.

Psychological Consultations with Distressed Caregivers

The following phone consultation, which evolved from our contact with one of the families in regard to the play session conducted with their child, is an example of the reaching-out potential of the procedure and the possibility of gradually building a relationship with parents that will help them help their children.

A Case Vignette: Sublimating Loss

The traumatic incident. About a year prior to our contact with the current family, their van, carrying the parents and their four children, was attacked by a barrage of gunshots fired from another car occupied by two Palestinian terrorists on a West Bank road. Both parents were killed and two of their four children were injured. The surviving children remained immobile in the van for a long time, fearing the return of the terrorists, until one of the children managed to find the parents' mobile phone and called for help. The four surviving children of this family moved in with relatives, who have six children of their own, and serve as their foster family.

Initial contact and its development. After hearing about our project, the foster mother initiated contact with us, sounding very ambivalent and cautious. She was not interested in referrals for therapy but was interested in learning more about the play of the younger children, since she was annoyed and concerned about their play; they were playing incessantly and repetitively the same aggressive make-believe play that she found impossible to witness. We agreed to see two of the younger children in a play session in a room adjacent to their classrooms: 5-year-old Shimon, who was in the attacked car, and 6-year-old Ron, who was one of the natural sons of the foster family.

The foster mother, after much encouragement through phone conversations, filled out questionnaires for us relating to the children's post-traumatic reactions and their behavior problems, but she chose not to respond to the questionnaires relevant to her own post-traumatic reactions and loss of psychosocial resources, arguing that she did not experience any trauma, hence this was irrelevant for her. We mailed her copies of the videotaped sessions with the children and extended an invitation to discuss what we saw, if and when she chose to do so. More than 6 months later she established phone contact with me, asking to discuss over the phone some worrisome issues concerning the children. I agreed and had a 50-minute session over the phone. I will focus here only on one of the two boys discussed.

Information from the play session: Shimon—5 years old. Shimon used the play session in a self-initiated, determined, intense, and continuous manner, with no disruptions or interruptions. While not displaying a wide range of affects, his affective tone was mostly sober and seemed appropriate to the content of his play. We saw him as an aware player dealing with his trauma by re-enactment and using mostly successful coping and soothing mechanisms. At times, however, these Cluster One soothing mechanisms lost their effectiveness and the child enlisted defense mechanisms such as splitting and identification with the aggressor, typical of Cluster Two (re-enactment without soothing).

Shimon immediately chose an art activity, which gradually took on a dramatic quality of a re-enactment. He drew a house with a red roof, a chimney, windows, and a door, which he purposefully colored in black. He then painted a wide area designated as a sky, and added four "baby butterflies" in the top part of the sky and two birds in its lower part. A distinct line in the sky separated the two areas: the lower area that, according to his explanation, could be hit by a rocket from the Arab homes, and the upper, safe zone. He explained that the butterflies managed to escape into the safety zone, were saved, and felt joyous and scornful of their attackers. But the rocket managed to hit the birds, which did not cross back the line in time, and killed them. The butterflies wanted to save the birds but could not do so, because they could not cross the line. He then announced that the butterflies started to cry, and began drawing rain-like tears, pouring down heavily from the sky onto the house.

He then turned to the play therapist, saying: "You know, my father and mother were killed and my older sister cried a lot, but I cried even more because I'm younger." He then added a black flower, painted the house door even darker, and announced that the drawing was finished.

In a following play segment he re-enacted a battle between dinosaurs and other animal figures with many killings. The smart ones, who were also the angry ones and the good ones, were those that triumphed.

Additional information. Shimon did not meet the criteria for PTSD diagnosis, although he showed some PTSD symptomatology, including re-experiencing through play, nightmares, and sleeping difficulties. Neither did he reach a clinical level of behavior disorders.

Intervention with the foster mother around Shimon. The foster mother appeared aware of Shimon's intelligence and social abilities. She was, however, concerned about his constant anger, mood swings, and explosiveness. The anger was not manifested in behavior difficulties, as he responded well to limit setting, but his tone when talking to his siblings and his play seemed to her an expression of constant anger. She was upset that she never saw him express any sadness over his losses.

As she reported in response to my question that she had not found the time to watch the play videotapes I had sent her, I told her about the play session. She was very surprised and touched when hearing about the drawing and the tears. She did not think until then that he liked to draw, and she had never seen him cry. I emphasized his extraordinary sublimation abilities, and I also explained about the connection he may have made in his play between strength, anger, and being smart, which helped him feel safer. In response to her question about ways of reducing the anger I suggested the introduction of a special drawing and story notebook, which she could use while sitting with him privately, paying attention to his drawings, and writing down his thoughts, fantasies, and feelings. She was apprehensive that this procedure may augment his anger, but she then could see how delineating a specific time and place for expressing his feelings and experiencing being listened to may be helpful to the child.

The foster mother then revealed a deeper concern, namely, that Shimon did not accept the finality of the death of his parents and was telling her that he was awaiting their revival when the Messiah arrives. I provided her with some educational input regarding the limitations in preschool children in understanding the concept of death, providing examples from other children. I thought that the idea of looking forward to the unknown time of the arrival of the Messiah, a time everyone was wishing for, could be viewed as a constructive one. She then shared her concern that this may hinder his attachment to her as a mother figure. She listened very attentively to my idea that children can be attached to more than one figure, and that a good previous attachment and memories of a close relationship may provide the basis for a good additional attachment.

I expressed my recognition of her sincere interest in building a meaningful relationship with the child, and I acknowledged her determination and coping ability in providing a caring and stable home for all the family children. I invited the mother to contact me by phone or to make an appointment whenever she needed to, and she has in fact responded to this invitation by requesting an additional phone consultation regarding the other videotaped child.

CLINICAL IMPLICATIONS FOR COPING AND RESILIENCE

The research data, together with the clinical observations gathered in conducting play sessions with 54 young children (4–7 years old), and especially those carried out with 29 children who had been directly exposed to terrorism, help bring into focus the question of the natural curative processes set forth via play and their essential ingredients. It is our impression that terrorist trauma may be processed in a different manner than trauma from familial abuse. Given a safe place and the presence of an attentive, containing, and validating adult, many children are able to draw on their inner resources (their secure attachment and healthy self-regulation and reflective abilities) and find means for constructing a congruent and empowering trauma narrative. This conclusion is supported by Saylor, Swenson, and Powell's report (1991) on the play and postdisaster adaptation of preschoolers exposed to Hurricane Hugo. Unlike most of the research that focuses exclusively on the risks of exposure to trauma, they noted positive changes in the children, in addition to such negative effects of the disaster as re-enactments, overgeneralization, and new fears. These changes included precocious concern for others, expanded insight, and advanced vocabulary. We agree with their conclusion that some of the more resilient children may be able to be supported by their parents—perhaps with some therapeutic guidance—if the parents themselves are coping well and may not need direct professional intervention.

Our data allow us to look at indicators of children's resilience, and to examine successful strategies that children use to sooth themselves and deal with the toxic materials of the trauma. The data analyses have shown that exposed children who show the best levels of adaptation manage to use re-enactment with soothing coping and defensive strategies and show a preponderance of "protection and care-taking themes," such as body function, help and caring, competence, feeding, grooming, rescue, resurrection, and protection.

Further qualitative analyses of the children's play revealed an array of specific mechanisms employed by the children in order to sooth themselves while re-enacting aspects of the traumatic experience, so as to achieve a reduction in the level of anxiety. The most useful mechanisms included:

Playfulness and amusement: Expressions of enthusiasm in regard to specific toys or evolving play ideas; changing the tone of voice in accordance with chosen roles; joking about mishaps (physically imitating the fall of the "slinky" while laughing); making up rhymes ("whatever comes out—makes me proud"); creatively exploring many ways of modeling the slinky into different shapes.

Affiliation with the adult: Sharing with the adults the play plan, meanings, and affects; requesting assistance; assigning roles ("you guess which song I am playing"); asking to reverse roles (i.e., asking the therapist to pretend that she is the baby and the child is her parent); using the adult for physical comforting (leaning one's head on the adult's knee when disappointed in lotto game); inquiring when the adult may be back for another visit.

Anticipation of danger and planning and constructing "environmental" protective measures: Building fences; blockading houses; blocking windows; preparing arrow-slits; constructing escape routes through steps, slides, and ladders; and planning a move to another country.

Increasing safety by confining dangerous characters: Entrapping the tiger in a cage; locking the bus door against the robber; throwing the bad guys in jail.

Devising magical protective measures: marking a drawing with a line in the sky above which the rockets cannot reach; activating magical forces like telepathy to know what others are planning.

Protecting the body by making it invincible: The soldier's body and heart are made of iron; he has 1000 lives; the hero has a magical body shield.

Using communication technology to enlist help (mostly cellular phones): Calling another truck on the cellular phone for a ride when one's truck breaks down; calling the police for help with a problem; father is calling someone to train together; child is calling mother to bring a new ball because the existing ball was punctured by a dinosaur; calling grandmother to buy milk; calling father to come home for dinner with the kids.

Appointing and enlisting protectors: Mother figure is appointed as prime minister and helps to prevent a disaster on a bus; a heavily armed cowboy is put in charge of protecting the other cowboys; dinosaurs are protecting the good ball players against the bad players; wild animals are added to protect the good soldiers in their camp.

The use of symbolic art to sublimate grief and to resolve guilt (see the above example of Shimon's play activity).

Bolstering of one's self-image by acknowledging or showing off one's achievements and talents, or by boasting about the advantages of one's group.

Using music for soothing: listening to the music from the adjacent classroom; humming; playing the flute; pretending that the play characters are making music; making up lyrics related to the play activity.

Engagement in altruistic and caretaking activities, such as feeding and caring for family members; feeding the therapist; giving immunizations to prevent disease; and offering the wounded medical care.

The following mechanisms employed by the children proved partially useful in soothing and advancing processing:

Attempts to figure out through play re-enactments the confusion regarding ab-
stract or complex questions, such as: What provides safety and what entails
danger? (Moving the soldier's camp a number of times to a safe area); Who
is alive and who is dead? ("Now he is more dead. . . .", "They were dead but
they are alive. . . ."); Who is the enemy and who is the protector? (marking
the bad guys as those with helmets).

Exploring language: Repeating and trying to figure out adult statements. For
example: A child re-enacts a scene of cowboys and Indians and explains
that the cowboy needs to be with his gun at all times because "no one can
survive in these 'territories' for more than a year" (alluding to a popular
adult statement about survival in the West Bank territories).

Making up language to express unusual experiences (such as those related to
morbid content), such as, "here is the 'Bloodery'"—where blood is sold.

Cognitive processing and intellectualization: Discussions of fairness and mo-
tives of cruel people; displaying extensive knowledge of a variety of dangerous animals and their hierarchy; making up riddles to feel in control;
displaying one's ability to outsmart the stronger but stupid enemy.

Play suppression and play interruptions: Announcing the need for a break
from an emotionally charged play theme ("I am tired of this; I will finish
it later"), or requests to leave the room to go the restroom or to check on
the waiting caretaker. These breaks away from a specific play reenactment
allowed some children to later return and complete the play. At times the
play remained interrupted, and the child could not engage further in any
play activity.

It should be noted that many of the exposed children who used protection and care-taking themes also enacted aggressive and revenge fantasies.
These included displays of physical power, destruction, killings, death, and
burial, as well as quite sadistic scenes of torture. Symbolic aggression is an
understandable, normal reaction to an experience of threat and is usually
considered important because it gives an alternative option to actual acting
out. It helps the child vent his or her anger against both "the enemy" and
also against his or her significant others who failed to protect him or her.
Play allows the child to transform the experience of helplessness, anxiety, and
vulnerability and to acquire a sense of assumed power and retaliation ability.

The freedom to express forbidden feelings may in itself, however, increase the child's anxiety rather than reduce it (Varkas, 1998). A child in the
aftermath of a traumatic event often needs active help from the adult in moving
beyond these feelings to a sense of being able to feel protected. Otherwise
such externalizing defense mechanisms as "identification with the aggressor"
and "omnipotent control" may be crystallized and lead to sadism, masochism,
chronic hypervigilance (Frankel, 2002), or risk-taking behavior (Glodich,
Allen, & Arnold, 2001).

CLINICAL IMPLICATIONS FOR PLAY THERAPY

Terr (1983, 1990) described traumatic play as dangerous, because if it does not progress and transform over time it creates more terror than was consciously there when the game started. Thus it may leave the child vulnerable and helpless. As we pointed out, our findings reveal a more differentiated picture, showing a spectrum of post-traumatic play patterns ranging from mostly adaptive and resilient through varying degrees and kinds of maladaptation. Only some of the traumatized children, especially those who exhibit predominantly "overwhelming re-experiencing," are similar to the ones described in Terr's work.

Our suggestion is that therapists tailor differential interventions to suit the individual needs of children, and that those may be based on the conceptualizations of their different predominant coping and defensive mechanisms (Chazan, 2003) and on the additional play indicators we found in this project to be significant in processing trauma. Developmental needs (Slade, 1994; Shelby, 2000; Drewes, 2001) as well as stage of trauma and safety issues (Herman, 1997) should also be considered. These considerations may help settle some of the controversial and ambiguous issues apparent in the current literature on play therapy with traumatized young children (Webb, 2004; Gil, 2002; Terr, 2003; Taylor & Chemtob, 2004). These issues include the degree of structuring and directivity of the therapist (Nader & Pynoos, 2000; Ryan & Needhan, 2001), the contribution and risk of psychodynamic interpretations of the play (Terr, 2003; Webb, 1991), and the relative emphasis on exploration, expression, and release of affects (Ogawa, 2004), on object relations (Gallagher, Leavitt, & Kimmel, 1995), on cognition (including correcting distortions and creating a coherent narrative) and behavior, such as overcoming fears and avoidance behavior (de Arellano et al., 2005).

Our findings demonstrate that almost all of the traumatized children we saw exhibited at least some abilities to process traumatic materials by balancing spontaneously re-enacting and soothing, provided there was a safe context and a holding environment. Therapists should be aware of and identify these mechanisms and patiently support and expand them.

When the child appears "stuck" in repetitious re-enactments without sufficient soothing abilities, or even more so, when these deteriorate into overwhelmed chaotic play, the therapist must deal with the question of how much time to allow the play to continue before taking steps to modify it, or help the child regulate his anxiety. Most of the diverse, currently accepted therapy treatments for PTSD include among their interventions relaxation and stress management as a major therapeutic component (AACAP, 1998). This "soothing" component consists of various techniques to monitor and regulate the patient's level of arousal to advance safely in the "imaginal" exposure and in the processing of traumatic memories without overwhelming the patient. Gil (1998), in addressing this question in relation to post-traumatic play, advocates the use of a range of interventions from least to most intrusive in such instances. Her ideas for interventions include asking the child to make some physical movement to interrupt rigid, constricted reactions (e.g., standing up, moving arms); making a verbal statement that encourages the child to disengage from the play and observe it; asking about the experience of the different characters; and actively wondering about additional possibilities ("what would happen if"). Terr (2003), who has previously advocated similar ideas with regard to therapeutically manipulating repetitive play through "corrective denouement," recently modified her ideas regarding "correction." She now maintains that suggestions may be made and clues given, but in the end a traumatized child should conceptualize the corrective solutions himself or herself.

Indeed, keeping in mind the variety of soothing and protecting mechanisms employed by individual resilient children in our project, the therapist's role may be viewed as that of monitoring the child's use of soothing mechanisms, by reminding and inspiring the child to access the mechanisms which are more fitting for him or her. These actions communicate to the child that he or she is both the player and the director of the play and that possibilities for help and protection can be created. Furthermore, the therapist needs to clearly communicate at times that he or she can serve as an untiring protector, both as a participant and as an observer of the child's play. Our data demonstrated that "awareness of oneself as player" (Chazan, 2002) is associated with soothing ability in play and with adaptation. This awareness may be seen as a precursor for the emergence of reflection, to use Slade's (1994) terms, that is, the point in treatment when the therapist and the child step out of the play together and can share reflections and symbolic meanings.

For children who seem overwhelmed (due to anxiety, depression, and hypervigilance) and therefore unable to use play to process the trauma, a very gentle approach seems warranted, aimed at building a sense of safety and trust. In these cases a direct reconstruction of the trauma, or interpretations of feelings or defenses, seem contra-indicated. Herman (1997) emphasizes the importance of both internal and external safety before the processing can proceed, affirming that without a reasonable sense of safety there is no way of thinking in a symbolic manner. In thinking about a young child whose inner equilibrium has been disrupted by trauma and whose ability to play has been compromised, we may use Winnicott's (1971) observation that "Psychotherapy has to do with two people playing together. The corollary of this is that where playing is not possible then the work done by the therapist is directed towards bringing the patient from a state of not being able to play into a state of being able to play" (p. 38).

Slade (1994) develops this idea further, noting that the literature has emphasized the therapist's role in offering interpretation and deciphering meaning, while neglecting his or her role in the process of creating meaning or make-believe. She argues that for immature children, or for children whose capacities for symbolization and abstraction are limited, interpretations of inner feelings and experiences may lead to denial and disorganization. She highlights the importance of the therapist's "simply playing" with the child, and his or her role in leading the child in learning to develop a narrative in play and in gradually integrating affect into it. This co-creation within a growing meaningful relationship helps the development of a reflective self-function. Our suggestion is that the same therapeutic needs may be evident in traumatized children, whose previous developmental achievements may be thwarted by the traumatic experience, which overwhelms their ability to process, represent, and integrate the traumatic experiences into existing schemas.

ADDITIONAL CONSIDERATIONS FOR TRAUMA PROFESSIONALS

Any discussion of interventions with a traumatized population is incomplete without some consideration of the experience of the professionals carrying out the intervention. We touch briefly on a couple of such issues only to emphasize our belief that they warrant more serious reflection and discussion.

Secondary traumatic stress reactions: The risk of negative effects to the psychological well-being of mental health workers due to being exposed to the traumatic experiences of others—termed secondary traumatic stress, compassion fatigue, or trauma counter-transference—has been stressed in recent literature (Figley, 1995; Stamm, 1995; Collins & Long, 2003). In our work we often experienced the witnessing of the children's trauma through their play as very emotionally taxing, and we found that we needed to space our exposure to be able to contain it. There were, however, moments when the level of traumatic exposure was unexpected (just as in a real traumatic event) and therefore emotionally more overwhelming. To demonstrate one such personal experience: A standard questionnaire relating to the parents' trauma exposure and PTSD, received by mail from one of the mothers in our project, caused me a number of sleepless nights. For this mother the structured format of the questionnaire did not suffice and she added a full handwritten page, which fell out as I opened the envelope. The page included a very detailed description of a terrorist shooting in her home, and how she thought that her surviving son was dead because her deceased daughter's brains had covered his face. Our play sessions with unexposed children proved to be a good antidote to the emotional burden of playing with the young children exposed to terrorism. Additional helpful supports involved sharing our work with colleagues, and reminding ourselves of our purpose to help those in more need than we are.

Ethical dilemmas: The ambivalence, suspicion, and apprehension with which this project was initially received by various community representatives evoked in me an array of "counter-transferential" feelings. Some psychological services were worried about being flooded by referrals from the project. Families were worried about possible recommendations for therapy. Boards of education were worried about the public image of their population. This anxiety was contagious and brought forth ethical questions for self-examination: Would the results of this project attack the convictions or tarnish the image of an ideologically committed, exposed population? Could they weaken their defense mechanisms? Could avoidance and denial be working in the service of adaptive coping? Or, conversely, could these reactions in a community suffering from prolonged exposure be viewed as expected post-traumatic effects, needing to be gently confronted and processed?

It was the initial support of a number of mental health workers who are more embedded in this community that helped me get started. The growing interest in the project, however, gives me much hope that we had indeed identified a valid need and a safe procedure for helping.

CONCLUSION

In line with Herman (1997), I believe that recovery can occur only within the context of relationships. This is particularly true for young children, who need to sooth the wounds of their trauma to process it successfully. We have demonstrated through our project how play can become a major arena for understanding the experience of children without intruding or traumatizing, for raising the awareness of parents to their children's inner world, and for therapeutic healing.

REFERENCES

Achenbach, T., & Edelbrock, C. (1983). *Manual for the Child Behavior Checklist and Revised Child Behavior Profile*. Burlington: University of Vermont Department of Psychiatry.

Allwood, M. A., Bell-Dolan, D., & Husain, S. A. (2002). Children's trauma and adjustment reactions to violent and nonviolent war experiences. *Journal of the American Academy of Child and Adolescent Psychiatry, 41*(4), 450–457.

Almqvist, K., & Brandell-Forsberg, M. (1997). Refugee children in Sweden: Posttraumatic stress disorder in Iranian preschool children exposed to organized violence. *Child Abuse and Neglect, 21*(4), 351–366.

American Academy of Child and Adolescent Psychiatry. (1998). Practice parameters for the assessment and the treatment of children and adolescents with posttraumatic stress disorder. *Journal of the American Academy of Child and Adolescent Psychiatry, 37*(Suppl.10), 4S–26S.

American Psychiatric Association. (1994). *Diagnostic and Statistical Manual of Mental Disorders* (4th ed., DSM-IV). Washington, DC: Author.

American Psychiatric Association. (2000). *Diagnostic and Statistical Manual of Mental Disorders* (4th ed., DSM-IV-TR). Washington, DC: Author.

Chazan, S. E. (2000). Using the Children's Play Therapy Instrument (CPTI) to measure the development of play in simultaneous treatment: A case study. *Infant Mental Health Journal, 21*(3), 211–221.

Chazan, S. E. (2001). Toward a nonverbal syntax of play therapy. *Psychoanalytic Inquiry, 21*(3), 394–406.

Chazan, S.E. (2002). *Profiles of play*. London: Jessica Kingsley Publishers.

Chazan, S.E. (2003). *Children's Play Therapy Instrument—Adaptation for trauma research (CPTI-ATR)*. Unpublished manuscript.

Chemtob, C. M., Nakashima, J. P., & Hamada, R. S. (2002). Psychosocial intervention for postdisaster trauma symptoms in elementary school children: A controlled community field study. *Archives of Pediatrics and Adolescent Medicine, 156*, 211–216.

Collins, S., & Long, A. (2003). Working with the psychological effects of trauma: Consequences for mental health-care workers: A literature review. *Journal of Psychiatric and Mental Health Nursing, 10*(4), 417–424.

de Arelano, M.A., Waldrop, A.E., Deblinger, E., Cohen, J.A., Danielson, C.K., & Mannarino, A.R. (2005). Community outreach program for child victims of traumatic events: A community-based project for underserved populations. *Behavior Modification, 29*(1), 130–155.

Drewes, A. A. (2001). Developmental considerations in play and play therapy with traumatized children. In A. A. Drewes, L. J. Carey, & C. E. Schaefer (Eds.), *School-based play therapy* (pp. 297–314). New York: John Wiley & Sons.

Figley, C. R. (Ed.). (1995). *Compassion fatigue: Coping with secondary traumatic stress disorder in those who treat the traumatized*. Philadelphia: Brunner/Mazel.

Frankel, J. (2002). Exploring Ferenczi's concept of identification with the aggressor: Its role in trauma, everyday life, and the therapeutic relationship. *Psychoanalytic-Dialogues, 12*(1), 101–139.

Gallagher, M. M., Leavitt, K. S., & Kimmel, H. P. (1995). Mental health treatment of cumulative/repetitively traumatized children. *Smith College Studies in Social Work, 65*(3), 205–237.

Galovski, T., & Lyons, J. A. (2004). Psychological sequelae of combat violence: A review of the impact of PTSD on the veteran's family and possible interventions. *Aggression and Violent Behavior, 9*, 477–501.

Gil, E. (1998). *Play therapy for severe psychological trauma* (videotape manual). New York: Guilford Press.

Gil, E. (2002) Play therapy with abused children. In F. W. Kaslow (Ed.), *Comprehensive handbook of psychotherapy: Interpersonal/humanistic/existential: Vol. 3* (pp. 59–82). New York: John Wiley & Sons.

Glodich, A. M., Allen, J. G., & Arnold, L. (2001). Protocol for a trauma-based psychoeducational group intervention to decrease risk-taking, reenactment, and further violence exposure: Application to the public high school setting. *Journal of Child and Adolescent Group Therapy, 11* (2–3), 87–107.

Goenjian, A. K., Karayan, I., Pynoos, R. S., Minassian, D., Najarian, L. M., Steinberg, A. M. et al. (1997). Outcome of psychotherapy among early adolescents after trauma. *American Journal of Psychiatry, 154*, 536–542.

Hazboun, V. (2003). A Psychotherapeutic view of violence. *Palestine-Israel Journal, 10*(4), 24–29.

Herman, J. (1997). *Trauma and recovery.* New York: Basic Books.

Hoven, C. W., Duarte, C. S., Lucas, C. P., Mandell, D. J., Cohen, M., Rosen, C., et al. (2002). *Effects of the World Trade Center attack on NYC public school students: Initial report to the New York City Board of Education.* New York: Columbia University Mailman School of Public Health—New York State Psychiatric Institute and Applied Research and Counseling, LLC.

Howe, M. L. (1997). Children's memory for traumatic experiences. *Learning and Individual Differences, 9*, 153–174.

Joshi, P. T., & O'Donnell, D. A. (2003). Consequences of child exposure to war and terrorism. *Clinical Child and Family Psychology Review, 6*(4), 275–292.

Kernberg, P. F., Chazan, S. E., & Normandin, L. (1998). The Children's Play Therapy Instrument (CPTI). *Journal of Psychotherapy Practice and Research, 7*(3), 196–207.

Klingman, A., & Cohen, E. (2004). *School-based multisystemic interventions for mass trauma.* New York: Kluwer Academic/Plenum.

Laor, N., Wolmer, L., Mayes, L. C., & Gershon, A. (1997). Israeli preschool children under Scuds: A 30 months follow-up. *Journal of the American Academy of Child and Adolescent Psychiatry, 36*, 349–356.

Lavi, T. (2003). *Psychological adjustment following exposure to extreme political violence: The contribution of exposure variables and personality constructs to the moderation of the pathogenic sequelae following exposure among Palestinian children.* Unpublished doctoral dissertation, Tel-Aviv University, Tel-Aviv, Israel.

Lerner, Y. (2003). Mental health services in the changing Israeli society. *Palestine Israel Journal. 10*(4) 42–48.

Manenti, A. (2003). (Moderator). Roundtable: Two traumatized societies. *Palestine Israel Journal, 10*(4) 64–77.

Marans, S., Mayes, L. C., & Colonna, A. B. (1993). Psychoanalytic views of children's play. In A. J. Solnit, D. J. Cohen, & P. B. Neubauer (Eds.), *The many meanings of play: A psychoanalytic perspective* (pp. 9–28). New Haven, CT: Yale University Press.

March, J. S., Amaya-Jackson, L., Murray, M. C., & Schulte, A. (1998). Cognitive-behavioral psychotherapy for children and adolescents with posttraumatic stress disorder after a single-incident stressor. *American Academy of Child and Adolescent Psychiatry, 37,* 585–593.

Nader, K., & Pynoos, R. S. (2000). Play and drawing techniques as tools for interviewing traumatized children. In C. E. Schaefer, K. Gitlin, & A. Sandgrund (Eds.), *Play diagnosis and assessment* (pp. 375–389). New York: John Wiley & Sons.

Ogawa, Y. (2004). Childhood trauma and play therapy intervention for traumatized children. *Journal of Professional Counseling; Practice, Theory and Research, 32*(1), 19–29.

Osofsky, J.D. (1995). The effects of exposure to violence on young children. *American Psychologist, 50*(9), 782–788.

Perrin, S., Smith, P., & Yule, W. (2000). Practitioner's review: The assessment and treatment of post-traumatic stress disorder in children and adolescents. *Journal of Child Psychology and Psychiatry and Allied Disciplines, 41,* 277–289.

Pine, D. S., & Cohen, J. A. (2002). Trauma in children and adolescents: Risk and treatment of psychiatric sequelae. *Biological Psychiatry, 51*(7), 519–531.

Rubin S. S. (1994). Playing and motherhood; or How to get the most out of avant-garde. In D. Bassin, D. Honey, & M. M. Kaplan (Eds.), *Representations of motherhood* (pp. 272–282). New Haven, CT: Yale University Press.

Ryan, V., & Needham, C. (2001). Non-directive play therapy with children experiencing psychic trauma. *Clinical Child Psychology and Psychiatry, 6,* 437–453.

Salmon, K., & Bryant, R. A. (2002). Posttraumatic stress disorder in children: The influence of developmental factors. *Clinical Psychology Review, 22,* 163–188.

Saltzman, W. R., Steinberg, A. M., Layne, C. M., Aisenberg, E., & Pynoos, R. S. (2002). A developmental approach to school-based treatment of adolescents exposed to trauma and traumatic loss. *Journal of Child and Adolescent Group Therapy, 11,* 43–56.

Saylor, C. F., Swenson, C. C., & Powell, P. (1991). Hurricane Hugo blows down the broccoli: Preschoolers' post-disaster play and adjustment. *Child Psychiatry and Human Development, 22*(3), 139–149.

Scheeringa, M. S., Peebles, C. D., Cook, C. A., & Zeanah, C. H. (2001). Toward establishing procedural criterion and discriminant validity for PTSD in early childhood. *Journal of the American Academy of Child and Adolescent Psychiatry, 40,* 52–60.

Scheeringa, M. S., & Zeanah, C. H. (2001). A relational perspective on PTSD in early childhood. *Journal of Traumatic Stress, 14,* 799–815.

Scheeringa, M. S., Zeanah, C .H., Drell, M. J., & Larrieu, J. A. (1995). Two approaches to the diagnosis of posttraumatic stress disorder in infancy and early childhood. *Journal of the American Academy of Child and Adolescent Psychiatry, 34,* 191–200.

Scheeringa, M. S., Zeanah, C. H., Myers, L., & Putnam, F. (2003). New findings on alternative criteria for PTSD in preschool children. *Journal of the American Academy of Child and Adolescents Psychiatry, 42,* 561–572.

Shelby, J. S. (2000). Brief therapy with traumatized children: A developmental perspective. In C. E. Schaefer & H. G. Kaduson (Eds.), *Short term play therapy for children* (pp. 69–104). New York: Guilford Press.

Silverman, W. K., & La Greca, A .M. (2002). Children experiencing disaster: Definitions, reactions, and predictors of outcome. In A. M. La Greca, W. K. Silverman, E. M., Vernberg, & M. C. Roberts (Eds.), *Helping children cope with disaster and terrorism* (pp. 11–33). Washington, DC: American Psychological Association.

Slade, A. (1994). Making meaning and making believe: Their role in the clinical process. In D. P. Wolf & A. Slade (Eds.), *Children at play: Clinical and developmental approaches to meaning and representation* (pp. 81–107). London: Oxford University Press.

Smith, P., Perrin, S., & Yule, W. (1999). Cognitive behaviour therapy for post traumatic stress disorder. *Child Psychology and Psychiatry Review, 4*(4), 177–182.

Stamm, B. H. (Ed.). (1995). Secondary traumatic stress: Self-care issues for clinicians, researchers and educators. Baltimore: Sidran Press.

Taylor, T. L., & Chemtob, C. M. (2004). Efficacy of treatment of child and adolescent traumatic stress. *Archives of Pediatric and Adolescent Medicine, 158,* 786–791.

Terr, L. (1983). Play therapy and psychic trauma: A preliminary report. In C. E. Schaefer & K. J. O'Connor (Eds.), *Handbook of play therapy* (pp. 308–319). New York: John Wiley & Sons.

Terr, L.C. (1990). *Too scared to cry.* New York: HarperCollins.

Terr, L.C. (2003). "Wild child": How three principles of healing organized 12 years of psychotherapy. *Journal of the American Academy of Child and Adolescent Psychiatry, 42*(12), 1401–1409.

Thabet, A.A.M., Abed, Y., & Vostanis, P. (2004). Comorbidity of PTSD and depression among refugee children during war conflict. *Journal of Child Psychology and Psychiatry, 45*(3), 533–542.

Varkas, T. (1998). Childhood trauma and posttraumatic play: A literature review and case study. *Journal of Analytic Social Work, 5*(3), 29–50.

Webb, N. B. (Ed.). (1991). *Play therapy with children in crisis.* New York: Guilford Press.

Webb, N. B. (Ed.). (2004). *Mass trauma and violence: Helping families and children cope.* New York: Guilford Press.

Wershba-Gershon, P. (1996). Free symbolic play and assessment of the nature of child sexual abuse. *Journal of Child Sexual Abuse, 5*(2), 37–57.

Winnicott, D .W. (1971). *Playing and reality.* New York: Basic Books.

Wirgen, J. (1994). Narrative completion in the treatment of trauma. *Psychotherapy,* *31*(3), 415–423.

Wright, M. O., Masten, A. S., Northwood, A., & Hubbard, J. J. (1997). Long-term effects of massive trauma: Developmental and psychobiological perspectives. In D. Cicchetti & S. L. Toth (Eds.), *Developmental perspectives on trauma: Theory, research, and intervention* (pp. 181–225). Rochester, NY: University of Rochester Press.

Yule, W. (2001). Post-traumatic stress disorder in children and adolescents. *International Review of Psychiatry, 13*, 194–200.

Yule, W., Perrin, S., & Smith, P. (1999). Post-traumatic stress reactions in children and adolescents. In W. Yule (Ed.), *Post-traumatic stress disorder—Concepts and therapy* (pp. 25–50). Cambridge, UK: Cambridge University Press.

CHAPTER 9

When a Benevolent Servant Becomes a Malevolent Dictator

A Dark Side of Nuclear Technology

Donna Macomber and Elena L. Grigorenko

Through the release of atomic energy, our generation has brought into the world the most revolutionary force since prehistoric man's discovery of fire. This basic force of the universe cannot be fitted into the outmoded concept of narrow nationalisms. For there is no secret and there is no defense; there is no possibility of control except through the aroused understanding and insistence of the peoples of the world. We scientists recognize our inescapable responsibility to carry to our fellow citizens an understanding of atomic energy and its implication for society. In this lies our only security and our only hope—we believe that an informed citizenry will act for life and not for death.

Albert Einstein, 1947

INTRODUCTION: THE ACCIDENT

Nuclear energy supplies over 16% of the world's electricity. Simply stated, nuclear energy generates electricity by boiling water to make steam, which then drives turbine generators. There are currently 440 nuclear reactors operating in 31 countries worldwide, the majority of which are located in the United States (104), followed by France (59), Japan (53), Russia (30), and the United Kingdom (27) (World Nuclear Association). In theory, nuclear energy has a distinct environmental advantage over fossil fuels in that it does not cause any pollution. Under normal circumstances, all waste is contained and managed. Because of the known hazards of radioactivity (inherent in nuclear energy, whose main source of fuel is uranium), the safety-driven design and operation of nuclear power plants is of utmost importance. However, practice does not always reflect theory.

On April 26, 1986, a catastrophic nuclear accident took place in Reactor No. 4 at the Chernobyl power plant in Ukraine. Operators were conducting an experiment to ascertain how long the generators would run without power in the event of a power failure. Therefore, they reduced the production of reactor power (Mould, 2000) and blocked the flow of steam to the generators. Unfortunately, a design defect in the reactor model made its operation at low power unstable. The extra buildup of steam resulted in a power surge and the operators manually disabled the safety system, as it would have interfered with the test. Realizing too late that the situation was serious, an operator activated the safety system. A power surge 100 times larger than the normal maximum operating level and an increase in temperature in the reactor resulted in two explosions—one destroyed the metal plate that sealed the top of the reactor and the second destroyed the building that housed it (Mould; Shcherbak, 1996). Radioactive particles were released into the atmosphere and prevailing winds carried them to the north, east, and west in a variable distribution pattern.

The first indication that an accident had taken place came from the Forsmark nuclear power plant in Sweden. High levels of radiation were detected on plant workers passing through the gate. The plant was evacuated and hours later it was determined that the problem was coming not from within the plant but from the east (Mould, 2000; Wroble & Baum, 2002). In response to worldwide pressure, the Soviet government issued a terse statement on the evening of April 28, 1986:

> An accident has occurred at the Chernobyl Atomic Power Plant as one of the atomic reactors was damaged. Measures are being undertaken to eliminate the consequence of the accident. Aid is being given to those affected. A Government Commission has been set up. (Mould, 2000, p. 45)

No other information was forthcoming at that time (Tonnessen, Mardberg, & Weisaeth, 2002). The Soviet government had implemented its long-proven tactic of keeping silent to avoid trouble (Rahu, 2003), which in turn exacerbated rumors and speculation about the magnitude of the incident. A media frenzy ensued and the death toll was estimated to be in the thousands. Area residents received little or no information about the accident and its consequences.

Precautionary measures, such as staying inside and eating canned food, were not made available to the public for nearly a week (Wroble & Baum, 2002).

Ionizing radiation can reach and harm the body via two pathways: external (e.g., radioactive clouds, material on the ground) and/or internal (e.g., inhalation of radioactive materials and/or ingestion of contaminated foods and water) (Becker, Robbins, Beebe, Bouville, & Wachholz, 1996). The Chernobyl reactor released plutonium, uranium, iodine-131 (I^{131}), strontium-90 (Sr^{90}), and cesium-137 (Cs^{137}) into the atmosphere (Brown, 2002; Shcherbak, 1996). The amount of cesium-137 released was equivalent to 200 times the combined cesium at Hiroshima and Nagasaki (Fusco & Caris, 2001; Mould, 2000).

Cesium-137 easily penetrates the soil, is absorbed by plants, and is then consumed by animals and humans through food and water (Fusco & Caris, 2001). The body mistakes cesium-137 for potassium, which is needed by every living cell; as a result, it accumulates in the muscles (Roche, 1996). Cells of the thyroid and other endocrinological organs (e.g., pituitary, pineal, and adrenal glands) also intensively incorporate cesium-137 (Fusco & Caris, 2001). Exposure to cesium-137 greatly increases cancer risks, and cases of extreme exposure can result in serious burns and even death (http://www.epa.gov/radiation/radionuclides/cesium.htm). Iodine-131 is absorbed by the thyroid gland, which controls growth (Roche, 1996); this isotope causes thyroid disorders and cancer of the thyroid.

The degree of radioactive contamination varied from region to region because of prevailing winds at the time of the accident. The highly contaminated 10 km zone around the Chernobyl plant (the "dead zone" or "exclusion zone") has been permanently deemed a restricted area. With the exception of those individuals who man security checkpoints, no one can occupy the dead zone, although an estimated 450–600 people live there illegally (Vickery, 2002) in complete isolation. Since 1992, elderly residents have been allowed to return to certain areas of the 30 km zone, but the return of children is strictly forbidden (Mould, 2000). Many elderly residents who were evacuated and relocated had difficulty making the transition to a new environment and have returned to their former homes, ignoring the hazards of continuous radiation exposure. As many as 200,000 people live in severely contaminated areas (Vickery, 2002) that still require monitoring because of high radiation levels (Bellaby, 2004). The food chain and water system are unfit for humans—land can no longer be farmed, forests can no longer be used, and rivers cannot be fished.

At the time of the accident, the 30 km region around the Chernobyl plant was declared uninhabitable, necessitating the evacuation and relocation of some 300,000 people. The evacuation was poorly organized and exemplified the lack of preparedness of organizations and individuals for such a disaster.

Residents were not allowed to take any personal belongings upon evacuation, as they were also deemed contaminated. Some families were relocated twice—initially from their homes and then again after relocation sites were declared contaminated. Even then, some were issued temporary relocation papers indicating that they could be relocated yet again (Wroble & Baum, 2002). With the exception of Prypiat—a satellite-town of the Chernobyl power station where most of the station's personnel lived—evacuees were for the most part rural people who produced their own food and lived in villages their families had inhabited for thousands of years (Fusco & Caris, 2001). After relocation they often found inadequate housing, unemployment, obstacles in obtaining healthcare, and difficulty making the transition from a rural to an urban culture (Roche, 1996).

The Republic of Belarus, northwest of Chernobyl, received the majority of radioactive fallout—an estimated 70%. Although some areas were evacuated, most of the radioactivity was dispersed in such a way that the level of contamination did not warrant relocation. Residents of these areas were left to live in the presence of constant lower-level radiation.

One account of the accident puts the health of millions at risk; others claim that although Chernobyl was, without question, a serious accident, the radioactive material released diluted quickly and therefore would have few appreciable direct health effects on human populations (Rytomaa, 1996). Although the list of nuclear accidents before Chernobyl is by no means short, the link between radiation and public health is still poorly understood.

The victims of Chernobyl, however, experienced this dearth of knowledge of the impact of radiation first-hand and on several levels. Specifically, because of the lack of monitoring, diagnosing, and preventive services, many people did not know whether they had been exposed to radiation, whether the exposure was sufficient to cause health problems, whether they would develop exposure-related diseases or conditions, and whether they would experience new exposures and of what magnitude (Wroble & Baum, 2002). These types of problems are referred to here as the direct impact of irradiation on public health. In addition, the radioactive contamination of water, soil, and food resulted in the loss of homes, personal property, community, lifestyle, and employment, as well as stigmatization and uncertain futures. These changes in turn resulted in elevated rates of physical and mental health problems—referred to here as the indirect impact of irradiation on public health. Our discussion of the consequences of Chernobyl is structured around these two types of impacts of irradiation—direct and indirect.

The discussion below is divided into sections so that particular groups that experienced (or still experience) both the direct and indirect effects of irradiation are featured in each section. The groups are described in order of their proximity to and involvement with the accident—liquidators (i.e., the people in charge of containing, minimizing, and cleaning up the consequences of the tragedy), laypeople who were acutely affected by high levels of exposure to the fallout (those who were evacuated from highly contaminated areas), laypeople who were and still are affected by low levels of radiation (those allowed to remain in lightly contaminated areas because of federal recognition of these areas as inhabitable), and people in other countries affected by the fallout.

LIQUIDATORS

Six firefighters were on duty at the reactor on the day of the accident and were the first responders to the site after the explosions. These individuals, although adequately trained, were not advised of radiation procedures with regard to this particular incident and had insufficient protective clothing (Fusco & Caris, 2001; Mould, 2000). All of them died of serious forms of acute radiation sickness.

Before and after the magnitude of the accident was realized, various firefighters, professionals, and military personnel were actively dealing with the consequences of the tragedy. Collectively, these people are referred to as *liquidators*. The fires were extinguished and the radioactive releases stopped 10 days after the accident. Overall, approximately 200 of the first emergency workers at the scene suffered acute radiation damage; 31 of those died (Rytomaa, 1996). Ayres (2004) also reports an official death toll of 31 workers at the plant, but claims that experts estimate the number to be closer to 7000 (in the immediate aftermath of the accident).

Liquidators were responsible for containment of the fire at the Chernobyl reactor, removal of radioactive material from the roof of the burning reactor, fighting retroactive fires, and cleanup operations (Fusco & Caris, 2001). Cleanup operations included the evacuation of residents from the 30 km zone, razing houses and buildings, exterminating livestock and wildlife, and burying contaminated materials. Reported estimates of the liquidators involved vary and range from 200,000 to as many as 800,000. In fact, Mould (2000) and Rytomaa (1996) state that as many as 650,000 liquidators were recruited from all 15 republics of the Soviet Union over the course of the cleanup operations. However, Belyakov (1999) states that a more realistic estimate would be 300,000 to 320,000 individuals. The highest increased health risk for those who worked in the 30 km zone was estimated to occur from 1986–1987, with the highest risk period from April to July (Ivanov, Tsyb, Gorsky, et al., 1997).

Although iodine-131 has a half-life of only 8 days, it caused substantial radiation exposure during the weeks immediately following the accident (Henshaw, 1996; Schwenn & Brill, 1997; Shcherbak, 1996), a common byproduct of which is thyroid cancer. Thyroid cancer can easily metastasize and spread to other parts of the body. Surgical removal of the thyroid can prevent the development of cancer; however, it necessitates lifelong thyroid hormone medication (Schwenn & Brill; Shcherbak; Sweet, 1996). Data from the Russian National Medical Dosimetric Registry (RNMDR)—the agency directly involved with health outcomes of irradiation (Ivanov, Tsyb, Gorsky, et al., 1997)—confirm 47 verified cases of thyroid cancers in liquidators. The RNMDR contains data on 432,276 individuals, including 167,862 liquidators. Twenty-eight thyroid cancers were detected in the emergency workers of 1986, 15 in emergency workers of 1987, and 4 in those from 1988–1990. In a later study of thyroid cancer incidence in approximately 100,000 liquidators living in six regions of Russia, Ivanov, Tsyb, Gorsky, and colleagues found a statistically significant increase of thyroid cancer in liquidators from 1986–1998 compared with the general male population (Ivanov, Tsyb, Petrov, et al., 2002). Participants lived in the northwest, Volgo-Vyatsky, Central Chernozemny, Povolzhsky, and North Caucasus regions, and the Urals of Russia.

It is difficult to present with certainty the actual quantity of external physical doses of radioactive exposure endured by the liquidators. Belyakov (1999) reports overexposed subgroups may have received doses as high as 0.25 Gy.[1] Ivanov et al. (2002) estimate that in 1986 liquidators received a mean dose of 1.68 Gy and in 1988–1990 they received 0.33 Gy. Ivanov and colleagues (2000) estimated radiation risks for non-cancer diseases among a cohort of 59,207 male liquidators for whom external gamma-radiation doses were known and health information was available as part of their registration in the RNMDR prior to January 1, 1992. In this cohort, the mean dose maximum was found in liquidators of 1986 (167 mGy) and the minimum in liquidators who entered the zone in 1988 and after (31 mGy). Data were the result of annual medical examinations entered into the RNMDR. With respect to the non-cancer diseases, dose estimates of radiation were stratified by age at time of arrival to the zone, year of arrival to the zone, and area of residence. The highest excess relative risk was found for cerebrovascular diseases, fol-

---

[1]Rem, Sv, and Gy are terms used to describe the relative biological measurements of radiation. The term used in the United States is rem (rad equivalent man), but the recommended units are described as grays (Gy) or sieverts (Sv). 1 Gy and 1 Sv are equal to 100 rem. For reference, according to the Idaho State University Radiation Information Network, the average person in the United States receives about 360 millirems (one thousandth of a rem) every year (http://www.physics.isu.edu/radinf/risk.htm).

lowed by endocrine diseases and metabolic disorders, essential hypertension, mental disorders, diseases of the nervous systems and sensory organs, and diseases of the digestive system, respectively (Ivanov et al, 2002). However, the study did not allow for associated risk factors such as obesity, high cholesterol, smoking, and alcoholism, and the authors note that the results were tentative and recommended further research. Worth mentioning is that similar detrimental health effects are often linked to excessive stress and anxiety.

The standardized mortality rate in Russia increased by 24% from 1990–1993, particularly in men aged 35–44 years, corresponding to the mean age of emergency workers in 1993 (Ivanov, Gorski, Maksioutov, Tsyb, & Souchkevitch, 2001). Between 1991 and 1998, 4,995 deaths of liquidators with documented external radiation doses in the range of 0.005–0.3 Sv were recorded: 515 due to malignant tumors; 1,728 due to cardiovascular diseases; 1,858 due to injuries, poisoning, or violent deaths; and 894 due to other causes. Contrary to other Russian and worldwide publications stating a significant mortality increase among emergency workers, however, Ivanov and colleagues found that mortality in the cohort of emergency workers did not exceed the spontaneous mortality level in corresponding age groups of the Russian population.

Loganovsky and Loganovskaja (2000) reported a significant increase in the incidence of schizophrenia in emergency workers compared with the general population (5.4 per 10,000 vs. 1.1 per 10,000) 3 years after the disaster. These workers did not have any preexisting psychiatric disorders, as those who did not pass a required medical examination were not hired as liquidators. Exposure to ionizing radiation is thought to cause brain damage, affecting the function of the limbic system, an area of dysfunction found by neurobiological studies to occur in schizophrenic patients (Loganovsky & Loganovskaja). The authors theorized that exposure to ionizing radiation caused damage to the limbic system and thus triggered a disposition to schizophrenia or schizophrenia-like symptoms. An EEG analysis of patients with acute radiation sickness (ARS) and 1986–1987 emergency workers revealed EEG changes, with spastic activity shifted to the left frontotemporal region (cortical-limbic overactivity) 3 to 5 years after irradiation (1989–1991), and organic brain damage with inhibition of the cortical-limbic system 10 to 13 years after irradiation (1996–1999) (Loganovsky & Yuryev, 2001). In 1996, these participants were diagnosed with "personality changes due to a general medical condition" according to the *Diagnostic and Statistical Manual IV* (American Psychiatric Association, 1994, pp. 173–174). Interpretation of the EEG results revealed a dysfunction of the left frontotemporal limbic system (1989–1991), and the alteration of brain wave activities indicating cerebral disorganization (1996–1991), which is thought to lead to schizophrenia (Loganovsky & Yuryev).

Among many liquidators, post-traumatic stress disorder (PTSD) was diagnosed utilizing criteria in the *Diagnostic and Statistical Manual of Mental Disorders–Revised* (DSM-III-R) (American Psychiatric Association, 1987). Symptoms of PTSD include persistent anxiety, exaggerated arousal, difficulty falling or staying asleep, hypervigilance, irritability, outbursts of anger, and difficulty concentrating or completing tasks. On returning home, the workers and their families noted and reported an increase in irritability (daily outbursts of anger such as shouting, verbal aggression, and throwing objects), and workers reported sleep disorders and difficulty concentrating (Tarabrina, Lazebnaia, & Zelenova, 2001). An additional study measured physiological activity using imagery in 13 Chernobyl workers diagnosed with PTSD (Tarabrina, Lazebnaia, Zelenova, Lasko, et al., 2001). Workers were asked to imagine personal traumatic situations associated with their time spent at Chernobyl while galvanic skin reflex, heart rate, and electromyograms of the left lateral frontalis muscle were measured. The left lateral frontalis muscle is located above the left eyebrow—the movement of which produces facial expressions. The authors found no increase in physiological activity in the workers diagnosed with PTSD and concluded that the lack of an increase in activity was due to the experience of an assumed and conceptual reaction to traumatic stimuli (invisible) rather than a direct perception (visible).

The following is a personal account of a liquidator involved in cleanup operations:

> *August 1993. Moscow.* You find it difficult to control yourself: everything is tense and wound up, and you have a lump in your throat. You just buried the second pilot of your team. He was flying with you to Chernobyl, and now he is no more. You feel an unpleasant heaviness in your chest, and it's difficult for you to breathe. Why did he die so early? Who is to blame? Who is responsible for what happened to him and for what is happening to all of you? You feel a pounding in your temples, and it feels as though your head were in a vice. (Tarabrina, Lazebnaia, & Zelenova, 2001, p. 52)

It is difficult to draw accurate conclusions regarding the effects of Chernobyl on the liquidators as a group. As stated previously, even the actual number of liquidators involved is undetermined. The liquidators are also a heterogeneous group: They were responsible for a variety of tasks in the cleanup operation, differed in their tenure in the contaminated zone, were from different organizational affiliations (e.g., military, police, reservists, scientists, laymen), varied in age, and were of different nationalities. The amount of radiation exposure for this group can only be estimated and any predisposition to physical diseases or psychological disorders is unknown. With the exception of acute radiation sickness for the first responders and enormous increases in thyroid cancer, morbidity rates as a direct result of Chernobyl appear to be inconclusive; however, several research studies indicate a degree of detrimental health effects. What is certain is that liquidators who were in the contaminated zone immediately after the accident suffered the most serious health consequences, and psychosocial effects appear to play an enormous role in the health and well-being of the Chernobyl liquidators.

LAYPEOPLE: RELOCATED AND NOT RELOCATED
As we mentioned earlier, there are two distinct categories of laypeople affected by the accident. The first is the people who lived and worked in areas that were recognized as uninhabitable as a consequence of the fallout. Those people were forcefully evacuated from these areas; however, quite a number of them, especially in rural areas, returned to their houses despite public health warnings. The second group is the people living in the areas affected by the fallout who were not relocated because the contamination danger was classified as acceptable by federal standards in the Soviet Union. Below we describe the available data on the impact of the Chernobyl accident on the health of these two groups.

Congenital Abnormalities and Health Risks in Russia
As previously stated, those residing in the 30 km area around the Chernobyl power plant received the highest doses of radiation prior to evacuation, particularly those residing in the Gomel Oblast[2] in the Republic of Belarus. In 2002, the First Deputy State Secretary at the Health Ministry of Ukraine reported that all people affected by Chernobyl (evacuees and residents of contaminated territories) had seen deterioration in their health status over the years (Breus, 2002). Yet, what specific conditions can be identified in conjunction with this generic statement?

Previous animal and human research has proven numerous detrimental effects of ionizing radiation on a developing fetus (see Grigorenko, 2001). An increase in birth defects and malformations was detected in the areas of Belarus that received the most radioactive contamination (Lazjuk, Nikolaev, & Novikova, 1997). Multiple congenital malformations, polydactyly (more

---

[2]An oblast is a subdivision of the larger country.

than the normal number of fingers or toes), and reduction limb defects were the most frequent—malformations that are most commonly associated with dominant chromosomal mutations. However, teratogenic (developmental) effects or chromosomal disorders such as Down syndrome were not found to have increased (Lazjuk et al.). Castronovo (1999) performed a descriptive analysis of birth defects and malformations in Belarus to evaluate the risks associated with fetal irradiation as a function of both the total dose (particularly from cesium-137 exposure) and post-conception time at irradiation. He found no evidence that radiation exposures in pregnant women produced excess teratogenic effects that can be attributed to Chernobyl. In another study, researchers monitored developmental anomalies and congenital malformations of newborns in the Republic of Belarus and in less-affected regions before and after the Chernobyl accident. Data revealed higher incidences of anomalies and malformations in contaminated rural regions of Belarus than in control areas (Feshchenko, Schroder, Muller, & Lazjuk, 2002).

Buzhievskaya, Tchiaikovskaya, Demidova, and Koblyanskaya (1995) analyzed the archives of the two largest obstetric hospitals in Kiev, Ukraine. Kiev is located approximately 90 km south of Chernobyl and received significantly less contamination than did areas north and east of the plant. Annual birthrates for Kiev were estimated at 33,000 for 1969–1990. The two hospitals studied accounted for 25% to 33% of all deliveries. These researchers found no mutations or teratogenic effects; however, the frequency of therapeutic abortions increased by a factor of 1.5. This was interpreted as a social consequence of Chernobyl.

Throughout the contaminated region, an unprecedented surge of thyroid cancer, especially in children, was found to be directly attributable to Chernobyl, and Belarusian scientists pointed to an increase in almost every type of cancer during the years after the accident (Fusco & Caris, 2001). Reported cases of thyroid cancer in children skyrocketed from 2 before the accident to approximately 1000 in the 10 years after (Bellaby, 2004). Iodine-131 is a major teratogenic agent because of its rapid intake via food and water by the thyroid gland, particularly in children under 3 years of age. Henshaw (1996) reported excess cases of thyroid cancer in children 3 to 5 years after the accident. In Belarus, Ukraine, and the southwest Russian Federation, there has been a 100-fold increase in the normal incidence of thyroid cancer (Rytomaa, 1996). From 1986–2001, 2071 patients who were under age 18 years at the time of the accident underwent thyroid surgery (Breus, 2002). Ivanov and colleagues (2003) examined reported cases of thyroid cancer in adolescents and adults aged 15–69 years in the Bryansk Oblast of the southwestern Russian Federation. Bryansk Oblast (east of Chernobyl) shares its borders with Belarus and Ukraine. From 1986–1998, 1051 cases of thyroid cancer in Bryansk Oblast were detected; 769 (73%) of these cases occurred between 1991 and 1998. Latest estimates report that about 2000 cases of thyroid cancer have occurred in children or adolescents because of Chernobyl fallout (Williams, 2001), and this epidemic will not reach its peak until 2006 (Ayres, 2004). The Chernobyl Thyroid Diseases Study Group of Belarus, Ukraine, and the U.S., and colleagues (2004) are currently conducting a study of a large cohort of individuals (over 25,000) who were under age 18 years at the time of the accident. The study began in Belarus in 1996 and in Ukraine in 1998 and screens participants for thyroid diseases every 2 years. The researchers screen not only for thyroid cancer, but other diseases of the thyroid as well, including "benign nodules, hypothyroidism, autoimmune thyroiditis, and hyperparathyroidism" (Chernobyl Thyroid Diseases Study Group et al., p. 491). This study aims to provide directly measured risk estimates of thyroid cancer from exposure to radioactive iodines, which are important for radiation epidemiology and public health.

An examination of cancer risk in the Kaluga Oblast in the western Russian Federation 10 years after the Chernobyl accident revealed no statistically significant effect of radiation on cancer morbidity, with the exception of thyroid cancer in women (Ivanov, Tsyb, Nilova, et al., 1997). An unfavorable trend of malignant tumors of the respiratory organs was also found in this region, but this was thought to be a fluctuation of spontaneous cancer rates and was not considered a result of exposure to ionizing radiation (Ivanov, Tsyb, Nilova, et al.). In this region, it appears that no increase in the incidence of non-thyroid cancers can be definitively attributed to the Chernobyl accident. Specifically, no increase in leukemia has been demonstrated, although the incidence of blood disorders in contaminated regions has increased (Henshaw, 1996; Rytomaa, 1996). This result raises questions regarding the findings of a small increase in childhood leukemia in Western Europe after Chernobyl (Hoffmann, 2002).

Individuals who resided in close proximity to the Chernobyl reactor and those who were unfortunate enough to be in the direct path of the most severe radioactive fallout have been found to suffer the most serious health consequences. Belarus underwent the highest increases in birth defects and malformations as well as increases in thyroid cancer. Similar increases were also found east of Chernobyl in northern Ukraine and the southwestern Russian Federation. However, occurrences of thyroid cancer and other ill health effects decreased as a function of distance from the reactor core. Interestingly, although researchers found no increase in birth defects or malformations in Kiev, an increase in therapeutic abortions occurred, which was thought to be an indirect consequence of the Chernobyl accident.

Intervention for the Health Effects of Exposure to Radioactivity

In terms of a response from psychosocial therapeutic and preventive services to people's needs, as previously stated, the period immediately after the Chernobyl accident can only be described as chaotic. Hundreds of thousands of individuals were forced to relocate to other cities. Their primary concern was survival and finding the basic needs of food, clothing, and shelter, as well as successful adaptation to a new environment. Exacerbating the problem, information regarding the accident was not forthcoming from the government, nor were proper precautions for prevention of further harm from radioactive fallout. Although there were some psychologists working with relocated people, services were mostly sporadic and asystematic.

One can assume that those who first responded to the accident were treated medically for radiation poisoning and the ill effects of contamination; however, because the government was reluctant to even admit that an accident had taken place, little is known about this or any further attempts to prevent additional damage to the health of those affected by the radiation.

As illustrated in previous sections, ill health effects after Chernobyl were found by many researchers; however, because of poorly kept health records prior to 1986, only the extraordinarily high occurrence of thyroid cancer in children can be scientifically attributed to the accident. In fact, the World Nuclear Association has reported that there is no evidence of a major public health impact attributable to the Chernobyl accident other than this enormous upsurge (http://www.world-nuclear.org). We address this epidemic here.

As a result of the accident, radioactive iodine was dispersed in gaseous or aerosol form and was most likely directly absorbed into the body via two pathways—through the lungs by inhalation, or through the food chain (it was deposited on plants and water, thus entering the food chain [Becker et al., 1996]). It was then most likely ingested by the public in milk, green vegetables, and other foods (Schwenn & Brill, 1997). The area surrounding Chernobyl was primarily rural and the residents typically raised diary cows for milk and grew their own vegetables. Becker and colleagues reported that direct thyroid radioassay measurements taken after the accident found the highest doses to the thyroid in children, thought mainly to be due to the consumption of contaminated cow's milk. Iodine-131 has a half-life of 8 days and most of the exposure to radioactive iodine occurred shortly after the accident (Schwenn & Brill). Once incorporated into the body, its effects depend on its retention (Rabin, 1986). The administration of potassium iodide (KI) can block further uptake of radioactive iodine into the thyroid gland, but this administration must be initiated shortly after exposure to radiation (Robbins, 1997; Schwenn & Brill; Sweet, 1996). Unfortunately, with the delay in information to the populace, success of the distribution of KI was limited and optimal administration doses were rarely achieved (Becker et al., 1996). In fact, subsequent surveys suggest that only 25% of the population received KI, often with varying and sometimes prolonged delays (Becker et al.; Robbins; Schwenn & Brill). Standard therapy for thyroid disease includes surgery, but even after thyroidectomy, recurrence is likely and a lifetime of maintenance therapy with a thyroid hormone is necessary (Schwenn & Brill; Sweet). This has been a crushing financial burden on a government already experiencing economic hardship (Robbins, 1997).

Rapid first aid, triage, and transportation to properly equipped medical facilities are essential for on-site victims (Rabin, 1986), and effective measures following a nuclear accident must include a well-organized evacuation plan, removal of local foods and milk from the food chain, distribution of potassium iodide, and the provision of substitutes for breast milk (Schwenn & Brill, 1997). Schwenn and Brill intimate that many incidences of thyroid cancer could have been prevented if not for the delay in the government response to the accident. The delay of an immediate, honest, and straightforward account of events generated mistrust in the government, and once information was forthcoming, the public was skeptical. In fact, the International Atomic Energy Agency (IAEA) 1990 Chernobyl project gave the people in less-contaminated areas a clean bill of health, but many people did not believe it (Sweet, 1996). The most important lesson to be learned from Chernobyl is the importance of quickly disseminating accurate information to the general public to avoid panic and severe secondary psychological consequences arising from feelings of betrayal and neglect by the federal government and fears about future health and well-being.

Psychosocial Effects

Because of its worldwide impact, Chernobyl is said to be the greatest technological disaster of the 20th century. A sense of control is expected with technological accidents like Chernobyl—not so with natural disasters like hurricanes, earthquakes, or floods (Baum & Fleming, 1996). Technological disasters differ from natural disasters in that they contaminate and pollute the environment; the danger is invisible, which produces panic; there is no standard for recovery (meaning no easily identified beginning, middle, and end to the crisis); the ill effects may be gradual and enduring; poor information causes greater stress and the information given may be a stressor; the hazards are persistent; and victims experience chronic loss of control (Brown, 2002). Uncertainty, lack of definition of the situation, and loss of control contribute to chronic stress and the potential for persistent mental and physical health problems in survivors of a technological disaster (Baum & Fleming). Immediately following the accident, the primary concern of the exposed population was the possibility of future increases in cancer and leukemia, particularly in children; however, psychosocial problems have become areas of principal concern (Mould, 2000).

Residents of the areas around Chernobyl who were evacuated and relocated were done so without prior notification and with no formal procedures in place. Government representatives (liquidators and Soviet army units) arrived in many towns and villages and ordered the public to board buses and other vehicles. Some families were separated and not reunited for several weeks. In some of the more remote areas of the contaminated region, this was the first report that a nuclear accident had even occurred. Evacuees required official documentation to relocate and such documentation was often delayed or, once received, found to be temporary. Reported numbers of evacuees range anywhere from 100,000 to 300,000 people. One can only imagine the chaos and the evacuees' mental state: the shock of learning of the accident; coping with the possibility of radiation contamination and its consequences; and being forced to abandon homes, possessions, communities, and lifestyles—in all probability never to return. Upon arrival in new areas, evacuees were subjected to further stressors such as inadequate housing, inaccessibility to health care, unemployment, adaptation to a new environment, and bearing the stigma of being "contaminated." This differs greatly from the altruistic and supportive community that often develops during and after a natural disaster (Weisaeth, Knudsen, & Tonnessen, 2002). Relocated families reported feelings of alienation, isolation, and stigmatization from the larger community (Wroble & Baum, 2002).

Persons exposed to invisible contaminants experience and dwell on several forms of uncertainty as they attempt to cope with the consequences. In addition to exposure uncertainty and dose uncertainty, the following are also part of the process (Vyner, 1988, p. 1100):

- Latency uncertainty (*Am I in the process of developing an as yet undetected disease?*)
- Etiological uncertainty (*Is my illness caused by a previous exposure?*)

- Diagnostic uncertainty (*Are my undiagnosable symptoms due to an expression of an as yet undiscovered contaminant-caused disease?*)
- Prognostic uncertainty (*If I am diagnosed, what will my future health status be?*)
- Treatment uncertainty (*How should I treat the exposure or the illnesses I develop subsequent to an exposure?*)
- Financial uncertainty (*Who should and who will pay for my health effects from radiation?*)

Vyner (1988) suggested that the cognitive appraisal of an invisible exposure such as radiation contamination has three stages: (1) determining the name of the threat and its potential consequences; (2) determining how to cope with the threats; (3) reassessment of (1) and (2) as a coping process unfolds and new information becomes available. Unfortunately, unavailable answers and slowly emerging new information regarding radiation exposure can have a negative impact on adaptation to and coping with a catastrophic event, and this may result in adverse psychological effects.

Leon (2004) reported on factors that are predictive of differences in emotional distress and in the manifestation of psychological and physical health problems following a disaster. These include:

- The extent of exposure to the traumatic event
- The amount of devastation
- Loss or injury of family, relative, and co-workers
- The overall impact on one's usual life activities (Leon, p. 8)

Psychological and social problems reported by Chernobyl survivors in various surveys include low self-esteem, a tendency to link all illnesses to Chernobyl, high personal anxiety, feelings of victimization, feeling that there is no future, feeling unable to influence the present or the future, reduced intellectual achievement, social tensions over eligibility for Chernobyl benefits, conflict between healthy living and the need to save or earn money by accepting the reality of radiation contamination, mistrust of government experts and information, and escapism through alcohol and drugs (Mould, 2000).

Adams and colleagues (2002) examined the association between exposure to Chernobyl fallout and psychological and physical well-being of mothers of young children 11 years after the incident. Mothers who were evacuated to Kiev from the contaminated zone were compared with mothers who had never lived in a contaminated area. Evacuees were found to be more distressed and perceived their physical health as poorer than did controls. However, they did not report more stress in their lives from environmental sources but were more reactive to those stressors.

Havenaar and colleagues (1996) conducted an epidemiological study of three risk groups (those living in areas with high levels of contamination, those evacuated from contaminated zones, and liquidators) aged 18–65 years in the Gomel Oblast of Belarus and found that affective disorders (e.g., dysthymia and depression not otherwise specified (NOS) and anxiety disorders (e.g., generalized anxiety) were the most frequent diagnosis reported for all groups (as per criteria of the DSM-III-R, American Psychiatric Association, 1987). All diagnoses for women were prevalent at a rate twice that of men, particularly anxiety disorders, and a higher incidence of psychological distress and minor psychiatric disorders was reported. For all groups, 8 out of 10 individuals reported excessive worry about the effects of radiation. In a subsequent study, Havenaar and colleagues (1997) compared adults from the area said to be the most severely affected by the accident, the Gomel Oblast just north of Chernobyl, to those in Tver, 500 miles away, 6.5 years after the accident. Psychological distress was exceptionally high in both regions, with a higher risk of psychiatric disorders demonstrated among women with children younger than 18 years in the exposed region. With regard to cognitive factors (in particular hazard perception, risk perception, and sense of control), these data are found to have played an important role in the occurrence of health complaints under conditions of stress. The analysis confirms that health problems reported by exposed individuals are entrenched in cognitive sets that guide people's health perceptions (Havenaar, de Wilde, van den Bout, Drottz-Sjoberg, & van den Brink, 2003). It should be mentioned here that the former Soviet Union was in the midst of momentous political, economic, and social upheaval during this time. Although the accident at Chernobyl alone did not collapse the Soviet Union, the government's incompetent reaction and delayed release of accurate information regarding the incident precipitated the Soviet collapse, and in itself caused a great deal of distrust of government officials and distress for those affected. It was found that those from the Gomel Oblast considered radiation exposure as the greatest health danger, whereas those living in Tver were more concerned about the political and economic situation at the time (Havenaar et. al., 2003).

Remennick (2002) examined the long-term health and psychosocial effects of survivors of the Chernobyl accident who immigrated to Israel. The study population consisted of adults (30–59 years old) who had resided in Israel for a minimum of 3 years. Immigrants from the Chernobyl-affected areas and those from other regions in the former Soviet Union were compared.

Chernobyl-affected immigrants reported depression, a sense of stigma, and cancer-related anxiety. They also experienced more severe occupational downgrading and were more disappointed with the results of their resettlement than were other immigrants. In a similar study, Cwikel and colleagues (2000) reported that exposed groups of Israeli immigrants from the former Soviet Union demonstrated higher mean scores of depression, somatization, anxiety, obsessive–compulsive style, and interpersonal sensitivity, particularly symptoms of PTSD. The cohort included immigrants from the former Soviet Union who arrived in Israel after 1989 from more exposed areas of Chernobyl, less exposed areas, and those who immigrated from other republics. A study of children aged 12–18 years who immigrated to Israel between 1989 and 2000 from highly exposed, mildly exposed, and unexposed regions of the former Soviet Union reported no relation between exposure to radiation and performance on tests of neurobehavioral and cognitive performance (Bar Joseph, Reisfeld, Tirosh, Silman, & Rennert, 2004). However, mothers who were pregnant at the time of the accident rated their children higher on attention deficit hyperactivity disorder (ADHD), irrespective of their location. The authors concluded that this was either a consequence of a distorted perception due to higher levels of anxiety and fear regarding radiation effects or a direct transmission of that fear and anxiety to their children (Bar Joseph, et. al). Foster (2002) reported that 261 survivors who immigrated to the New York tri-state area in the United States 15 years after the accident and who had lived closer to the disaster and had greater exposure to it reported higher levels of anxiety and posttraumatic reactions than did those who had lived farther away from Chernobyl.

Survivors of other nuclear accidents or incidents have reported similar complaints. The most serious commercial power plant accident in U.S. history took place on March 28, 1979, at Three Mile Island (TMI) in Pennsylvania. Radioactivity was released into the atmosphere but led to no deaths or injuries to workers or residents of the nearby community, or forced evacuations. A study by Baum and Fleming (1993) compared four groups: (1) individuals who lived within 5 miles of TMI, (2) those who lived within 5 miles of an undamaged plant, (3) those who lived within 5 miles of a traditional coal plant, and (4) those who lived more than 5 miles from any power plant. More than 5 years after the accident, those who resided within 5 miles of the plant reported greater levels of somatic distress, anxiety, depression, and decreased concentration (Baum & Fleming). Studies of atomic bomb survivors in Hiroshima and Nagasaki reported similar findings. Yamada and Izumi (2002) and Ohta and colleagues (2000) found that Hiroshima and Nagasaki survivors' psychological and mental health was still negatively affected—17 to 20 and up to 50 years later. The degree of radiation exposure, disassociation to sites of these disasters, and/or the passage of time had no effect in alleviating the fears of the victims of nuclear events. Similarly, researchers compared the self-perception and health of women affected by the Chernobyl catastrophe and a demographically comparable group of women affected by the Three Mile Island catastrophe 10–11 years after the accidents (Bromet & Litcher-Kelly, 2002). In both groups, when compared with the general population, women showed elevated levels of subclinical symptoms and stronger links between the perception of danger and mental health (i.e., women who attributed greater danger to the catastrophe reported poorer mental health).

Approximately 5 years after the Chernobyl accident, a considerable number of children presented to Kiev clinics with symptoms of fatigue, pallor, inattention, abdominal pain, headache, and poor school performance. They were diagnosed with vegetative dystonia originating from the accident (Stiehm, 1992). Symptoms of vegetative dystonia closely resemble chronic fatigue syndrome (a mysterious disease affecting many in the U.S.). Of course this angered parents, especially after learning that their children had secondary effects of radiation. It was believed that this "epidemic" was in fact psychological fallout from the accident, as it occurred too many years after Chernobyl to be attributed to acute radiation exposure and too soon to be an early manifestation of cancer (Stiehm). However, diagnosis of vegetative dystonia is not accepted in the West, where the symptoms may be diagnosed as PTSD, anxiety, depression, or somatoform disorders (Loganovsky & Yuryev, 2001).

The most crucial period for fetal brain development occurs between 8–15 and 16–25 gestational weeks. Thus, radiation exposure during this time period is particularly harmful. Otake and Scholl (1998) reviewed brain damage and growth retardation among prenatally exposed atomic bomb survivors. Reevaluation of data from the Radiation Effects Research Foundation (RERF, Hiroshima and Nagasaki, Japan) revealed a high correlation between gestational age at time of irradiation and severe mental retardation and seizures. The researchers also noted a decline in average IQ scores and school performance. The significant increase in the frequency of severe mental retardation was found only in the periods of 8–15 and 16–25 weeks after conception, with 80% of the resultant severely mentally retarded cases developing in the 8- to 15-week period. Nyagu, Loganovsky, and Loganovskaja (1998) compared children of mothers who lived in contaminated areas surrounding Chernobyl while pregnant with pregnant mothers who lived in the Kharkov region (so-called clean zones approximately 300 miles southeast of Chernobyl). Contaminated areas were defined as the 30 km exclusion zone, strictly controlled zones (15 Ci/km^2),[3] and moderately contaminated areas (1–15 Ci/km2). The researchers found a significant increase in mental retardation and of borderline to low-range IQ in 6- to 8-year-olds irradiated in utero as a result of the Chernobyl disaster. These children also demonstrated emotional and behavioral disorders. Children ages 6–7 and 10–11 years who suffered prenatal irradiation were reported to have more psychological impairments and increased occurrences of specific developmental speech–language disorders, emotional disorders, and disorders of social functioning compared with age-matched control children whose mothers continually lived in uncontaminated rural areas of Belarus (Kolominsky, Igumnov, & Drozdovitch, 1999). A moderate correlation between high personal anxiety in parents and emotional disorders in children was also demonstrated. The study was conducted using the database of the Republican Health Centre of Radiation Medicine in 1992–1993 and in 1996–1997. In a similarly designed study, Igumnov and Drozdovitch (2000) reported children exposed to radiation in utero exhibited marked phobic anxiety; again, a moderate correlation was determined between high personal anxiety of parents and emotional disorders in the children. The children studied were born of mothers who lived in settlements with cesium-137 soil deposition densities that ranged from 100 to 14,500 kBq/m$^{-2,4}$ compared with randomly selected children whose mothers lived in areas of Belarus with cesium-137 soil deposition densities ranging from 0.2 to 200 kBq/m^{-2}. The authors concluded that the origin of borderline intellectual functioning and emotional disorders in the exposed group is associated with unfavorable social–psychological and sociocultural factors (low education of parents, evacuation and relocation, and difficulties adapting) (Igumnov & Drozdovitch).

In Kiev, an area considered to have low radioactive fallout, 10- to 12-year-old evacuees who were in utero or infants at the time of the Chernobyl accident were compared with age-matched, non-evacuee controls in two studies. No differences between the two groups were found on measures of mental health and behavior (Bromet et al., 2000), verbal IQ, memory, school performance, parent and teacher ratings of attention, and perception of school grades by mother and child (Litcher, Bromet, Carlson, Squires, & Goldgaber, 2000). Physical examinations and routine blood tests were also normal

---

[3]Ci = Curie. A Curie is a unit of radioactivity equal to 3.7×10^{10} disintegrations per second.

[4]kBq = 1,000 becquerel. A becquerel is a measurement of radioactivity that corresponds to one disintegration per second. According to Western standards, soil contaminated with cesium levels above 50,000 Bq/square meter is unsuitable for agriculture, particularly for livestock farming (WISE News Communique, http://www.antenna.nl/wise/326-7/3259.html).

(Bromet et al.; Litcher et al.). Evacuee children did, however, rate themselves lower in perceived scholastic competence (Bromet et al.), and children with greater Chernobyl-focused anxiety performed slightly worse on measures of attention than did children with less Chernobyl-focused anxiety (Litcher et al.). In these studies, evacuee mothers rated their children's well-being as significantly worse than that of non-evacuees and reported significantly more somatic symptoms in their children despite normal physical examinations and blood tests. Litcher and colleagues reported that evacuee mothers indicated their children had memory problems more frequently than did control mothers. Houts, Tokuhata, Bratz, Bartholomew, and Sheffer (1991) interviewed women who were pregnant during the Three Mile Island crisis. These women reported being extremely disturbed about their pregnancy and tended to rate their children as less healthy than controls. Other than the mothers' report, the children's health status was unknown at the time of the study.

Empirical studies of the effects of the Chernobyl accident on the surrounding population have some or all of the following limitations: (a) small participant samples, (b) difficulty identifying all individuals exposed to radiation, (c) inaccurate or absent measurements of radiation exposure, (d) difficulty attaining matched controls, (e) lack of information about prior functioning, and (f) difficulty determining causal pathways (Baum & Fleming, 1993; Grigorenko, 2001). However, stress, anxiety, and subclinical depression seem to be recurring themes. Parents express a great deal of negative affect regarding the safety, welfare, and future of their children after Chernobyl. These attitudes are not unfounded and cannot help but have a detrimental effect on their children's development.

Evacuee children are at greater risk for anxiety and depressive disorders known to increase in adolescence. Creasey and colleagues (1997) found that 6- to 8-year-olds exhibit angry negative affect when confronted with maternal distress, and display avoidant coping strategies in response to paternal sadness. A relationship has been demonstrated between mild forms of parental distress and preschool children's behavior styles (West & Newman, 2003). Parental depression has been found to result in increased interpersonal conflict and internal and external behavior problems in 3- to 5-year-olds, and mild parental anxiety can result in negative temperament and emotion regulation (focus and sustaining attention) (West & Newman, 2003). Anxiety disorders and impairment have a reciprocal relationship—impairment leads to continued exacerbation of anxiety symptoms, which in turn worsens impairments (Pynoos, Steinberg, & Piacentrini, 1999). Adolescents who experienced Chernobyl were found to have distorted views of life caused by the traumatic event, which had exerted a negative influence on their emotional well-being

(Kronik, Akhmerv, & Speckhard, 1999). In fact, adolescents who were impacted by the Chernobyl disaster estimated their life expectancies to be on average 12 years shorter than teenagers who were unaffected (Mould, 2000).

The psychosocial trauma of Chernobyl was inflicted primarily on the parents and only secondarily on the children, even though children are the focus of their parents' anxiety. Anxious parental responses to trauma and fears of recurrent trauma increase a young child's post-trauma distress (Pynoos et al., 1999); conversely "witnessing parents constructively cope with their negative affect may serve as an important social reference for the developing child" (Creasey et al., 1997, p. 53). Children can cope with hazardous environments as long as parents are not pushed beyond their stress limits. Once that point is exceeded, however, the development of young children deteriorates swiftly and markedly (Garbarino, Kostelny, & Dubrow, 1991).

> We are the children of Chernobyl,
> We want to live, to laugh, to grow, to love
> But we are doomed.
> We have no future.
> We plead with you mothers and fathers
> Help us.
> Help us
> Will you hear?
> Unite to work for a better cause
> You are people and you are not of stone.
> Help us. Please? (Roche, 1996, p. 45)

This poem was written by schoolchildren from the contamination zone in Ukraine and is illustrative of an environment of despair and hopelessness. Post-Chernobyl children live in a world that has little resemblance to their pre-Chernobyl life. They cannot visit certain areas of their country that may have once been familiar to them or experience the natural world as they once did, and they must be wary of their natural surroundings. Many children suffer from terminal or chronic illnesses and must undergo painful and frightening surgeries or treatments; others suffer from psychological and/or developmental impairments. Numerous children exhibit signs and symptoms of post-traumatic stress disorder and self-report low self-esteem and/or low levels of scholastic ability and health. Untreated parents who are extremely stressed, depressed, and anxious can affect how a child will cope with a traumatic event (Lubit, Rovine, DeFrancisci, & Eth, 2003). Inability or difficulty in coping by parents has a watershed effect on these children, who seem to have little hope for a promising future. Early identification of children affected by trauma and treatment by experienced mental health professionals for both parents and children can alleviate long-term effects.

Intervention for the Psychosocial Effects of Chernobyl

The International Federation of Red Cross and Red Crescent Societies, together with the national Red Cross societies of Belarus, Ukraine, and Russia, have been running the Chernobyl Humanitarian Assistance and Rehabilitation Programme (CHARP) since 1990 to address the basic health needs of those living in the highly affected regions of the three countries (Revel, 2001). Because this was the first nuclear disaster of this magnitude, health effects on the population were unclear, and the need for more accurate information was given precedence. Over time, however, the need for psychological support programs became evident. People living in the most contaminated areas reported feelings of anxiety, depression, and pessimism, and many somatic complaints such as headaches, stomach pains, and fatigue. However, it was not until 11 years later that support programs were put into place in Belarus (Revel, 2001). Tkachenko and Vlasov (1995) claim that it was only after the findings of their research study that psychological services for children and their families began to be developed. Their study involved elementary and middle school-aged children from the Bryanskaya Oblast. Mental development, personality formation, attention, memory, thinking, height, weight, jumping ability, ability to perform physical work, personal and family medical history, and cardiovascular, respiratory, and central nervous system (CNS) function were investigated in approximately 1100 first- to third-graders, and in approximately 1000 fifth- to ninth-graders. Sweet (1996) reported that the United Nations Educational, Scientific, and Cultural Organization (UNESCO) set up centers among relocated people and in contaminated areas to provide consultations and training for adults and play centers for children, fostered the creation of support groups, and organized social events to start re-knitting a social fabric. CHARP has mobile units that travel to the remote rural areas of the six most affected regions of Belarus, Ukraine, and Russia, and claims to have assisted more than 2.8 million people—90,000 of whom have received social and psychological assistance (Revel, 2001). Hundreds of thousands of lives were disrupted by Chernobyl, and "to move successfully beyond a traumatic event, one must incorporate in the mind what has been a terrifying, overwhelming, and hurtful experience" (Kronik, Akhmerv, & Speckhard, 1999, p. 588). Radiation-induced fear has a much longer half-life than the radioactive particles released into the atmosphere that night in 1986, and although efforts have been made to satisfy the need for psychological support groups in the most affected areas, Revel notes that there is still much to be done to address this problem. In addition to basic needs such as food, water, and shelter as well as immediate medical attention, psychosocial services are also essential after an accident like Chernobyl—the lack of such services made a complex situation even more difficult in 1986 and for years after.

IMPACT ON NEIGHBORS

Many other countries, though distant from the epicenter of the accident, were affected by the fallout and deserve consideration. Below we briefly review literature relevant to this group.

Concerns in Western Europe

Measurable radioactive fallout from Chernobyl was found throughout Western Europe, and fearfulness of the effects of radiation on the public resulted. Ionizing radiation cannot be appreciated by the senses and individuals are completely dependent on others for information as to the extent of the damage and its consequences. The lack of information from official sources raised questions regarding the health threat to Western Europeans. Only generalizations and estimations regarding the health effects of the fallout became available. A notable decrease in birthrates in the early months of 1987 in Sweden, Finland, and Greece was found (Rytomaa, 1996), and an increase in the rate of induced abortions performed in Denmark during the months following Chernobyl was noted, especially in the regions with the most measured increase in radiation (Knudsen, 1991). However, this increase in radiation was so low that risk of a rise in birth defects was not expected, and the abortions were more the result of fear regarding the accident than of the accident itself. Induced abortions in Sweden and Greece also escalated (Rytomaa). Tonnesen and colleagues (2002) reviewed survey data from 12 European countries two and a half years after the accident. A significant relationship was found between the level of fallout in the 12 countries and the number of respondents who took countermeasures. The only consistent reaction found across Europe was public outcry about the lack of information from authorities.

Hoffman (2002) reviewed data from the European Childhood Leukemia and Lymphoma Incidence Study (ECLIS, April 13, 2004) for the period after the accident and found a small but statistically significant increase in childhood leukemia after Chernobyl. A peak in the incidence of Down syndrome in the cohort of children conceived around the days of the highest contamination was reported in Berlin. The data also revealed temporal clusters of Down syndrome in 1987 in Scotland and Sweden, and Norway reported an increase in spontaneous abortions (miscarriages) 1 year after the accident. Germany reported a peak in perinatal mortality in 1989. However, Dolk, Nichols, and the EUROCAT Working Group (1999) found that Chernobyl had no detectable impact on the prevalence of congenital anomalies in Western Europe after calculating expected congenital anomalies from 1980–1985 as a baseline. The authors reviewed data from population-based congenital anomaly registers in 16 regions in Belgium, Czechoslovakia, Denmark, France, Ireland, Italy, Luxembourg, the Netherlands, and United Kingdom. They did detect, however, an increase in Down syndrome in the late 1980s, but deemed this increase unrelated to Chernobyl.

CONCLUSION

It is clear that the nuclear accident in Chernobyl resulted in detrimental health impairments and negative psychosocial impacts on the population of the former Soviet Union immediately affected by the fallout. The most severe health impact affected those professionals who were on-site during the accident, the liquidators who immediately responded to the accident, and those who resided in closest proximity to the reactor site. It is also apparent that the impact was greater on those individuals subjected to long-term irradiation, even at lower levels, than short-term, although substantial, irradiation. The evidence also suggests that the fallout affected the health of people in Western Europe, although this evidence is substantially weaker and cannot be confidently attributable to Chernobyl (Hoffmann, 2001).

What we have illustrated here are examples of the direct and indirect effects of the nuclear accident. Direct effects include thyroid cancer in children and adults, birth defects and malformations, mental retardation and decreased IQ in children, schizophrenia, cardiovascular disease, and various other physical disorders. The indirect effects include increases in therapeutic abortions in affected regions of the former Soviet Union and Western Europe, stress, anxiety, depression, low self-esteem, decreased perceptions of health, and symptoms of PTSD as well as the multitude of difficulties resulting from adaptation to a new environment. These indirect effects have been found to be consistent among individuals who resided nearest to and farthest from the reactor site as well as those who immigrated to other countries—even many years after the incident. In 2000, the United Nations Scientific Committee on the Effects of Atomic Radiation (UNSCEAR) reported clear evidence of the non-radiation-related psychological disorders described here as well as a substantial increase of suicide during the first six and a half years following the accident (Rahu, 2003). From the lesson of Chernobyl, it is clear that, if a radioactive disaster were to happen again, a critical element of the response would be psychosocial intervention: therapy by clinicians knowledgeable about the impact and consequences of irradiation, who can work hand-in-hand with heath practitioners and services engaged with relocating people, since evacuation and relocation are likely with radioactive accidents. To our knowledge, there is no summative statement of requisite nuclear accident-related psychosocial services. Unfortunately, the services provided to the victims of the Chernobyl accident were so limited that it is impossible to generalize much from these experiences.

Chernobyl still employs about 4000 workers; however, they live approximately 50 miles away from the plant (Ayres, 2004). The plant is still seen as a threat to the area because of the deterioration and possible collapse of the hastily built sarcophagus[5] (Kasper, 2003). The U.S. and European governments have contributed billions of dollars to a repair project, and a new steel shield is scheduled to be completed by 2007 (4/13/04). *Moscow News* reports that work to repair the sarcophagus began in mid-February of 2005 (http://www.mosnews.com/news/2005/02/18/Chernobyl.shtml).

With a worldwide increase in the demand for energy, the use of nuclear power is expected to rise. Painstaking efforts must be made to safely construct and operate nuclear power plants, and a thorough analysis of the wide range of consequences of another accident must be made. As stated previously, there are 440 active nuclear reactors worldwide, with many more in various stages of construction or planned for the future (World Nuclear Association). Nuclear accidents are not new to modern civilization, and it is unlikely that Chernobyl will be the last. In a post-9/11 world, extensive measures have been undertaken to protect against terrorist attacks on nuclear power plants; however, it is questionable whether there is a comprehensive plan in place should such an attack take place. Official preparatory planning and exercises in crisis management are in order (Weisaeth, Knudsen, & Tonnessen, 2002). As with natural disasters, public health programs should be in place to provide disaster relief for victims, including more effective psychological services. A plan for long-term follow-up should also be implemented to monitor the physical and mental health effects of radioactive fallout. Perhaps these programs should be implemented by an international agency such as the World Heath Organization (WHO), as nuclear disasters know no borders and can have a worldwide impact. Nuclear energy can be an efficient and economical method to satisfy increasing power demands, but it can also jeopardize

---

[5]A shield was put into place over the Number 4 reactor to contain radioactive debris and further contamination.

the physical health and quality of life of human and animal populations. A respectful balance is in order.

ACKNOWLEDGMENT

Preparation of this essay was supported by a grant under the Javits Act Program (Grant No. R206R00001) as administered by the Institute for Educational Sciences, U.S. Department of Education. Grantees undertaking such projects are encouraged to express freely their professional judgment. This chapter, therefore, does not necessarily represent the position or policies of the Institute for Educational Sciences or the U.S. Department of Education, and no official endorsement should be inferred.

We express our gratitude to Ms. Robyn Rissman for her editorial assistance and to the editors of this book for their helpful comments.

The contact addresses for the authors are: Donna Macomber, Yale University, PACE Center, PO Box 208358, New Haven, CT 06520–8358 (or via e-mail at donna.macomber@yale.edu), and Dr. Elena L. Grigorenko, Yale University, PACE Center, PO Box 208358, New Haven, CT 06520–8358 (or via e-mail at elena.grigorenko@yale.edu).

REFERENCES

Adams, R. E., Bromet, E. J., Panina, N., Golovakha, E., Goldgaber, D., & Gluzman, S. (2002). Stress and well-being in mothers of young children 11 years after the Chornobyl nuclear power plant accident. *Psychological Medicine, 32*, 143–156.

American Psychiatric Association, Committee on Nomenclature and Statistics. (1987). *Diagnostic and statistical manual of mental disorders (DSM-III-R)* (3rd revised ed.). Washington, DC: Author.

American Psychiatric Association. (1994). *Diagnostic and statistical manual of mental disorders (DSM-IV)* (4th ed.). Washington, DC: Author.

Ayres, S. (2004, April 23). 18 years on, Chernobyl residents live and die by the nuclear plant. *Cox News Service.*

Bar Joseph, N., Reisfeld, D., Tirosh, E., Silman, Z., & Rennert, G. (2004). Neurobehavioral and cognitive performances of children exposed to low-dose radiation in the Chernobyl accident. *American Journal of Epidemiology, 160*, 453–459.

Baum, A., & Fleming, I. (1993). Implications of psychological research on stress and technological accidents. *American Psychologist, 48*(6), 665–672.

Becker, D. V., Robbins, J., Beebe, G. W., Bouville, A. C., & Wachholz, B. W. (1996). Childhood thyroid cancer following the Chernobyl accident: A status report. *Endocrinology and Metabolism Clinics, 25*(1), 197–211.

Bellaby, M. D. (2004, November 14). Chernobyl sees population growth: Some accuse the government of ignoring high radiation levels. *Telegraph Herald (Dubuque, IA).*

Belyakov, O. V. (1999) Notes about the Chernobyl liquidators [Online]. Retrieved October 24, 2002, from http://www.belyakov.info/lhp/notes.pdf

Breus, A. (2002, May 2). Ukraine says public health worse for Chernobyl-affected. *Nucleonics Week, 43*(18), 21.

Bromet, E. J., Goldgaber, D., Carlson, G., Panina, N., Golovkha, E., Gluzman, S. F., et al. (2000). Children's well-being 11 years after the Chornobyl catastrophe. *Archives of General Psychiatry, 57,* 563–571.

Bromet, E. J., & Litcher-Kelly, L. (2002). Psychological response of mothers of young children to the Three Mile Island and Chernobyl nuclear plant accidents one decade later. In J. M. Havenaar, J. G., Cwikel, & E. J. Bromet (Eds.), *Toxic turmoil. Psychological and societal consequences of ecological disasters* (pp. 69–84). New York: Kluwer Academic Press.

Brown, J.S., Jr. (2002). *Environmental and chemical toxins and psychiatric illness* (pp. 27–65). Washington, DC: American Psychiatric Publishing.

Buzhievskaya, T. I., Tchaikovskaya, T. L., Demidova, G.G., & Koblyanskaya, G. N. (1995). Selective monitoring for a Chernobyl effect on pregnancy outcome in Kiev, 1969–1989. *Human Biology, 67*(4), 657–672.

Castronovo, F.P., Jr. (1999). Teratogen update: Radiation and Chernobyl. *Teratology, 60,* 100–106.

Chernobyl Thyroid Diseases Study Group of Belarus, Ukraine, and the USA, Stezhko, V. A., Buglova, E. E., Danilova, L. I., Drozd, V. M., et al. (2004). A cohort study of thyroid cancer and other thyroid diseases after the Chornobyl accident: Objectives, design and methods. *Radiation Research, 161,* 481–492.

Creasey, G., Ottlinger, K., DeVico, K., Murray, T., Harvey, A., & Hesson-McInnis, M. (1997). Children's affective responses, cognitive appraisals, and coping strategies in response to negative affect of parents and peers. *Journal of Experimental Child Psychology, 67,* 39–56.

Cwikel, J. G., Abdelgani, A., Rozovski, U., Kordysh, E., Goldsmith, J. R., & Quastel, M.R. (2000). Long-term stress reactions in new immigrants to Israel exposed to the Chernobyl accident. *Anxiety, Stress, and Coping, 13,* 413–439.

Dolk, H., Nichols, R., & EUROCAT Working Group. (1999). Evaluation of the impact of Chernobyl on the prevalence of congenital anomalies in 16 regions of Europe. *International Journal of Epidemiology, 28,* 941–948.

Environmental Protection Agency. Retrieved March 11, 2005, from http://www.epa. gov/radiation/radionuclides/cesium.htm

Feshchenko, S. P., Schroder, H. C., Muller, W. E., & Lazjuk, G. I. (2002). Congenital malformations among newborns and developmental abnormalities among human embryos in Belarus after Chernobyl accident. *Cellular and Molecular Biology, 48*(4), 423–426.

Foster, R. M. P. (2002). The long-term mental health effects of nuclear trauma in recent Russian immigrants in the United States. *American Journal of Orthopsychiatry, 72*(4), 492–504.

Fusco, P., & Caris, M. (2001). *Chernobyl Legacy.* Millbrook, NY: deMO.

Garbarino, J., Kostelny, K., & Dubrow, N. (1991). What children can tell us about living in danger. *American Psychologist, 46*(4), 376–383.

Grigorenko, E. L. (2001). The invisible danger: The impact of ionizing radiation on cognitive development and functions. In R.J. Sternberg & E.L. Grigorenko (Eds.), *Environmental effects on cognitive abilities* (pp. 255–283). Mahwah, NJ: Lawrence Erlbaum.

Havenaar, J. M., de Wilde, E. J., van den Bout, J., Drottz-Sjoberg, B. M., & van den Brink, W. (2003). Perception of risk and subjective health among victims of the Chernobyl disaster. *Social Science & Medicine, 56,* 569–572.

Havenaar, J. M., Rumyantzeva, G., Van Den Brink, W., Poelijoe, N., van den Bout, J., van Engeland, H., et al. (1997). Long-term mental effects of the Chernobyl disaster: An epidemiologic survey in two former Soviet regions. *American Journal of Psychiatry, 154*(11), 1605–1607.

Havenaar, J. M., Van Den Brink, W., Van Den Bout, J., Kasyanenko, A. P., Poelijoe, N. W., Wohlfarth, T., et al. (1996). Mental health problems in the Gomel Region (Belarus): An analysis of risk factors in an area affected by the Chernobyl disaster. *Psychological Medicine, 26*(4), 845–856.

Henshaw, D. (1996). Chernobyl 10 years on: Thyroid cancer may be the only measurable health effect. *British Medical Journal, 312*(7038), 1052–1053.

Hoffmann, W. (2001). Fallout from the Chernobyl nuclear disaster and congenital malformations in Europe. *Archives of Environmental Health, 56*(6), 478–484.

Hoffmann, W. (2002). Has fallout from the Chernobyl accident caused childhood leukemia in Europe? *European Journal of Public Health, 12,* 72–76.

Houts, P. S., Tokuhata, G. K., Bratz, J., Bartholomew, M. J., & Sheffer, K. W. (1991). Effect of pregnancy during TMI crisis on mothers' mental health and their child's development. *American Journal of Public Health, 81*(3), 384–386.

Idaho State University Radiation Information Network. Retrieved March 17, 2005, from http://www.physics.isu.edu/radinf/risk.htm.

Igumnov, S., & Drozdovitch, V. (2000). The intellectual development, mental and behavioural disorders in children from Belarus exposed in utero following the Chernobyl accident. *European Psychiatry, 15,* 244–253.

Ivanov, V.K., Gorski, A.I., Maksioutov, M.A., Tsyb, A.F., & Souchkevitch, G. (2001). Mortality among the Chernobyl emergency workers: Estimation of radiation risks (preliminary analysis). *Health Physics, 81*(5), 514–521.

Ivanov, V. K., Gorski, A. I., Maksioutov, M. A., Vlasov, O. K., Godko, A. M., Tsyb, A., et al. (2003). Thyroid cancer incidence among adolescents and adults in the Bryansk region of Russia following the Chernobyl accident. *Health Physics, 84*(1), 46–60.

Ivanov, V. K., Maksioutov, M. A., Chekin, S. Yu., Kruglova, Z. G., Petrov, A. V., & Tsyb, A. F. (2000). Radiation–epidemiological analysis of incidence of non-cancer diseases among the Chernobyl liquidators. *Health Physics, 78*(5), 495–501.

Ivanov, V. K., Tsyb, A. F., Gorsky, A. I., Maksyutov, M. A., Rastopchin, E. M., Konogorov, A. P., et al. (1997). Thyroid cancer among "liquidators" of the Chernobyl accident. *British Journal of Radiology, 70,* 937–941.

Ivanov, V. K., Tsyb, A. F., Nilova, V., Efendiev, V. F., Gorsky, A. I., Pitkevich, V. A., et al. (1997). Cancer risks in the Kaluga oblast of the Russian Federation

10 years after the Chernobyl accident. *Radiation Environment Biophysics, 36,* 161–167.

Ivanov, V. K., Tsyb, A. F., Petrov, A. V., Maksioutov, M. A., Shilyaaeva, T. P., & Kochergina, E. V. (2002). Thyroid cancer incidence among liquidators of the Chernobyl accident. *Radiation Environment Biophysics, 41,* 195–198.

Kasper, K. (2003). Chernobyl: Facts and fiction. *Health Physics, 84*(4), 419–420.

Knudsen, L. B. (1991). Legally induced abortions in Denmark after Chernobyl. *Biomedicine & Pharmacology, 45*(6), 229–231.

Kolominsky, Y., Igumnov, S., & Drozdovitch. (1999). The psychological development of children from Belarus exposed in the prenatal period to radiation from the Chernobyl atomic power plant. *Journal of Child Psychology and Psychiatry, 40*(2), 299–305.

Kronik, A. A., Akhmerv, R. A., & Speckhard, A. (1999). Trauma and disaster as life disrupters: A model of computer-assisted psychotherapy applied to adolescent victims of the Chernobyl disaster. *Professional Psychology: Research and Practice, 30*(6), 586–599.

Lazjuk, G. I., Nikolaev, D. L., & Novikova, I. V. (1997). Changes in registered congenital anomalies in the Republic of Belarus after the Chernobyl accident. *Stem Cells, 15*(S2), 255–260.

Leon, G. R. (2004). Overview of the psychosocial impact of disasters. *Prehospital and Disaster Medicine, 19*(1), 4–9.

Litcher, L., Bromet, E .J., Carlson, G., Squires, N., & Goldgaber, D. (2000). School and neuropsychological performance of evacuated children in Kiev 11 years after the Chernobyl disaster. *Journal of Child Psychology and Psychiatry, 41*(3), 291–299.

Loganovsky, K. N., & Loganovskaja, T. K. (2000). At issue: Schizophrenia spectrum disorders in persons exposed to ionizing radiation as a result of the Chernobyl accident. *Schizophrenia Bulletin, 26*(4), 751–773.

Loganovsky, K. N., & Yuryev, K. L. (2001). EEG patterns in persons exposed to ionizing radiation as a result of the Chernobyl accident: Part 1: Conventional EEG analysis. *Journal of Neuropsychiatry and Clinical Neurosciences, 13,* 441–458.

Lubit, R., Rovine, D., DeFrancisci, L., & Eth, S. (2003). Impact of trauma on children. *Journal of Psychiatric Practice, 9*(2), 128–138.

MosNews.com. *Repair of leaking Chernobyl sarcophagus begins.* Retrieved February 18, 2005, from http://www.moscownews.com/news/2005/02/18/Chernobyl.shtml

Mould, R. F. (2000). *Chernobyl record: The definitive history of the Chernobyl catastrophe.* Bristol, England: Institute of Physics Publishing.

Nyagu, A. I., Loganovsky, K. N., & Loganovskaja, T. K. (1998). Psychophysiologic aftereffects of prenatal irradiation. *International Journal of Psychophysiology, 30,* 303–311.

Ohta, Y., Mine, M., Wakasugi, M., Yoshimine, E., Himuro, Y., Yoneda, M., et al. (2000). Psychological effect of the Nagasaki atomic bombing on survivors after half a century. *Psychiatry and Clinical Neuroscience, 54,* 97–103.

Otake, M., & Scholl, W. J. (1998). Review: Radiation-related brain damage and growth retardation among the prenatally exposed atomic bomb survivors. *International Journal of Radiation Biology, 74*(2), 159–171.

Pynoos, R. S., Steinberg, A. M., & Piacentini, J. C. (1999). A developmental psycho-pathology model of childhood traumatic stress and intersection with anxiety disorders. *Biological Psychiatry, 46,* 1542–1554.

Rabin, S. M. (1986, November 15). Medical intervention in a nuclear accident. *Hospital Practice,* 137–152.

Rahu, M. (2003). Health effects of the Chernobyl accident: Fears, rumours, and the truth. *European Journal of Cancer, 39,* 295–299.

Remennick. L. I. (2002). Immigrants from Chernobyl-affected areas in Israel: The link between health and social adjustment. *Social Science & Medicine, 54,* 309–317.

Revel, J. P. (2001). Meeting psychological needs after Chernobyl: The Red Cross experience. *Military Medicine, 166*(12, Suppl. 2), 19–20.

Robbins, J. (1997). Lessons from Chernobyl: The event, the aftermath fallout: Radio-active, political, social. *Thyroid, 7*(2), 189–191.

Roche, A. (1996). *Children of Chernobyl.* London, U.K.: HarperCollins

Rytomaa, T. (1996). Ten years after Chernobyl. *Annals of Medicine, 28,* 83–87.

Schwenn, M. R., & Brill, A. B. (1997). Childhood cancer 10 years after the Chernobyl accident. *Current Opinion in Pediatrics, 9,* 51–54.

Shcherbak, Y. M. (1996). Ten years of the Chernobyl era. *Scientific American, 274*(4), 44–49.

Stiehm, E. R. (1992). The psychologic fallout from Chernobyl. *American Journal of Diseases of Children, 146,* 761–762.

Sweet, W. (1996). Chernobyl's stressful after-effects. *IEEE Spectrum, 33,* 26–34.

Tarabrina, N. V., Lazebnaia, E. O., & Zelenova, M. E. (2001). Psychological characteristics of post-traumatic stress states in workers dealing with the consequences of the Chernobyl accident. *Journal of Russian and East European Psychology, 39*(3), 29–42.

Tarabrina, N. V., Lazebnaia, E. O., Zelenova, M. E., Lasko, N. B., Orr, S. F., & Pitman, R. K. (2001). The psychophysiologcial reactivity of workers dealing with the aftermath of the accident at the atomic power station at Chernobyl. *Journal of Russian and East European Psychology, 39*(3), 43–68.

Tkachenko, A. S., & Vlasov, V. N. (1995). Psychological service: Help to children and teenagers from Bryanskaya oblast. *Psikhologicheskiy Zhurnal, 16*(5), 122–128.

Tonnessen, A., Mardberg, B., & Weisaeth, L. (2002). Silent disaster: A European perspective on threat perception from Chernobyl far field fallout. *Journal of Traumatic Stress, 15*(6), 453–459.

Vickery, T. (2002, April 26). Ukrainians remember Chernobyl, but are more troubled by poverty. *Associated Press Worldstream.*

Vyner, H. M. (1988). The psychological dimensions of health care for patients exposed to radiation and the other invisible environmental contaminants. *Social Science Medicine, 27*(10), 1097–1103.

Weisaeth, L., Knudsen, O., Jr., & Tonnessen, A. (2002). Technological disasters, crisis management and leadership stress. *Journal of Hazardous Materials, 93,* 33–45.

West, A. E., & Newman, D. L. (2003). Worried and blue: Mild parental anxiety and depression in relation to the development of young children's temperament and behavior problems. *Parenting: Science and Practice, 3*(2), 133–154.

Williams, D. (2001). Lessons from Chernobyl. *British Medical Journal, 323,* 643–644.

World Information Service on Energy (WISE), Nuclear Monitor and News. Retrieved March 18, 1990, from http://www.antenna.nl/wise/326–7/3259.html

World Nuclear Association. Retrieved from http://www.world-nuclear.org

Wroble, M. C., & Baum, A. (2002). Toxic waste spills and nuclear accidents. In A. M. La Greca, W. K. Silverman, E. M. Vernberg, & M. C. Roberts (Eds.), *Helping children cope with disasters and terrorism* (pp. 207–221). Washington, DC: American Psychological Association.

Yamada, M., & Izumi, S. (2002). Psychiatric sequelae in atomic bomb survivors in Hiroshima and Nagasaki two decades after the explosions. *Social Psychiatry & Psychiatric Epidemiology, 37,* 409–415.

CHAPTER 10

Advancing Healing and Reconciliation[1]

Ervin Staub and Laurie Anne Pearlman

In this chapter, we describe an approach to promoting post-genocide psychological recovery, reconciliation, the development of positive relations between groups, and a peaceful society. We describe a number of projects we conducted in Rwanda between 1999 and 2004 in which we developed and evaluated this approach. We have used components of this approach with varied groups. These include staff of local and international non-governmental organizations (NGOs) whose work ranges from community-building to reconciliation, leaders and field staff from survivor organizations, journalists, high-level national leaders, trauma counselors, commissioners of the Rwandan National Unity and Reconciliation Commission (NURC), and others.

In the course of describing this work, we discuss some issues important in reconciliation and the prevention of new violence, such as a shared understanding of history (or collective memory). We comment on some current conditions in Rwanda that appear to either facilitate or create problems for reconciliation

[1]We are grateful for the support of our work by the John Templeton Foundation (1999–2000), United States Institute for Peace (2001–2002), Dart Foundation (2001), United States Agency for International Development (2002–2004), and a small private donation. We are also grateful to the National Unity and Reconciliation Commission of Rwanda, which co-sponsored our seminars/workshops starting in the summer of 2001. We thank our many associates in Rwanda, especially Fatuma Ndangiza, Aloisea Inyumba, Alphonse Bakusi, Alphonsine Mutabonwa, and Athanase Hagengimana, and U.S. associates who sometimes volunteered their time: Vachel Miller, Alexandra Gubin, and Adin DeLaCoeur.

213

and the building of a peaceful society. We also offer observations along the way about how outsiders or third parties might be most helpful in these processes.

Our work has been a response to a fundamental question that arises in the aftermath of genocide or intractable, violent conflict: After such violence, how can groups that continue to live together build a better, non-violent future? Although the approach we describe here was developed and used in Rwanda, it seems applicable to other places where violent conflict, mass killing, or genocide has taken place.

In recent years, especially since the activity of the Truth and Reconciliation Commission in South Africa, the necessity for reconciliation between groups in the aftermath of violence and ways to promote it have received a great deal of attention (Lederach, 1995, 1997). It has become apparent to many observers that violence between groups often resumes (de la Rey, 2001), even when it has ended with peace treaties and agreements. Segments of one or both of the groups may find the agreements unacceptable, and/or deep feelings of insecurity, hurt, anger, and hostility may remain. The resumption of violence seems an even greater danger when genocide ends with victory by the victim group over the perpetrator group, as in Rwanda.

Reconciliation is a change in attitude and behaviors toward the other group. We define it as mutual acceptance of each other by members of groups, and the processes and structures that lead to or maintain that acceptance (Staub & Pearlman, 2001). Although structures and institutions that promote and serve reconciliation are important, the essence of reconciliation is a changed psychological orientation toward the other. Reconciliation implies that victims and perpetrators do not see the past as defining the future. They come to accept and see one another's humanity and see the possibility of a constructive relationship.

Following great violence between groups, especially genocide, reconciliation is a profoundly difficult challenge. It can only develop gradually, with likely setbacks along the way (Staub & Bar-Tal, 2003). Truth and justice have already become part of conventional thinking as requirements for reconciliation (see Proceedings of Stockholm International Forum on Truth, Justice and Reconciliation, 2002). Montville (1993) has suggested that healing from past wounds is important to reconciliation; we see it as an essential aspect of reconciliation.

THE IMPACT OF VICTIMIZATION ON SURVIVORS AND PERPETRATORS

The impact of genocide on survivors is enormous. Their perception of themselves and of the world is deeply affected. They feel diminished, vulnerable.

The world looks dangerous and people, especially those outside one's group, untrustworthy (Staub, 1998). These psychological disruptions may give rise to intense trauma symptoms such as nightmares, flashbacks, and emotional numbing, as well as disruptions in survivors' world view, relationships with self and others, and identity (McCann & Pearlman, 1990a; Pearlman & Saakvitne, 1995). Because identity is rooted in part in group membership, even members of the victim group who were not present when the genocide was perpetrated may be greatly traumatized (Staub). In Rwanda, this means "returnees," mainly children of Tutsi refugees from earlier violence who came back from neighboring countries after the genocide to devastated families and community. This traumatization may be especially likely since these returnees were not accepted and integrated in the countries of their former refuge, which strengthened their identities as Tutsi from Rwanda. Some of them came back as part of the Rwanda Patriotic Army (RPA), the mainly Tutsi army that entered from Uganda in 1990 and initiated the civil war. In 1994, the RPA defeated the government and ended the genocide. Others came in their wake.

The psychological consequences of victimization include extreme sensitivity to new threat. When conflict with another group arises, it may be more difficult for survivors to take the perspective of the other and consider the other's needs. Without corrective experiences, they may believe they need to defend themselves even when violent self-defense is not necessary. In response to new threat or conflict they may strike out, in the process becoming perpetrators (Staub, 1998). Healing from psychological wounds, from the trauma that can result from victimization, is important to prevent such defensive violence and to enhance the capacity of the group for reconciliation.

Often perpetrators have endured victimization or other traumatic experiences as part of the cycle of violence. Their unhealed psychological wounds have contributed to their actions. Of course, the extent of their victimization may be substantially less than that of those they have harmed, which is certainly the case in genocide. Nonetheless, unless others acknowledge their injuries and address them, they may be unable to shift from a defensive stance of self-justification to a position of accepting responsibility for their actions, which would pave the way for reconciliation.

Sometimes past trauma is fixed and maintained in collective memory; it becomes a "chosen trauma" that continuously shapes group psychology and behavior (Volkan, 1997). This seems to have been the case with Hutus in Rwanda. The first author had the opportunity to conduct a prison interview with the person who was Justice Minister during the genocide. As other Hutus have done, she referred to the group's experience under Tutsi rule before 1959 (actually Belgian rule, the Belgians using the Tutsis to rule in their behalf) as "slavery." Although this statement may also be self-justification, this period does seem to be a chosen trauma in Hutu collective memory.

In addition, as recent studies have shown, people who engage in intense violence against others tend to be psychologically injured by their own actions (MacNair, 2002; Rhodes, Allen, Nowinski, & Cillessen, 2002). To protect themselves from empathic distress, guilt, and shame, perpetrators often distance themselves from victims. This distancing begins to develop in the course of the evolution of increasing discrimination and violence that usually precedes genocide (Staub, 1989). The lessening of empathy and compassion easily extends to other people as well. When the violence has ended, perpetrators often continue to blame victims and hold on to the ideology that in part motivated, and to them justified, their violence, in order to protect themselves from the emotional consequences of their actions. Those members of the perpetrator group who did not participate in planning or executing the genocide but were passive bystanders to it are likely to be similarly, although presumably less intensely, affected. Healing from the psychological consequences of their own or their group's actions may enable people to see the humanity of the victims, to feel empathy, regret, and sorrow, and to become open to apology and reconciliation.

To summarize, healing from wounds that result from being harmed (see also Montville, 1993), having harmed others, or being a member of a group that has harmed others (Staub & Pearlman, 2001) seems important for reconciliation. Reconciliation is important to prevent a continuing cycle of violence, especially between groups that continue to live together. As healing begins, reconciliation becomes more possible.

Healing and reconciliation are interdependent, especially when groups that have engaged in violence against each other continue to live together. Healing is essential both to improve the quality of life of wounded people and to make new violence less likely—an overarching goal of our work in Rwanda. At least some limited degree of safety is needed for healing to begin (Herman, 1992; McCann & Pearlman, 1990a). Widespread severe poverty, the gacaca (community justice process), the release of many prisoners in 2003, the development of a constitution, democratic elections, and the continuing violence in the Congo have significant impact on people in Rwanda today. Nonetheless, healing processes are underway in the country, and apparently, many people feel safe enough to engage in such processes. As reconciliation begins, it increases the feeling of security and perhaps actual security, which makes further healing easier. Progress in one realm fosters progress in the other in this cycle.

PROMOTING HEALING AND RECONCILIATION IN THE COMMUNITY

In this section, we describe an intervention we developed to promote community healing and reconciliation, and we briefly describe an experimental evaluation of its effects. Our goal was to develop an intervention that people without advanced professional training could deliver, that facilitators could use with groups, and that could readily be integrated into other programs for healing, reconciliation, and community-building.

Developing a group, rather than an individual, intervention seemed essential for a number of reasons. First, the genocide affected most of the population of about 8 million in Rwanda, making an individual approach to healing impractical. Second, the genocide was a community disaster, and healing as part of a group, in the community of others, seems more appropriate and potentially more effective. A group approach also seems more appropriate to Rwandan culture which, like many African cultures, is community—rather than individual oriented (Wessells & Monteiro, 2001). Further, one of the consequences of victimization is disconnection from other people (Saakvitne, Gamble, Pearlman, & Lev, 2000), and group healing can help people reconnect with others. Social support or connection is an important antidote to trauma, at least in the U.S. (Wortman, Battle, & Lemkau, 1997). Finally, reconciliation between groups requires the engagement of the whole population, and involving more people in interventions is essential.

Our intention has been to offer both information (content) and a way of delivering it (process) that others can use to *augment* their ongoing work. This approach acknowledges the expertise of local staff, allows for cultural adaptation of the material, leaves control in the hands of the local facilitators, and allows each user to identify his/her own specific goals (e.g., healing, reconciliation, forgiving, group coexistence, improved adaptations to daily life).

Terminology. In the following description, we define several terms. Facilitators or facilitator-participants are the people who attended our seminars in 1999 and in the training-of-trainers in 2003–04. These people were professional helpers with various backgrounds and positions. Some were trained trauma counselors, others public educators for the national unity and reconciliation commission, still others front-line staff in local NGOs; a few were staff of religious organizations. They facilitate a variety of types of groups in the community, and were participants in our seminars; hence the (interchangeable) names, facilitators and facilitator-participants.

In describing our research, we use the term "integrated groups" to describe the experimental groups in which facilitators integrated our material with their usual approach to healing, reconciliation, and/or community-building.

In our first project in 1999, we conducted a 2-week seminar/workshop in Kigali with about 35 Rwandese staff of local and international NGOs that engage in healing and community building. About two thirds of the participants were Tutsi, one third Hutu. These participants would eventually facilitate groups in the community (we therefore refer to them below as facilitator-participants). Our local collaborators recruited them, mainly from organizations with which we made contact on our first trip in January 1999.

We developed a workshop based on theory, research, and experience with complex trauma and violence (Allen, 2001; Herman, 1992; McCann & Pearlman, 1990a; Pearlman & Saakvitne, 1995; Esterling, L'Abate, Murray, & Pennebaker, 1999; Saakvitne et al., 2000; Staub, 1989, 1998, 1999, 2003). The workshop included brief psycho-educational lectures with extensive large- and small-group discussions after each lecture, and an experiential component that gave participants opportunities to apply the material to their personal experience. Our objective was to provide participants with information that they could later use in their work with groups in the community, as well as opportunities to reflect on and process some of their own genocide-related experiences.

Staff from local NGOs who attended a one-day meeting with us in January 1999 identified five elements as potentially useful in their fieldwork. These elements became the basis of much of our later work in Rwanda. We describe the five elements below.[1]

1. *Understanding the effects of trauma and victimization and avenues to healing.*

There is some tendency among professionals who provide assistance in the wake of psychosocial disasters to distinguish and contrast approaches focusing on trauma and on community building. From our perspective, the two approaches are not contradictory but can be integrated and can support each other. Our approach blends an understanding of complex psychological trauma with a community-centered approach to recovery.

Understanding psychological trauma, including both the symptoms of post-traumatic stress disorder (PTSD) (American Psychiatric Association, 1994) and the profound effects of traumatic experiences on the self, perceptions of people and the world, and one's spirituality, can contribute to healing (Allen, 2001; Rosenbloom & Williams, 1999; Saakvitne et al., 2000; Staub, 1998). Experiencing senseless, violent cruelty toward oneself and one's group diminishes self-worth. Realizing that the way one has changed is the normal

---

[1]The mini-lectures we developed to share these ideas are available on our website, http://www.heal-reconcile-Rwanda.org

consequence of extraordinary, painful experiences can ease people's distress and open the possibility for further healing.

Providing people with a framework for recovery offers hope, a fundamental aspect of healing (Saakvitne et al., 2000). Traumatized people often carry their pain and sense of danger into the present. Engagement with their painful experiences—remembering the events and feeling the emotions related to what happened—under empathic, supportive conditions, can help people move constructively into the future. It can also help them gain new trust in, and reconnect with, people.

Trauma specialists have found that another aspect of healing is creating a story of one's experience that makes sense of it. By symbolizing or representing traumatic experiences through narratives, dramatizations, or art, people can create meaning (Harvey, 1996; Herman, 1992; Lantz, 1996; Newman, Riggs, & Roth, 1997; Pennebaker & Beall, 1986), such as trying to prevent such suffering by others (Higgins, 1994). Indeed, some research has found that traumatic experiences stimulate a search for meaning (Tokayer, 2002).

Encouraging people to talk about their painful experiences, or exposure, can overcome the avoidance that maintains trauma symptoms (Foa, Keane, & Friedman, 2000). Although there is some disagreement about the need for survivors to talk about their traumatic experiences (Bonnano, Noll, Putnam, O'Neill, & Trickett, 2003), the preponderance of clinical and empirical evidence suggests that doing so is helpful for many survivors. Survivors of sudden, traumatic loss also require a framework for understanding traumatic grief and the need for mourning (Rando, 1993).

We provide a broader understanding of the psychological aftermath of traumatic experiences, "beyond PTSD," helping people understand the behavioral, cognitive, emotional, interpersonal, spiritual, and physiological sequelae of violence. We also convey to workshop participants that trauma does not imply psychopathology or dysfunction. Furthermore, communities can use a neighbor-to-neighbor approach to address trauma: We support people in participating actively in their own recovery. This framework seems to have energized and empowered the people with whom we worked in Rwanda.

2. *Understanding genocide.* People often see genocide as incomprehensible evil. People also often see their own suffering as unique. Learning about similar ways that others have suffered and examining the psychological and social roots of such violence can help people see their common humanity with others. It can mitigate negative attitudes toward oneself, and even toward perpetrators, helping victims to see perpetrators (as well as passive bystanders) as human beings, in spite of their horrible actions. This experience should make reconciliation with members of a perpetrator group more possible. We

hypothesized that exploration of the influences that lead to genocide, based primarily on the conception developed by Staub (1989, 1996, 1999, 2003) and enriched by other conceptions (see, for reviews, Chorbajian & Shirinian, 1999; Totten, Parsons, & Charny, 1997), would contribute to both healing and reconciliation. (For a description of some of the factors leading to genocide, see the section "Working with National Leaders" below.)

In our brief lectures about the origins of genocide, we did not discuss how the influences we noted apply to Rwanda (see, however, Staub, 1999). Instead, we presented the concepts and their application to other genocides (Staub, 1989), and then asked the participants to apply them to Rwanda. They did so very effectively.

3. *Understanding basic psychological needs.* The frustration of basic psychological needs by social conditions is one cause of groups turning against other groups (Burton, 1990; Kelman, 1990; Staub, 1989). We hypothesized that understanding basic psychological needs could contribute to understanding the origins of genocide and its impact on people, and could further promote healing. Traumatic experiences frustrate or disrupt basic needs (McCann & Pearlman, 1990a; Pearlman, 2003), and healing promotes the fulfillment of those needs. Basic psychological needs on which we focus include security or safety, trust, esteem, positive identity, feelings of effectiveness and control, positive connections to other people, a comprehension of reality and of one's own place in the world, and transcendence (or spiritual needs) (McCann & Pearlman; Pearlman & Saakvitne, 1995; Saakvitne et al., 2000; Staub, 1989, 2003).

4. *Engagement with experience.* We planned to have participants engage with what happened to them during the genocide by first writing (Pennebaker & Beall, 1986), or if they were unable to write, drawing something about their experiences. The next step would be to discuss these experiences in small groups. However, while these facilitator-participants all could write, 50% of the population in Rwanda cannot, and many of the people in the community with whom our participants worked have never held a pen or pencil. So instead, we invited the facilitator-participants to reflect privately upon what they experienced during the genocide. Many of them expressed a preference to engage in the exercise in this way.

We discussed the importance of empathic responding to others' experiences, and provided some limited training in it. We demonstrated lack of response, inappropriate responses such as offering advice or immediately beginning to tell one's own story, as well as appropriate empathy. We also invited discussion of culturally appropriate responses. In small groups, participants then told their stories, and often cried with others in this process.

We worked with a mixed group, both Hutus and Tutsis. Given the realities in Rwanda—the genocide by Hutus against Tutsis with the Tutsis now in power—it may not be surprising that the Hutus, who participated actively in the workshop in general, did not tell the "stories" of their experiences during the genocide. Still, we believe that hearing the painful stories of Tutsis—stories that mainly focused on what happened to the victims, hardly mentioning perpetrators—could promote empathy in Hutus and contribute to reconciliation. The empathic participation of Hutus in the small groups may have further helped Tutsis toward healing and reconciliation. Scholars at the Stone Center have written about the central role of empathy in healing and connection (Jordan, Walker, & Hartling, 2004).

5. *Vicarious traumatization*. Vicarious traumatization (VT) is a transformation in the self of the helper that comes about through incomplete or interrupted empathic engagement with trauma-survivor clients and a sense of commitment or responsibility to help (McCann & Pearlman, 1990b; Saakvitne et al., 2000; Saakvitne, Pearlman, and the Staff of the Traumatic Stress Institute, 1996). Although research findings are mixed, the preponderance of evidence suggests that VT may be more common in helpers with a personal trauma history than those without such a history (Arvay, 2001). We introduced the notion to our Rwandese facilitator-participants, most of whom may be considered "wounded healers," who immediately grasped the VT concept. They seemed grateful for this acknowledgment of the challenges of their work and relieved by the normalization of their experience. They collaborated enthusiastically to explore work-related stressors as well as to share possible coping strategies and ways of addressing and transforming their VT.

Informal Observations

The information we provided in our workshop about the origins of genocide and mass killing, exemplifying principles by reference to various cases, and the discussions that followed, in the course of which participants applied the principles to the genocide in Rwanda, had a visibly powerful impact on participants. Learning that people elsewhere had suffered similarly and coming to understand how certain influences contribute to genocide seemed to help participants feel that they were not outside history and human experience. They seemed moved and rehumanized by the understanding that what had happened in their society is a human, albeit horrific, process. One woman said, "If this has happened to other people, then it doesn't mean that God abandoned the people of Rwanda." Echoing several others, another person said, "If we can understand how this happened, we can act to prevent it in the future." In applying their new knowledge of the influences leading to genocide to what happened in Rwanda, participants seemed to gain a deep, *experiential understanding* of the roots of genocide in their country.

Two aspects of the trauma material we presented seemed to provide some relief to participants. The idea that the widely varied behavioral, emotional, cognitive, interpersonal, and spiritual adaptations they experienced and observed in others are normal responses to abnormal events was depathologizing. The additional notion that traumatized people can be effective in their lives seemed to provide hope. It also may have provided permission for people to acknowledge their pain without fearing that others would see them as "crazy."

Our informal observations, along with the results of our formal evaluation (described briefly below and in detail in Staub, Pearlman, Gubin, and Hagengimana, in press), suggested that Tutsis' orientation to Hutus became more positive as they came to understand that perpetrators acted in response to societal, cultural, and psychological forces. Such an understanding may help people to realize that preventing mass violence requires inhibiting the social processes that lead to it, which profoundly shape and form potential perpetrators. Our formal research results suggested that the material also helped the Hutu seminar participants, who presumably did not actively harm others,[2] to have a way of understanding the horrible events of the genocide.

We intended our facilitator-participants to use the new material with groups in the community, in combination with their traditional methods or approaches, the latter presumably reflecting their understanding of the community and its history and needs (see Wessells & Monteiro, 2001). Part of the seminar focused on integrating our approach with the facilitators' own quite varied approaches, and we encouraged them to develop further this *integrated approach* in their work with groups in the community.

Measuring Impact

There has been a great deal of research on the effects of contact between members of different groups in overcoming prejudice or devaluation (Pettigrew & Tropp, 2000). However, the evaluation of interventions to reduce conflict between groups is mostly informal anecdotal, rather than systematic, research (Ross & Rothman, 1999). We conducted an experimental study to assess the impact of our intervention—not on the people in our seminar, but

[2]This assumption is based on the likelihood that most accused perpetrators were either in jail or had fled the country by this time.

on members of community groups they subsequently facilitated (Staub et al., in press).

Following the seminar, some of the facilitator-participants integrated our approach with their own, in their work with community groups comprising the different segments of the community: Tutsis, among them women who were tortured through rape; widows; HIV-affected persons; Hutus; and Twa (about 1% of the population). For our research purposes, these were the experimental groups. Other staff from the same organizations who had not participated in the workshop used their usual or traditional approach with equally diverse community groups. Both types of groups (integrated and traditional) were newly created for the purpose of the study, meeting 3 hours, twice a week, for 3 weeks. Participants were 194 people, with approximately 60% self-identified as Tutsi, 16% as Hutu or Twa, and 23% providing anomalous identifying information, with some changes in self-identification across measurements. There were about 16 people in each of the research groups. The organizations for which our facilitators worked, with the assistance of our Rwandan research associates, assigned participants to treatment and control groups. As far as we know there was no selection bias in assigning them to groups. However, since we had no direct control over the assignment and it cannot, therefore, be considered a random assignment, we attempted to control for any pre-treatment group differences statistically.

The activities of the groups were of the kind the facilitators normally conducted. Some focused on healing, others on community building (talking about their difficulties and providing support to each other in the course of agricultural work), with the seminar material integrated into these activities in the experimental groups. Control groups were also created, which were simply evaluated for changes over time. Both the integrated and traditional groups filled out questionnaires before they began to meet, about a month later (just after facilitators stopped working with them), and 2 months after that. Members of the *control* groups filled out the same questionnaires at about the same times.

We found that trauma symptoms decreased in the integrated groups led by the facilitators who participated in our seminar both over time and in comparison to the other groups. Symptoms increased somewhat in both the traditional groups led by facilitators who did not participate in our seminar and the control group. We also found an increase in positive orientation toward the other group in the groups led by facilitators we trained, both over time and in comparison to the other groups. The elements of this positive orientation included (a) seeing the genocide as having complex origins (rather than simply resulting from the evil nature of the perpetrators or from bad leaders), (b) expressing willingness to work with the other group for important goals (e.g., a better future), and (c) expressing willingness to forgive the other group if its members acknowledged what they did and apologized for the group's actions (see Staub, 2003; Staub et al., in press).

In summary, relatively limited participation in groups led by facilitators who participated in our seminars contributed to both healing and a more positive attitude by groups toward each other. We subsequently further developed elements of this approach, which we used in our work with varied groups.

WORKING WITH NATIONAL LEADERS

We conducted two seminar/workshops, both organized in collaboration with the National Unity and Reconciliation Commission (NURC), with high-level national leaders. The 35 participants in a 4-day meeting in August 2001 were government ministers, members of the Supreme Court, heads of national commissions (electoral, constitutional), the heads of the national prison system and of the main Kigali prison, an advisor to the president, leaders of religious organizations, and commissioners of the NURC. In January 2003, the 60 to 70 participants in a 1-day seminar were a similar group, with more government ministers, both the president and vice-president of the Supreme Court, heads of political parties, and members of parliament. Although both of these seminars were mixed, the current leadership is predominantly Tutsi and there were more Tutsi than Hutu leaders present.

We designed the 2001 seminar to advance leaders' understanding of the impact of genocide both on themselves and on the people of Rwanda, and to consider avenues to healing that leaders might promote. Two important purposes were to provide an understanding of (1) how genocide and mass killing originate and (2) policies and practices in the society that might reduce the likelihood of renewed violence and promote positive relations between groups in Rwanda, in the hope that leaders would advance such policies and practices. The social context was the planned gacaca, or community justice process, and leaders expressed concern that one undesirable byproduct of the process would be retraumatization. Probably their unexpressed concern, and our strong concern, was also that the testimonies of horrible actions in front of the gacaca would create renewed anger in both groups, and possibly renewed violence.

As in our previous work in Rwanda, in the second leaders' seminar, we suggested that both difficult economic and political conditions and group conflict are starting points for the evolution of group violence (Staub, 1989; 1999; 2003; Staub & Bar-Tal, 2003). By January 2003, the context included the release of large numbers of prisoners earlier that month, and the experience of some pilot work with gacaca. We discussed the important roles of scapegoating, destructive ideologies, devaluation of members of another group, unhealed wounds from past traumatic experiences, excessive respect for authority, the importance of pluralism, the gradual evolution of increasing violence, and the role of bystanders—both people inside a group and outside groups and nations. We provided leaders with a form to help them shape and evaluate policies and practices. One endpoint of each of the dimensions on part one of the form shows influences that would make violence between groups more likely, whereas the other endpoints would make it less likely. For example, these dimensions included devaluation vs. humanizing people, unhealed wounds vs. healing of wounds, monolithic society vs. pluralism, overly-strong respect for authority vs. moderate respect.

The group members identified and discussed policies and practices from the standpoint of these dimensions. For example, how might new decentralization policies affect people's sense of obedience to authority? What is the impact of providing special help to needy survivors of the genocide, but given highly limited resources, not to needy members of the perpetrator group? They considered whether particular practices would make violence more or less likely and what they could do to shape such practices to reduce the likelihood of future violence. We also discussed avenues to reconciliation following violence, such as truth, justice, healing from past wounds, significant contact between groups as they work together for shared goals, and the creation of a shared history in place of different and conflicting views of history.

The group in 2001 intensely discussed and, together with the facilitators, applied this understanding of the origins of genocide and prevention of violence in Rwanda. The group discussed the challenges of addressing harmful elements of culture, such as a hierarchical society with great respect for authority, which serve them as leaders. These elements, including obedience to orders to kill, appear to have contributed in a variety of ways to the genocide in Rwanda, (Des Forges, 1999; Mamdani, 2002; Staub, 1999).

The meaning of group. Guided by a government policy of "unity" and the strong commitment of individual leaders to this policy, the use of the terms "Hutu" and "Tutsi" has been strongly discouraged and people rarely used these terms in 2001. In response to our discussion of devaluation of the "other group," seminar participants stated that there were no groups in Rwanda. They stated that the Belgian colonizers artificially created divisions. Although there is not enough research and experience to offer much guidance, our understanding of the impact of victimization, group relations, and reconciliation suggests that acknowledging feelings of hostility between groups and working to overcome them is more likely to lead to reconciliation and peace than is asserting unity and not addressing such feelings. In the former Yugoslavia, for example, the government discouraged exploration of the mass killing that took place during World War II by the Croat republic allied with Nazi Germany. Thus, the deep wounds, fear, and hostility between groups that were likely to remain were not addressed. With such exploration, perhaps the violence of the 1990s would have been avoided.

In our discussions, participants moved toward acknowledging that, whether or not there is a biological basis for the differentiation between Hutu and Tutsi, there has been differentiation socially (in terms of interpersonal behaviors such as discrimination) and psychologically (in terms of seeing themselves and others as belonging to one group or the other). A high-status participant said at one point, "I wonder what they say about each other in their homes."

Although the reasons are unclear, our strong impression is that the terms Hutu and Tutsi were used more in 2003 than during the preceding few years. In 1999, Rwandese people did not use the terms at all, and we were strongly advised by our Rwandese cultural consultants to follow suit. By 2003, participants in our leaders' seminar were able to engage in extensive, if emotionally charged, discussions about this issue. They discussed addressing the different experiences the two groups had before, during, and after the genocide, and the deep feelings that have developed toward the "other" as relevant to understanding the origins of genocide and to healing and reconciliation.

Creating a shared history of Rwanda. After violence, each group tends to see the other as at fault. Each blames the other for its own violent acts, claims and sees these acts as necessary reactions to the other's actions or to the danger the other represents (Bar-Tal, 2002). Conflicting views about what happened can rekindle hostility and violence.

Especially when groups live together, creating a history that is acceptable to both sides may be central to reconciliation (Bar-Tal, 2002; Cairns & Roe, 2002; Penal Reform International, 2004; Staub & Bar-Tal, 2003). A French–German commission of historians did this after World War II, with a focus on showing that the two countries had not always been implacable foes (Willis, 1965). In our first leaders' seminar, some participants expressed the belief that history is objective, that there is only one correct factual account of events. Predominantly, however, the group recognized that there can be different perspectives on historical events and agreed that creating a shared history acceptable to all groups in Rwanda is important. They noted that the government had just convened a commission to create a history to be taught in the schools. The hope was that this history curriculum would lay the groundwork for a more peaceful future. In our seminar small-group discussions, a group considering how such a history could be created attracted many participants, who had many ideas about how to achieve it. These included each group taking the role of the other in describing history, as well as the recognition of earlier peaceful coexistence. However, in the end many participants expressed skepticism that it would be possible to create such a history at this time, in light of the feelings generated by the recent genocide. In July 2003, the creation of such a history for the schools was still in progress. (The history of Rwanda as it is taught in the ingando, or reeducation camps, is outlined in the Penal Reform International report of May 2004.)

In our subsequent seminars/workshops in Rwanda, we introduced elements of an approach to the creation of a shared history. Using our approach to understanding the roots of genocide, we attempted to make past historical events comprehensible, identifying the social and psychological forces that led to discrimination and violence. By bringing understanding and empathy to historical events and actions, we hoped to help people acknowledge their own group's blameworthy actions and begin to accept the other group.

For example, in the second leaders' seminar, one of the participants referred to the "genocide" in 1959. At that time, there was a Hutu uprising against Tutsi rule, with about 50,000 Tutsis killed. In response to this comment we said that, as we understood it, what happened in 1959 was mass killing but not genocide (see Staub, 1989, and Staub & Bar-Tal, 2003 for a discussion of this distinction). We noted that the Belgian colonizers elevated the Tutsis, who ruled in their behalf. The situation of the Hutus was extremely bad and the societal arrangements unjust. We also acknowledged the difficulty in correcting unequal relations between groups and that, lamentably, attempts to correct such injustice commonly include violence (Davis, 1969). We also noted that under the Hutu rule that followed, there was discrimination and violence against the Tutsis. Had the Hutus created more just social arrangements, the subsequent evolution toward genocide would have been less likely. In the daily anonymous written evaluations that we collect in all of our seminars, one participant wrote that this was the first time that he or she learned that the violence in 1959 was not a genocide, that it was a response to injustice. This participant thanked us for the information.

Challenges of the gacaca as a vehicle for justice and reconciliation. At the time of our leaders' seminar in 2001, there was great concern about the potentially harmful impact of the upcoming gacaca, or community justice process. The leaders asked for our help in promoting the potential positive value of this process. We responded by initiating a seminar with community leaders and a public education campaign, which we describe below.

In the gacaca process, the populace elected 250,000 people from the general population in October 2001. These people would serve as judges, in panels of 19, in about 9000 locations around Rwanda. Their task was to judge the large majority of the approximately 115,000 people who were in jail since 1994, accused of perpetrating the genocide. The gacaca law requires the population to be present and participate. The process moves from identifying the crimes committed—ranging from property theft to rape, murder, and the planning of violence—to establishing what community members know about the crimes committed in that community, to judging alleged perpetrators. In the course of this process, people give and hear testimonies about killing, rape, and atrocities of many kinds. Communities gather in the fields each week to engage in this process.

The gacaca pilot process resulted in several changes. Changes were made in the areas of organization, categorization of crimes, moral damages, and sentences. Penal Reform International (PRI) has described and commented on those changes and presented a preliminary analysis of gacaca (PRI, 2004).

Members of our group agreed that, although it could have great potential positive effects, the gacaca process was likely to reactivate trauma for everyone. It might also generate renewed hostility in both groups. They expressed concern that everyone—witnesses, alleged perpetrators, judges, families of victims, people who knew alleged perpetrators as neighbors and now see them as enemies, and so on—would need support. The participants requested our help in shaping the gacaca process to promote reconciliation. It is our belief that people need preparation in advance, support during the process, and opportunities to process their experience afterwards in order to minimize retraumatization.

WORK WITH LOCAL COMMUNITY LEADERS

In June 2002, we facilitated a 4-day seminar/workshop with approximately 35 Rwandese community leaders from around the country. They were high- and mid-level leaders and staff primarily from Ibuka (the main survivor organization, of which several constituent associations were represented, such as Avega, a widows' organization, and Profemmes, an umbrella organization for women's associations throughout the country), the Ministry of Health, and the NURC. Participants included regional representatives, directors of central medical facilities, commissioners from the NURC, people in leadership roles in the assistance of widows, and others.

Our purpose was to help participants to lessen the potential negative effects and promote the potential positive effects of the gacaca, which was in its pilot phase. We, as the facilitators, and the NURC, which organized the workshop, agreed that the purposes of the gacaca process—justice, healing, and reconciliation—might be advanced if people had ways of understanding how genocide comes about. In addition, understanding psychological trauma and healing might help to minimize the retraumatization that seemed likely to occur as a result of the gacaca hearings and to enable people to support each other in the process. Before we addressed these goals in the seminar, we asked participants to describe the positive effects of the gacaca they anticipated and hoped for, and the negative effects they feared.

The anticipated positive effects included:

- The truth will be established (how relatives were killed, who should be punished).
- The process will create justice.
- Everyone will be involved in the process.
- The whole population will respect the decisions made because they will have taken part in the process.
- When perpetrators are punished, reconciliation will be possible.
- The problems between the two groups will be resolved.
- As the prisons empty, the economic burden on the country will diminish.
- The country can develop as it resolves problems.
- Over time, the effects of trauma will diminish.
- People will find out where their relatives died and can bury them with dignity, which will enable them to mourn properly.
- As circumstances in the country improve, exiles will return.

In addition, we suggested and the group agreed to the following:

- Innocent people can go home.
- Those sentenced and their relatives will know their fate and can turn to the future.
- The whole society will gain closure.

The potential negative effects resulting from the gacaca that people anticipated or feared included the following:

- Retraumatization may occur as people give or hear testimonies.
- Some people may give biased, untrue testimony.
- Some won't tell the truth because, as Christians, they believe they should love their enemy and God will punish them if they accuse people.
- In some cases there won't be witnesses because so many have been killed and others have moved to a different district and won't be found.
- In many cases victimized people live elsewhere, and it will be difficult for them to reach places where they are to testify.

- Witnesses' security won't be ensured.
- Many perpetrators are poor and it will be difficult for survivors to get compensation.
- Taking property of perpetrators for compensation will create problems for their children.
- Hatred will increase between families that testify and the guilty.
- Families may be killed out of revenge or have to flee the country because they testified.
- Conflict will develop within families with mixed ethnic origin as they accuse each other of perpetration.
- Some of those released may take revenge.
- People will find out about women who were raped.
- There can be corruption, protection of people in high positions.
- Some people who have been involved in the genocide may now hide as judges.
- The gacaca judges at the cell administrative level will categorize people and, as many of them have little education, some people will escape punishment.
- People will spend a great deal of time on the gacaca and they won't have time to work, reducing productivity in the country.
- Some people will get psychologically ill because of the stress and there may not be enough response from the ministries.
- Some perpetrators may testify without any spirit of repentance, just telling of their "heroic" deeds.
- Trauma may occur among people who committed genocide who feel ashamed because of their terrible crimes.

Some potential negative effects that we added, to which the group agreed, were as follows:

- There may be new trauma as people learn about something (e.g., rape) that happened to them or that was done by someone close to them.
- There may be renewed anger and rage by survivors, especially if they see perpetrators not sufficiently punished.
- There may be hostility from members of the perpetrator group who were not perpetrators, as they feel constantly accused in the course of testimonies about horrible acts by members of their group.

One additional element from this meeting seems important to note. In discussing past history, the group rejected the notion that there was significant dominance by and conflict between Tutsis and Hutus in the pre-colonial period, even though historical analyses indicate this (see Mamdani, 2002). Their attitude stands in contrast to our experience in a seminar in 2003 that was part of training trainers in our approach. Here, the widely respected Vice President of the NURC referred to such conflict in opening our seminar. Participants accepted this then and in later discussions. This may have been due to a different group composition, respect for the person who made the comment and his position, or the group members' participation in a previous seminar with us that prepared them to acknowledge a more complex truth. However, our experience in 2004 with the listener group interviews for our public education campaign (see below) revealed continuing rejection by people in the community of the notion that there was conflict between Tutsis and Hutus before colonization. In contrast, a report by Penal Reform International (2004) describes comments by prisoners who were released in early 2003 and then went through a reeducation ("sensitization") camp before they returned to their communities. Some of the prisoners objected to the presentation of history in the camp, according to which the Belgians created differences and difficulties between Hutus and Tutsis, as a significant distortion of the truth. Here we have an example of conflicting views of history that, because of their apparent importance to members of the two groups, need to be addressed as part of the process of preventing future violence.

Our 2001 and 2003 groups to some degree engaged with the question, "What aspects of the truth are important for reconciliation?" For example, it was evident that survivors of genocide need their suffering truthfully represented and acknowledged. This helps them heal and feel more secure; it conveys that the world does not simply accept such events as normal, and that steps can be taken to promote justice (Staub & Pearlman, 2001). The discussions also suggested that passage of time after victimization and appropriate preparation are required before people who suffered a genocide are ready to consider and acknowledge that their own group may have also perpetrated harm. (Acknowledgement by perpetrators of their harm-doing is even more difficult.) Our experience also suggests to us that directly presenting particular views of history, as we did in the seminar with community leaders, is less useful than exploring them in the course of discussion. This exploration is best done in the framework of understanding how certain historical events and conditions developed, which we did in our other seminars.

In his 2004 book, Gibson reported research from South Africa. His findings on the relationship between truth and reconciliation suggest that for some groups (whites, colored South Africans, and those of Asian origin), truth and reconciliation are positively related. But among black South Africans, truth appeared to contribute little to reconciliation. Thus, the relationship between truth and reconciliation may depend on victim/perpetrator group affiliation. If that were true in Rwanda, it would suggest the need for different approaches to the two groups. It may be that the apparent success of our approach is enhanced by our emphasis on its integration into facilitators' and others' usual way of doing things, which may include special considerations for the context in which they are working.

SEMINARS FOR JOURNALISTS

The way media report events can have many significant effects. It can intensify group differences and hostility or help people understand others' actions (Staub, 1989, 1999). It can limit pluralism or enhance the expression of varied views. We conducted two seminars for journalists and included journalist participants in two other week-long seminars.

The purpose of the first seminar, in August 1999, was to inform reporting by journalists, by helping them understand trauma and the roots of violence between groups. The 1-day seminar included about 35 journalists. The purpose of the second, 2-day seminar, in June 2002, was to help the 40 journalist participants develop constructive ways to report on the gacaca, and thereby promote healing and reconciliation. Understanding the origins of the events—robbery, rape, murder, killing of neighbors, and so on—investigated in the gacaca could help journalists report on them in ways that generate comprehension among the Rwandan public. Understanding psychological trauma and healing might help them gather information and report to the public in ways that are less likely to retraumatize people or create new trauma. An understanding of retraumatization could help reporters inform people about the ways they can support each other as individuals and as members of communities as they are exposed to the gacaca proceedings. We thought that our seminar might also lessen the retraumatization and vicarious trauma of journalists themselves that is almost certainly generated as they are exposed to stories of great violence and cruelty in the course of interviewing highly traumatized people (McCann & Pearlman, 1990b; Figley, 1995; Pyevich, 2002; Saakvitne et al., 1996).

Following a lecture and extensive discussion of the origins of genocide, we asked the participants to generate news stories. As an example, we applied information about the roots of genocide to understanding how a young man might have become a member of the Interahamwe, the militia composed of young men that did a great deal of the killing. In this example, we noted the difficult economic conditions in Rwanda and the lack of prospects for

young men; the political parties creating youth arms, which provided connection and community as well as identity for such young men (fulfilling
basic psychological needs); the history of devaluation of Tutsis and the strong
propaganda against them at the time; the power of the political group they
joined over them; as well as other elements. We suggested and they developed other story ideas: how a man came to kill his own son, someone who
tried to save lives and was killed, children of rape, a perpetrator confessing
at gacaca with no sign of remorse, and others. They worked in small groups,
each group working with one scenario or story idea.

The next day, following a lecture on psychological trauma, retraumatization, and healing, participants continued in their groups on the story they
began the first day, now including this new material. In addition to discussing ways to create stories that promote healing and reconciliation, in the large
group the journalists discussed the related issue of reporting details in depth,
with the possibility of contributing to renewed hostility and retraumatization,
or reporting fewer details but perhaps not fulfilling their role as journalists.
They expressed the belief that part of their role was to promote constructive social change, but also expressed concerns about how much freedom
they had in reporting. The group discussed limitations by the government on
their freedom to report and the government's concerns about what may be
considered incitement to violence. One well-respected Rwandese journalist
challenged the group's self-imposed limitations on what they might report,
leading to a lively discussion.

We are continuing to work with journalists on a project we have initiated, led by Radio la Benevolencija, to develop extensive radio programs for
Rwanda on the themes we have described here (sponsors include the Dutch
government, the Belgian government, and USAID). Radio is the primary means
for the population in Rwanda to receive information. The radio programs,
which began broadcasting in May 2004, include stories ("soap dramas") with
embedded information, direct informational/educational programs, and relevant art such as poetry and stories created by listeners. Grassroots activities
will aim to foster community discussions about the informational content
and transform this into action. The aims are to inform the population about
the origins of genocide; help them understand the perpetrators who are tried
by the gacaca or are released from prison; and inform people about trauma,
retraumatization and healing, thereby helping them find ways to assist and
support each other and to protect themselves from retraumatization.

This public education campaign includes two research elements. The
first element is based in a series of listener groups. The then-local senior
producer of this project, Suzanne Fisher, organized a representative sample

of participants who met with Rwandan research assistants and engaged in discussions of their attitudes toward and understanding of the information and themes to be broadcast in the radio programs (Fisher, in press). Fisher has taken care to include people who represent the diverse backgrounds of persons now living in Rwanda in the research: Tutsi who were in Rwanda during the genocide, Tutsi who returned from the diaspora during and after 1994, prisoners, who generally are Hutus, Hutus who did not actively participate in the killing, and Twa. These groups are being queried over time to provide comments to the radio team about how the programs are being received. Radio personnel refer to such a process as "formative research," as it shapes the programs on an ongoing basis.

The second research is an outcome study (which radio personnel refer to as "summative research"). A Yale University researcher has designed a systematic, controlled study to assess the impact of these radio programs on the population (Paluck & Green, 2004).

ISSUES AND CONTEMPORARY SOCIETAL/POLITICAL PROCESSES IMPORTANT TO RECONCILIATION

Ultimately, the effectiveness of our work and that of all third parties in post-conflict situations depends on the social and political context within which one conducts it. For example, development efforts to mitigate the extreme poverty in which most of the population lives, the vast public health disaster posed by the approximately 15% rate of HIV infection in Rwanda, and the approximately 50% literacy rate would undoubtedly promote reconciliation. We discuss here a few additional issues we regard as important.

During the genocide, some Hutus spoke out against the killings or publicly attempted to protect Tutsis and were consequently killed (Des Forges, 1999). Others successfully saved lives by hiding Tutsis, or even by stopping those who came to take a Tutsi away (Staub & Pearlman, 2001). Acknowledging such heroic rescue could help Hutus feel that others do not blame and devalue them as a group. In our 2001 leaders' seminar, we discussed the potential contribution to reconciliation of acknowledging and honoring Hutus who had tried to help Tutsis. Participants thought it might be too early for such an acknowledgment, that it would be too difficult psychologically, given the deep psychological wounds of Tutsis. We again discussed this issue in the community leaders' seminar in 2002, where participants had similar feelings. In our January 2003 seminar, the head of commemoration in Ibuka, who was also present in the 2002 seminar, reported that Ibuka was now planning to include such acknowledgments in future genocide commemorations. This did happen in the commemoration of the genocide in April 2003 and 2004. Among the likely influences promoting this was a book published by African Rights in 2002 about heroic helpers, *Tribute to Courage*.

An even more difficult issue is the acknowledgment by Tutsis of violence against Hutu civilians. Such violence took place in the course of the civil war. It was also an aspect of fighting infiltrators who came into Rwanda to kill Tutsis for several years after the genocide (Des Forges, 1999). Unknown numbers of Hutus were killed among those who escaped from Rwanda into Zaire (now the Congo) after the genocide was ended by RPF victory over government forces, when Rwandan forces helped Kabila's rebel forces overthrow Mobutu, the long-term ruler of Zaire

Unless others in some way acknowledge their "truth," people will hold on to their own version of history, which blames the other. As we have mentioned, we discussed in the seminar the exploitation of Hutus by Tutsis during the colonial period. Although we also introduced the issue of violence against Hutus, there was no significant discussion of this issue. The development of an inclusive history, a description of the past that includes multiple perspectives, and a complex exposition of the many factors that contributed to and supported these actions seems important to promote reconciliation. Others have shared this observation (Gibson, 2004).

Contemporary social processes will also contribute to or impede reconciliation. Many of these processes have been highly positive in Rwanda. These include the repatriation of Hutus who left the country after the genocide was ended by the RPA victory and their reintegration into society and even into the army; the gacaca; the release of prisoners in 2003—those old and sick, those who had confessed, and others who had already spent as much time in prison as their punishment would have been, given the crimes of which they were accused; decentralization, consisting in part of local elections; educational and other processes in reconciliation; efforts to improve the educational system, including free primary schools starting in 2003 and new universities; the development of a new constitution; and more.

Other processes such as free speech and the national elections (held in the fall of 2003) have been more problematic. The Tutsi minority, about 14% of the population, may justifiably have feared the outcome of totally free elections that might have brought Hutu leadership to power only 9 years after the genocide. The international community was most likely unwise to pressure Rwanda, which desperately needs the financial support of this community, to hold elections at this time (Uvin, 2003). Continued decentralization, increased free expression and pluralism, and the building of civil society before elections would probably have contributed more to democratization at this time.

Given the existing situation, certain restrictions or limitations on the free expression of ideas (certainly limiting hate speech and ideologies of hate like those that preceded the genocide) may be required to ensure the safety of the minority, and even as a protection of the majority from those who would initiate new violence. The more openly such limitations and the reasons for them are discussed, the less likely that they will create additional conflict between groups.

But open discussion can take place only if the limits created are reasonable. There are sections in the newly adopted constitution that can give the government power to limit free expression, depending on how they are interpreted. Moreover, in 2003, the Mouvement Democratique Republicain (MDR), one of the major parties, was the object of parliamentary investigation, accused of being "divisionist," and banned by the government. Leaders are often seen as limiting opposition to protect their interests. But the experience of intense victimization, particularly genocide, may lead to such a strong sense of vulnerability that any opposition can be seen as extremely dangerous. Since members of a group who are not present at the time of a genocide are also deeply affected (Staub, 1998), this is likely to be true of the Tutsi leaders who have returned from other countries. We have talked to survivors and returnees who were genuinely afraid of the party representing the Tutsis, the Rwandan Patriotic Front (RPF), losing the election and of what might happen as a result. Many in the general population were fearful because, in the past, the existence of political parties and elections were connected to violence. Even members of opposition parties expressed fear, and some supported the current president, Paul Kagame, because they value the stability and security that his government has brought.

Although the actions of the leadership are understandable in these terms, they are nevertheless problematic for the future democratic process. In addition to banning the MDR, several individuals, members of the MDR and others, have disappeared, their fate unknown (Human Rights Watch, 2003). In addition to the meaning of this as a human rights violation, intimidating participants in the political process is likely to restrict the movement toward democracy. Most recently, members of an independent human rights organization, Lipradhor, left the country, presumably afraid when the parliament asked that the organization be banned (Penal Reform International, 2004). The absence of pluralism is one of the influences contributing to violence between groups (Staub, 1989, 2003), and thus signals a potential turn away from a healthy society.

The election of Paul Kagame and the Tutsi-dominated RPF could enhance feelings of security and pave the road to democracy. However, government actions so far have not shown this. For this to happen, the involvement of the international community as an active bystander that speaks out about problematic policies and practices, as well as a constructive, supportive force, will be of great importance.

Finally, it is important to understand that reconciliation and the creation of a peaceful society have been challenged by many upheavals that Rwanda has experienced not only before and during the genocide, but also in its aftermath. Fighting infiltrators in the northwest of the country, the war in the Congo, the return of a huge number of refugees, recent hostilities with Uganda, the release of 22,000 prisoners in early 2003, the adjudication of property claims between members of the different groups, the gacaca, the creation of a constitution, and new political parties are on a partial list of the many processes that have psychological effects that must be managed if they are not to contribute to a renewed cycle of violence.

CONCLUSIONS

Our work in Rwanda has aimed to contribute to healing from psychological wounds, fostering reconciliation, and helping to prevent violence and building a peaceful society. One major issue is the evaluation of the benefits of such work; another is, if there are benefits, how they can be maximized.

The experimental evaluation of our first project showed positive effects, as summarized above. Less formal and more anecdotal indicators suggested that our later work also had positive effects. In anonymous evaluations that we conducted each day and at the end of each seminar/workshop, participants overwhelmingly said that their experiences were very useful to them. Frequently, they commented that all Rwandans should receive the information they gained.

We organized our first project in collaboration with a local NGO, le Mouvement Chretien pour l'Evangelisation, le Counselling et la Reconciliation (MOUCECORE). Our later seminars, in collaboration with the NURC, were all formally opened and closed by high-level officials. In introducing a seminar with journalists, the speaker, who had participated in our first leaders' seminar a year earlier, gave a detailed and highly accurate summary of the key points from that seminar. In conversations with participants in our prior seminars, including leaders, we have heard them express ideas and discuss policy matters using concepts and orientations we have presented and developed in our seminars. The continued interest of the NURC, leaders, and journalists in working with us is another positive indicator. Not long after the January 2003 leaders' seminar, a BBC interviewer asked the head of the NURC, who participated in the seminar, what the curriculum in the reeducation camps for released prisoners would include. She replied that they intended to teach them about the origins of genocide, about the psychological damage to both survivors and perpetrators as a result of the genocide, and the need for everyone to heal.

An important and often difficult issue for those who engage in third-party efforts is to extend the benefits of their work beyond the small numbers of people with whom they work directly (Ross & Rothman, 1999). We have worked with leaders whose willingness and interest in working with us has been astounding, and with facilitators who work with groups in the community, in order to maximize the reach of our work. In addition, in January and June 2003 and in January 2004, we conducted seminars that are part of training trainers in our approach. The creation of the public education campaign mentioned earlier is another way to extend whatever beneficial influence our approach might have.

The success of limited interventions like ours will depend on the political and social processes in the country. By working with leaders and journalists, by extending the reach of these efforts through radio programs and training trainers, we hope to have some positive influence on these processes. But of course the social and political processes depend on many factors. The challenges to the creation of a viable social, political, and cultural system are great in Rwanda. Some of the challenges include the psychological consequences of past history and the genocide; the destruction of basic infrastructure, social institutions, and culture (such as the justice system and communal relations) in the course of the civil war and genocide; social problems like profound poverty and HIV/AIDS; and the social upheavals mentioned above.

The more the government ensures security, allows the expansion of pluralism, and succeeds in ensuring that people can expect just relations between groups (Leatherman, DeMars, Gaffney, & Vayrynen, 1999), the more hope people will have for a better future. Improving economic conditions in the country would also help. The international community, whose passivity in the face of the genocide (Powers, 2002) was so extreme that it might be regarded as evil (Staub, 1999), could help in this realm. The indications are, however, that passivity, sadly the rule in the face of mass killing and even genocide (Staub, 1989), will again characterize the behavior of the international community.

A final issue is the relevance of the approach we have developed to other places and times. Information about the impact of violent victimization and other traumatic experiences and about avenues to healing; coming to understand roots of violence against one's group and oneself as part of the group, as well as one's group's violence against others and the nature of one's own role in it (as perpetrator, passive bystander, and so on); and engagement with painful experiences under supportive conditions are important for promoting healing and reconciliation between groups in many places around the world. Presumably this approach or elements of it could be applied to the Israeli–Palestinian conflict, to reconciliation and peace-making among Sunni and Shiite Moslems and Kurds in Iraq, with their history of antagonism, as well as to Serbs, Croats, and Muslims who lived in the former Yugoslavia. We invite and encourage others to use the material we have developed, to adapt it to other situations, and to assess its effectiveness. Our approach has always been to offer, not to impose; to augment, not to replace; to collaborate, not to dominate. Such a stance seems more likely than its converse to open more doors and ultimately to assist more people.

REFERENCES

African Rights. (2002). *Tribute to courage.* Kigali, Rwanda: Author.

Allen, J.G. (2001). *Traumatic relationships and serious mental disorders.* West Sussex, U.K.: John Wiley & Sons.

American Psychiatric Association. (1994). *Diagnostic and statistical manual of mental disorders* (4th ed.). Washington, DC: Author.

Arvay, M.J. (2001). Secondary traumatic stress among trauma counsellors: What does the research say? *International Journal for the Advancement of Counselling, 23,* 283–293.

Bar-Tal, D. (2002). Collective memory of physical violence: Its contribution to the culture of violence. In E. Cairns & M.D. Roe (Eds.), *Memories in conflict.* London: Macmillan.

Bonnano, G., Noll, J., Putnam, F., O'Neill, M., & Trickett, P.K. (2003). Predicting the willingness to disclose childhood sexual abuse from measures of repressive coping and dissociative tendencies. *Child Maltreatment, 8*(4), 302–318.

Burton, J. W. (1990). *Conflict: Resolution and prevention.* New York: St. Martin's Press.

Cairns, E., & Roe, M.D. (2002). *Memories in conflict.* London: Macmillan.

Chorbajian, L., & Shirinian, G. (1999). *Studies in comparative genocide.* New York: St. Martin's Press.

Davis, J.L. (1969). The curve of rising and declining satisfactions as a cause of some great revolutions and a contained rebellion. In H.D.Graham & T.R. Gurr (Eds.), *Violence in America.* New York: Bantam Books.

de la Rey, C. (2001). Reconciliation in divided societies. In D.J. Christie, R.V. Wagner, & D.D. Winter (Eds.), *Peace, conflict, and violence: Peace psychology for the 21st century* (pp. 251–261). Upper Saddler River, NJ: Prentice Hall.

Des Forges, A. (1999). *Leave none to tell the story: Genocide in Rwanda.* New York: Human Rights Watch.

Esterling, B.A., L'Abate, L., Murray, E.J., & Pennebaker, J.W. (1999). Empirical foundations for writing in prevention and psychotherapy: Mental and physical health outcomes. *Clinical Psychology Review, 19*(1), 79–96.

Figley, C. R. (1995). Compassion fatigue as secondary traumatic stress disorder: An overview. In C.R. Figley (Ed.), *Compassion fatigue: Coping with secondary traumatic stress disorder in those who treat the traumatized* (pp. 1–20). New York: Brunner/Mazel.

Fisher, S. (in press). *Tuning into different wavelengths: Listener clubs for effective Rwanda Reconciliation Radio.* Manuscript in preparation.

Foa, E.B., Keane, T.M., & Friedman, M.J. (Eds.). (2000). *Effective treatments for PTSD: Practice guidelines from the International Society for Traumatic Stress Studies.* New York: Guilford Press.

Gibson, J.L. (2004). *Overcoming apartheid: Can truth reconcile a divided nation?* New York: Russell Sage Foundation.

Harvey, M. (1996). An ecological view of psychological trauma and trauma recovery. *Journal of Traumatic Stress, 9,* 3–23.

Herman, J. (1992). *Trauma and recovery: The aftermath of violence from domestic abuse to political terror.* New York: Basic Books.

Higgins, C. (1994). *Resilient adults overcoming a cruel past.* San Francisco: Jossey-Bass.

Human Rights Watch. (2003, May). *Preparing for elections: Tightening control in the name of unity* [Briefing paper].

Jordan, J.V., Walker, M., & Hartling, L.M. (Eds.). (2004). *The complexity of connection: Writings from the Jean Baker Miller training institute.* New York: Guilford Publications.

Kelman, H. C. (1990). Applying a human needs perspective to the practice of conflict resolution: The Israeli-Palestinian case. In J. Burton (Ed.), *Conflict: Human needs theory.* New York: St. Martin's Press.

Lantz, J. (1996). Logotherapy as trauma therapy. *Crisis intervention and time-limited treatment, 2*(3), 243–253.

Leatherman, J., DeMars, W., Gaffney, P.D., & Vayrynen, R. (1999). *Breaking cycles of violence: Conflict prevention in intrastate crises.* Bloomfield, CT: Kumarian Press.

Lederach, J. (1995). *Building peace: Sustainable reconciliation.* Tokyo: United Nations University.

Lederach, J.P. (1997). *Building peace: Sustainable reconciliation in divided societies.* Washington, DC: United States Institute of Peace Press.

MacNair, R.M. (2002). *Perpetration-induced traumatic stress: The psychological consequences of killing.* Westport, CT: Praeger Publishers/Greenwood Publishing Group.

Mamdani, M. (2002). *When victims become killers.* Princeton, NJ: Princeton University Press.

McCann, I.L., & Pearlman, L.A. (1990a). *Psychological trauma and the adult survivor: Theory, therapy, and transformation.* New York: Brunner/Mazel.

McCann, I.L., & Pearlman, L.A. (1990b). Vicarious traumatization: A framework for understanding the psychological effects of working with victims. *Journal of Traumatic Stress, 3*(1), 131–149.

Montville, J.V. (1993). The healing function in political conflict resolution. In D.J.D. Sandole & H. Van der Merve (Eds.), *Conflict resolution theory and practice: Integration and application.* Manchester, U.K.: Manchester University Press.

Newman, E., Riggs, D.S., & Roth, S. (1997). Thematic resolution, PTSD, and complex PTSD: The relationship between meaning and trauma-related diagnoses. *Journal of Traumatic Stress, 10*(2), 197–213.

Paluck, E.L., & Green, D.P. (2004, May/June). *Overview and working plan for the La Benevolencija impact evaluation study: The impact of Musekeweya: Changes in knowledge, attitudes, and behaviors. A randomized controlled trial.* Unpublished manuscript.

Pearlman, L.A. (2003). *Trauma and attachment belief scale manual.* Los Angeles: Western Psychological Services.

Pearlman, L.A., & Saakvitne, K.W. (1995). *Trauma and the therapist: Countertransference and vicarious traumatization in the treatment of incest survivors.* New York: Norton.

Penal Reform International. (2004, May). *Research report on the Gacaca VI. From camp to hill, the reintegration of released prisoners.* PRI Rwanda. BP 370. Kigali, Rwanda.

Pennebaker, J.W., & Beall, S.K. (1986). Confronting a traumatic event: Toward an understanding of inhibition and disease. *Journal of Abnormal Psychology, 95,* 274–281.

Pettigrew, T.F., & Tropp, L.R. (2000). Does intergroup contact reduce prejudice? Recent meta-analytic findings. In S. Oskamp (Ed.), *Reducing prejudice and discrimination.* London: Lawrence Erlbaum Associates.

Powers, S. (2002). *A problem from hell: America and the age of genocide.* New York: Basic Books.

Proceedings of Stockholm International Forum on Truth, Justice and Reconciliation. (2002).

Pyevich, C.M. (2002). *The relationship among cognitive schemata, job-related traumatic exposure, and PTSD in journalists.* Unpublished doctoral dissertation, University of Tulsa, Oklahoma.

Rando, T.A. (1993). *Treatment of complicated mourning.* Champaign, IL: Research Press.

Rhodes, G., Allen, G.J., Nowinski, J., & Cillessen, A. (2002). The violent socialization scale: Development and initial validation. In J. Ulmer & L. Athens (Eds.), *Violent acts and violentization: Assessing, applying, and developing Lonnie Athens' theories* (vol. 4, pp. 125–144). Elsevier Science.

Rosenbloom, D.J., & Williams, M.B. (1999). *Life after trauma.* New York: Guilford.

Ross, M.H., & Rothman, J. (1999). *Theory and practice in ethnic conflict management: Theorizing success and failure.* New York: Macmillian.

Rutagengwa, T. (2004, November). *La Benevolencija radio listening clubs rapport de feedback sur les episodes 22, 23, 24 et 25.* (We report on listening club feedback on episodes 22, 23, 24, and 25.) Unpublished manuscript.

Saakvitne, K.W., Gamble, S.G., Pearlman, L.A., & Lev, B.T. (2000). *Risking connection: A training curriculum for working with survivors of childhood abuse.* Lutherville, MD: Sidran Foundation & Press.

Saakvitne, K.W., Pearlman, L.A., & the Staff of the Traumatic Stress Institute. (1996). *Transforming the pain: A workbook on vicarious traumatization.* New York: Norton.

Staub, E. (1989). *The roots of evil: The origins of genocide and other group violence.* New York: Cambridge University Press.

Staub, E. (1996). The cultural-societal roots of violence: The examples of genocidal violence and of contemporary youth violence in the United States. *American Psychologist, 51,* 17–132.

Staub, E. (1998). Breaking the cycle of genocidal violence: Healing and reconciliation. In J. Harvey (Ed.), *Perspectives on loss.* Washington, DC: Taylor and Francis.

Staub, E. (1999). The origins and prevention of genocide, mass killing and other collective violence. *Peace and Conflict: Journal of Peace Psychology, 5,* 303–337.

Staub, E. (2003). *The psychology of good and evil: Why children, adults and groups help and harm others.* New York: Cambridge University Press.

Staub, E., & Bar-Tal, D. (2003). Genocide, mass killing and intractable conflict: Roots, evolution, prevention and reconciliation. In D. Sears, L. Huddy, & R. Jarvis (Eds.), *Handbook of political psychology.* New York: Oxford University Press.

Staub, E., & Pearlman, L.A. (2001). Healing, reconciliation, and forgiving after genocide and other collective violence. In S. J. Helmick & R.L. Petersen (Eds.), *Forgiveness and reconciliation: Religion, public policy and conflict transformation* (pp. 195–217). Radnor, PA: Templeton Foundation Press.

Staub, E., Pearlman, L.A., Gubin, A., & Hagengimana, A. (in press). Healing, reconciliation, and the prevention of violence after genocide or mass killing: An intervention and its experimental evaluation in Rwanda. *Journal of Clinical and Social Psychology.*

Tokayer, N. (2002). Spirituality and the psychological and physical symptoms of trauma. (Doctoral dissertation, University of Connecticut, 2002). *Dissertation Abstracts International, 63,* 1052.

Totten, S., Parsons, W. S., & Charny, I. W. (Eds.). (1997). *Century of genocide.* New York: Garland Publishing.

Uvin, P. (2003). *Wake up. Some policy proposals for the international community in Rwanda.* Unpublished manuscript.

Volkan, V. (1997). *Blood lines: From ethnic pride to ethnic terrorism.* New York: Farrar, Straus and Giroux.

Volkan, V.D. (1998). Tree model: Psychopolitical dialogues and the promotion of co-existence. In E. Weiner (Ed.), *The handbook of interethnic coexistence*. New York: Continuum.

Wessells, M., & Monteiro, C. (2001). Psychosocial intervention and post-war reconstruction in Angola: Interweaving western and traditional approaches. In D.J. Christie, R.V. Wagner, & D.D. Winter (Eds.), *Peace, conflict and violence: Peace psychology for the 21st century* (pp. 262–275). Upper Saddler River, NJ: Prentice Hall.

Willis, F.R. (1965). *France, Germany, and the New Europe, 1945–1963*. Palo Alto, CA: Stanford University Press.

Wortman, C. B., Battle, E., & Lemkau, J. P. (1997). Coming to terms with the sudden traumatic death of a spouse or child. In A. J. Lurigio, W. G. Skogan, & R. C. Davis (Eds.), *Victims of crime: Problems, policies and programs*. Newbury Park, CA: Sage.

CHAPTER 11

The Firehouse Project

New York City Post 9/11

Laura Barbanel, Warren Spielberg, Rachelle Dattner,
Elizabeth Goren, Ian Miller, Tom McGoldrick, and Nina Thomas

On September 11th, the worst terrorist attack on U.S. soil occurred. Its impact reverberated throughout the country, but most specifically in and around New York City, a major site of the attack. It was frightening, and 6 months later people were still feeling the effects psychologically (Silver, Holman, McIntosh, Poulin, & Gil-Rivas, 2002). It had caused special pain for those who lost loved ones; often there was no knowledge of how the individual died or why. There were no bodies to retrieve. First responders, including firefighters, New York City police, and Port Authority police were particularly affected, both because of their role in the rescue efforts and in the losses that their departments sustained. It was also a time when psychology and psychologists were called on to work in places and in contexts in which they do not typically function. Psychologists were called on to develop new techniques and new models.

This chapter describes the "Firehouse Project," developed by two of us (LB & WS) in conjunction with the counseling services of the Fire Department of New York City (FDNY), which each of the authors participated in from its inception. Paragraphs marked with initials note each author's personal experiences with the project.

This paper is based, in part, on a presentation: The Firehouse Project, at the American Psychological Association Division 39, 23 Annual Spring Meeting, Miami, March 2004.

In December 2001, each of us was assigned to a firehouse that had been affected (i.e., lost members), four in Manhattan and two in Brooklyn. Each of us became the resident firehouse counselor or "shrink."

The goals of the Firehouse Project were to bring didactic, clinical, and referral services directly to firefighters. In March, the FDNY expanded the program to include nearly every house (63 in all) that had lost members. The captain of the house had to agree to have a "counselor" in order for it to take place. Theoretically, clinicians were welcome in the house. That did not mean that all of the firefighters welcomed them. The program as we developed it and worked in it lasted approximately 2 years. The design was simple, although each of us carried it out a bit differently. Each of us was assigned to a firehouse and visited the firehouse approximately once a week for a few hours (some did more and some less). Initially we were expected to do a psycho education group. After the first time, some of us continued to sit with the men in a group at the kitchen table; others did less of the group discussion and more one-on-one (as the firefighters called it). In general, we all did a lot of hanging around, waiting to be called on. Each of the authors had previously worked in the area of trauma and in some other post-9/11 work.

Firefighters faced many new issues. Death is not unknown to them, but the enormity of the numbers lost here was unprecedented. Firefighters wished to offer solace to the families of the deceased, as was their tradition, but they were fearful of being overwhelmed by the enormity of the needs of the families of their fallen comrades. They were attending memorials, wakes, and funerals for months, working down at the World Trade Center (WTC) site, cleaning up, which meant looking through the rubble for body parts. This meant spending little time with their own families, who were complaining about their absence. Visitors, presumably seeking to be of help and comfort to them but also at times becoming a burden, were inundating their firehouses. The firefighter became the symbol of 9/11 and many wanted to be near them, to touch them, to give and to receive solace from them. The tradition of always being welcoming to visitors was being strained. Considered heroes by the public, many firefighters felt they had failed. After all, they had not been able to save their own, nor even recover all of the bodies. They felt that the department and the city had failed them. If they had had better radios, more would have been saved, fewer would have perished. In addition to the losses they experienced, senior men were being transferred and retiring, so that the individual houses were changing manpower very quickly and dramatically. If they did not lose their buddies through death, it was through transfer and retirement. They were angry, mournful, and overwhelmed by it all. They did not have the psychological tools to deal with what they were feeling.

GENERAL ISSUES

Culture

General agreement exists among firefighters that problems are best kept in the house among the brothers and sisters and that discussing weakness is not a good idea. "Protective shields" that have served them over the years are the bonds of family, which includes the greater family of the house and the "brothers" more generally, the feeling of having a job with a purpose, and the rituals and traditions of the department (Taylor & Wolin, 2002). All three of these create a connectedness that serves to heal and reassure. After 9/11 these shields were no longer working. The family was shattered, the purpose was clouded by what was seen as defeat on the job, and the traditions, particularly the mourning rituals, were breaking their hearts.

Clinicians assigned to firehouses came with their own cultural mores as well. Each of the authors is a trained psychoanalyst, more typically working in a context where individuals come to see us based on referral or position. We live in a context in which introspection and revealing one's vulnerability is viewed as strength.

As we entered the firehouses we were coming into someone else's home. And the firehouse is considered a home, with a kitchen, bedrooms, and the floor where the fire fighting apparatuses are. There are officers who are the parents, and there are younger and older siblings. Although we were invited, the prohibition on communicating with strangers was strong. We felt both welcome and unwelcome from the first day to the last. This ambivalence toward psychology and psychologists was one of the greatest problems in the work. "I talk to my priest, not my shrink" was a comment heard in the houses. Gender was another important cultural issue. The firehouse, despite having an occasional woman firefighter, is essentially a male enclave. At the time of our project there were 22 women in the FDNY out of 11,500 firefighters. The women among us were responded to differently than the men, but we do not know how to describe that difference in the work. Some men were clearly more comfortable with a male counselor; some seemed to feel that it was easier to speak to a woman. Clearly, understanding male psychology and male group psychology in particular is important (Spielberg, 1993) to this work.

Although there were some glaring differences in the cultures from which the firefighters and the clinicians came, there was also a crucial similarity: Both groups consider themselves "helpers."

Confidentiality

The issue of confidentiality, a cornerstone of clinical work as we practice it, had to be looked at differently. Since we were told things on the run and in an informal context, it wasn't clear what could be said to whom. In our work we typically operate with great care and attention to confidentiality. What then does one do with a communication that is shared leaning up against a fire truck? Or told with three men sitting at a kitchen table? Does that mean the others know? When a guy tells you he is going out on leave or getting engaged or that his wife is pregnant, is that common knowledge? When someone tells you about a fight he has been in with another guy in the kitchen, if it comes up, do you acknowledge knowing it or not?

Structural Issues

Most of us were in houses that consisted of two companies, a ladder (or truck) and an engine. The truck finds the fire; the "truckees" find the survivors and work in the building of the fire. The engine members pump the water and put out the fire. There is always some rivalry between the two companies. The question of whose job is harder or more important, comes up all of the time. Each company has its own officers, its own characteristics, its own nickname, its own history and mythology. The "house," typically composed of a ladder and a truck, is the greater family. When we first arrived, companies were taken "out of service" for our group sessions. After a while this was deemed inappropriate and/or impolitic. So group sessions became more scattered and at times more chaotic.

Can you run a group when the bells are ringing; members of the house come in and out of the room? Can you run a group when you have a class clown, when only a few show up, and others have some reason (excuse?) not to be there? This became even more complicated because each time you arrived you could be seeing a different complement of firefighters, because of the complex work schedules they have.

Working with the firefighters in groups seemed an appropriate method, since the disaster happened to them as a group; it was a community disaster. Furthermore they were used to the group as their shield and their strength. It seemed the apt place for healing. And yet, individuals had their own trauma, their own issues. Each man or woman had his or her own story. The balance between the group and individual needs had to be determined.

Context

The political and social meaning of the World Trade Center attack weighed on the firefighters. The loss of 343 of their colleagues was enormous. They were considered the symbol of the atrocity and were made weary by it. They could not show vulnerability both for themselves and for the communities that expected so much of them.

Countertransference

Each of us chose this work with idiosyncratic reasons, be it our personal history of trauma or our need to be part of history. We wanted deeply to be accepted and helpful. We worried when we felt unwanted. We seemed to be on the lookout for signs of our effectiveness and feared we were not wanted much of the time. The lack of a clear therapeutic stance in protected clinical settings, such as those with which we were all familiar, created anxiety for us. These anxieties persisted even after the positive feedback of the project. It is not surprising then that one of the major countertransferential reactions we had to deal with was the fear that we were "not helpful and not wanted."

BEGINNINGS

Each of us was escorted on our first visit by a "peer counselor" who was supposed to introduce us and smooth our way into the firehouse. In some instances the peer stayed around; in others he left immediately. We introduced ourselves, told them a bit about the effects of trauma and why we were there. We had captive audiences in the first session, since the firefighters were called together by their officers. The intention was to provide some information on the psychological residue of trauma, to normalize the symptoms that many of them were experiencing. Some comparisons were made to the Oklahoma bombing. One of us got stony silence from his group; others had delivered a lot of complaints and anger, at the department for being let down in the tragedy, at the city for them not having a work contract. When asked about sadness, most drew a blank. In one group an officer said, "We don't talk about sadness, because anger is strong, sadness is weak." Each of us after the first session felt drained and challenged, knowing what we were supposed to do, but not quite sure how to do it.

It became clear that to be accepted we could not be aloof or anonymous. We had to be real; we had to be ourselves. These men and women judge individuals by their character, not by their role. They are uncomfortable with therapeutic neutrality or pretense, but wish to know those with whom they work. In this project we came to their work/homes and tried to entice groups of individuals, who did not know us or ask us to come, to open up to us. We had to learn about the job, from knowing about the apparatuses to knowing about the customs. We had to fit into their lives.

In contrast to stereotypes, however, we frequently found that many of them were able to self-disclose, were interested in learning about their psychological selves, and were ready to help and share their feelings with those they trusted. That, however, happened only when it was clear that we were part of the family. Although we were never truly a member of the family, there was a point at which each of us became trusted enough for openness, something that would not have been possible when we first arrived. We became the "inside-outsiders." We ate with them, celebrated with them, mourned with them. Somehow each of us broke through in his or her own way.

Some of us continued to do the groups with psycho educational content: anger management and relationships. The content varied depending on the individuals that participated. Some of us mostly "hung round," waiting to be needed. In that respect our position mimicked their own; after all, while the majority of the time at their job was not responding to emergencies, it was critical that they be there, ready when the emergency did occur.

These issues were so perplexing and in some ways so out of the realm of our ordinary experience that we felt an urgent need to meet and talk about them. Thus the group of us met monthly to discuss what we were doing and to gather support. We met in each other's homes, perhaps recreating the firehouse kitchen and the firehouse family. We worried about our effectiveness working with a group that is typically resistant to enterprises like psychotherapy, but mostly we worried about being needed and being helpful.

LB

The example that demonstrated this most dramatically to me was that of Evin, a lieutenant that I had spoken to briefly over the first few months. On the day of the closing of the WTC site, which was a day of some note in the firehouse, there was a breakfast and the families of the deceased were invited. I was there, standing around with a coffee cup in my hand. Evin came into the kitchen, saw me, and with a rather stern, morose look on his face said rather gruffly, "Oh, you're here. I need to talk to you." I assumed he wanted to tell me, since he was an officer, that I was no longer needed. We went outside to the street (the door to the house was open), leaned against the truck, and he started to tell me that his marriage was falling apart and the reasons for it. We spoke, or I should say I listened, for a half hour. And like a family when some members are busy, nobody came to interrupt. His gruffness was not for me but for the benefit of his men, lest they think he was needy and had to speak to the shrink.

PROCESS

It became clear that a variety of approaches were necessary, both group and individual. Firefighters were suffering from anger at their losses and from what they perceived as their mistreatment; they needed to memorialize, they were in conflict over the expression of survival guilt and their family pressures, and they needed to heal. There was a need for each of them to develop an individual narrative and to attempt to make some sense out of what was senseless.

EG

Managing the roller coaster of anger, sorrow, and helplessness was an on-going countertransference challenge. The guys in my house referred to our groups as "bitch sessions" and, although some of the men found the unrelenting resentment demoralizing after a while, others found relief in simply feeling heard by someone from the outside. They felt helpless in grief, in their doomed rescue efforts, in their ability to console each other and the grieving families, or to do anything to prevent another catastrophe. I felt helpless to relieve their pain. All I could do was listen and try to absorb what they were saying, without putting so much distance between me and them that they would feel alienated, or so little distance that they would have to take care of me. Our strongest bond was our shared identity as helper.

RD

In my initial approach, I found myself relying in the firehouse on my dual heritage—that of a Jew familiar with *Shiva* rituals, and that of a psychoanalyst trained to contain intense expressions of feeling. I would typically go into the kitchen of the firehouse without an agenda, and wait until someone spoke to me. Sometimes I felt I was simply "shooting the breeze," but invariably someone would show up and pour his heart out or ask for a referral or advice. The sequence was predictable. They would start by asking for advice on dealing with a child. For example, frequent nightmares, or a 5-year old terrified that his Afghani classmate would harm him.

IM

Sometimes I worked with individuals standing next to fire trucks almost certain to be called out to work within the next 10 minutes. Interestingly, during these talks, especially in the beginning, we each looked forward, with scarce eye contact. In a setting where social conviviality was the norm, this felt significant to me. Each of these men could look squarely at one another, in a joke, in anger at some worldly event, in telling his official "story" of 9/11. Yet, here, leaning back on the rig, the lack of visual contact reminded me of the qualitative change from patients' use of a chair to the use of a couch. Very spontaneously, without instruction, these firemen had located the freedom of the couch within their physical space. As with analytic patients, I felt myself present for these firemen in my use as witness, even as I remained unknown to them except in a comment of clarification, summation, or requested guidance.

Memorials
RD

Apart from the demands of the constant visitors, there were many memorial activities. One that stands out was held on a glorious spring day, 1 year and 9 months after 9/11. All the firefighters, and the wives and children of the deceased, gathered on the roof of the *Intrepid*, the aircraft carrier moored in the Hudson River, a short walk from the firehouse. The occasion was the dedication a bas-relief sculpture destined for the outside wall of the firehouse.

The relief's image was derived from Michelangelo's *Pieta*, reflecting the sentiment that, like Christ, the firefighters had died for us. There were strong religious overtones to many of these observances—consistent with the overwhelmingly Catholic upbringing of the firefighters. At each gathering there was a priest in attendance, and sometimes a rabbi as well. A movement is under way to canonize Father Michael Judge—the much loved FDNY chaplain who died administering last rites and was the first identified fatality of 9/11.

After all the funerals and memorial services, there were relentless requests that they attend a vast array of commemorations. Many families of the deceased firefighters made demands: from attendance at a street naming to the request that a dead firefighter's locker be preserved as a shrine in the firehouse so that the widow and children could come and pay homage. As time went by, the firemen began to articulate their exhaustion with these events and expressed resentment that their own needs and those of their own families were being overlooked.

In addition to the names on the shirts and pictures on the walls, various other forms of markings memorialized the fallen firefighters. The most personal memorial observances were the tattoos acquired by many of the men. These tattoos have multiple functions: they are intended to be badges of pride of belonging to a particular community; they bring an interior wound to the surface of the body; and they are emblems of loss.

All of the tattoos I saw contained the following: the firehouse code 5–5–5–5—representing the four sets of bells that signal the death of a firefighter; 55–8087—the box number which is the designation of the location of the World Trade Center; the date 9/11/2001; and, around the periphery of the insignia, which depicts the twin towers framed by an American flag, the initials of all the men who perished from their firehouse. That the vocabulary of these tattoos is instantly recognizable by all firefighters—and not by others—underscores their function as a sign of membership in a select brotherhood.

On another level, the tattoo provides a link with the dead, by offering up the body of the survivor as the site of a memorial. It is also a vehicle of identification with the dead by having submitted the body to a painful procedure in which the living flesh is forever altered. Some of the firefighters with whom I spoke about their tattoos seemed both relieved and slightly disappointed that the procedure was not as painful as they had anticipated.

Another kind of marking extended the boundaries of the brotherhood to include soldiers in Iraq. The firehouse is, after all, a quasi-military setting, and many of the men served in the military before joining the Fire Department. They were thrilled to have partnered with their "brothers" in Iraq. A squadron of F-18 Super Hornets dedicated their deployment to this firehouse. Each of the squadron's jets—the first Super Hornets deployed for combat by the Navy—has painted on it the name of a deceased firefighter from the firehouse. The squadron's pilots have patches that bear the insignia of the firehouse, and the firefighters have the squadron's patches.

Each group has told the other how honored they were to be so linked. The essence of this link seems to be that the pilots would avenge the deaths of the firefighters. One man at a firehouse objected: he believed firefighters live to *save* lives—he felt the names of the firefighters on these "killing machines" were an improper memorial. He was courageous to express this unpopular opinion, and was for this expression maligned and heaped with contempt by the others. This pressure to conform is one of the downsides of the tight brotherhood.

TM

I arrived at the house and a number of members were sporting elaborate tattoos with the names of their fallen brothers. The tattoos were raw, painful looking, and in unnaturally bright colors that would eventually fade over time. Each of the newly marked discussed in gruesome detail the tattooing process. This led to a series of stories abut people scarring themselves for someone they love. A burly lieutenant stated: "I know a guy who got his long-awaited transfer to Rescue 2. He decided to brand himself with R2."

A firefighter asked, "What if he gets transferred?" I thought of the permanency of the tattoos, their rawness, their fading, and the possibility of switching allegiances. I stated: "Scars fade. The pain grows less. But it is always there." The lieutenant stated: "I will never get over what they did to our brothers. That will always be with me like this tattoo."

WS

As the mourning process deepened over the winter, the men that I saw moved from a numbed, frozen guilt to a more therapeutic depression (Balint, 1953). A memorial wall was constructed, and only then was some other construction in the house done.

Firefighters are resilient people. Their group cohesiveness and prescribed mourning rituals served them well in dealing with the traumatic events of 9/11. The Fire Department rituals will go on—the brass plaques installed for fallen firefighters 1 year after their deaths remain on the walls, a yearly memorial service is held for the fallen at the Firefighters Memorial, and the annual commemorations in each firehouse will continue to be a comfort and a gathering place for the survivors.

From Heroes to Zeros

There are "no heroic acts left to be performed," Joe McGuiness pronounced to a disillusioned post-Vietnam America in his book (McGuiness, 1976, p. 21). Since then, thanks to technology, real-life death and destruction have become part of what Susan Sontag referred to as the routine small screen entertainment (Sontag, 2003) that we see to which we have become inured. That is, until September 11th, when the whole world became virtual eyewitnesses, cyberspectators in real time of nearly 3000 people vaporized incomprehensibly in a matter of moments when the World Trade Center collapsed. In our collective grief and vulnerability we watched those final moments and the rescue turned recovery effort replayed over and over, watching firefighters journey into and re-emerge from the destroyed World Trade Center, the area that came to be called Ground Zero. Haunted by these images in a disembodied nightmare, we made these men, who bore the imprint of a reality we could only imagine, into our culture's mythological heroic figures, whom we endowed with supernatural power and knowledge, appointing them the standard bearers of truth. Initially we needed to feel through our contact with them the crushing reality of what had happened, to brush them as they brushed death. Then, when we needed to distance ourselves from our collective pain and defeat, when we needed to move on, we turned away from these men, heroic but real, humanly flawed individuals whose struggles continue to this day. As firehouse clinicians brought into houses that had suffered what the department euphemistically termed "sustained losses," we became the inside-outsiders, privileged with the role of bearing witness and traversing a developing breach between the world at large and the firefighters through the survival and healing process.

From the comfort of our living rooms, we could idealize and feel for our heroes, at an emotionally safe distance from the visceral actuality these men embodied to their very core. When the firefighters closed the doors to their firehouses to mourn in private, we were content to corral these trauma carriers away from contagion, and to seal off our sense of defeat, so that we could once again feel an America endowed with life and power. Inside the firehouse, the pain congealed into isolation, alienation, and anger; the anger organized and masked less acceptable feelings of fear and powerlessness.

EG

A clever cynicism took hold in my house, expressed in comments like, "It'll pass. Today we're heroes, but soon we'll be back to being zeroes. They'll honk when we block the streets and complain that we don't work hard enough for our big pensions. When the dust settles, we'll be as interesting as the next bit on the 11 o'clock news." Some insisted that the public was using them to rubberneck and assuage their own guilt.

And somewhere along the line that did change. Article after article about firefighter's failings started appearing in 2003 and 2004, articles about DWI firefighters, about brawls in the firehouses, about sexual misconduct (Jacobson, 2004). It culminated with the mayor, in his expression of anger at firefighters' criticism of the fire commissioner, claiming firefighters should "look in the mirror" and "stop drinking on the job, using drugs . . . ." (Wilson & McIntyre, 2004). Two years before that, no New York City mayor would have dared to criticize the NYC firefighters in this way. Would the articles have been written? We can speculate as to whether firefighters are "misbehaving" to a greater extent than they did prior to 9/11, or whether the misconduct was a product of the disorganization of 9/11, or whether it was the media's need to discredit the former heroes.

EG

The 2-year anniversary ceremony came; the one dedicated to the men who were there that day and who had worked at Ground Zero. There, after the ritual honoring of badges, the guys broke into a spontaneous round of applause to the one man who had spearheaded the surviving company's escape from the building moments before the collapse. Through their crisis of faith and doubts about their own heroism, they too still seemed to want to believe that at least one among them had been a hero.

Survival Guilt

WS

Robert Lifton (1979) explicated the dynamics of survivors. I have found Lifton's distinctions between static and animated guilt to be useful in this context. When I first arrived in the house, many were numb, stuck in rage, and grappling with negative identifications of cowardice and helplessness. These "static" and frozen states coincided with a deep resistance to acknowledging their feelings and sharing them with others. Some were close to the fallen men, had trained with them, identified with them and their "deadness" (Smith, 1971). Men who were relieved to be alive could not voice their relief at being alive out of fear of offending the dead. Was their survival itself an act of cowardice?

LB

Billy was a shy firefighter in his mid-thirties, who was known, however, for his angry outbursts. As a chauffeur (driver) he would often get into near fights with taxi drivers who were in the truck's way (taxi drivers are the natural enemies of urban firefighters) in a way that belied his mild manners and shy demeanor. As I was conducting a group on anger management, he whispered to me on the side a question about his anger at his children. He said he would like to see me privately. We arranged it quietly in a way that nobody else would know. In our private sessions, he told me his life story. Abandoned by his father, he was raised by his mother in a neighborhood where he was one of the few of his ethnic background. He became a firefighter out of a wish "to help." He had married his childhood sweetheart and had two school-age boys at the time. He found that he was getting impatient with his boys around particularly issues related to homework. We spoke a great deal about his two children, his wish to be a good father, and his own difficulty with schoolwork. He had felt enormous stress at work since 9/11: the depression, the vying for who could do more for the widows, for the firehouse in general. He felt bad about not having been there on 9/11. He was off that day. But he felt a terrible loss. One of the guys who had been killed was a special friend of his. Two days before his friend had been killed Billy had had a terrible fight with him. He could not get that out of his mind. He wept. He said, "He was such a great guy. I know he knew that the fight didn't mean anything, that I loved

him and would do anything for him. I think he would have forgiven me."
I concurred quietly.

Billy did not come to see me after that, but about a month later I saw him
on the apparatus floor. He said, "Doc, thanks for your help. I have become
more patient with my kids."

EG

Tim Jones (all names here are fictitious) and I were standing awkwardly without
the security of drinks in our hand at a local bar holding a fundraiser for the
firehouse widows and their children. He began, "I was on the roster for that
morning. I was supposed to be there. But I had a death in my family had and I
wanted to go to the wake. Stevie Jones was my mutual partner. So I called him
real early that morning and asked if he could cover for me." The mutual partner
is the one the firefighter looks to first and counts on when he needs a favor. Stevie understood his mutual partner's need and offered to take Tim's place on the
11th. " 'No problem,' he said to me. 'Gotcha covered, buddy.' I think he said,"
Tim told me, and then went on. "So you see, it was a Jones for a Jones. How can
I not feel . . . I don't know . . .?" "Guilty?" I said, tossing the obvious therapeutic
balloon into the air. "Yeah, I guess . . . don't know." Of course he was gripped
with guilt, but we both knew that survivor guilt was the facile, oversimplified
explanation, an easy out for me, and a way for me to feel I understood.

Though he didn't say anything to me at that moment, Jones wasn't going
to let himself or me off the hook that easily. For him, there was no escape,
no relief from what Robert Jay Lifton (1979) calls the death immersion, its
shroud hung over his home and his firehouse, whose doors were draped in
black, above flags which hung at half mast, makeshift memorials with donations flowing in from a well-meaning public that needed to help. Tim proceeded to explain that his mother was afflicted with the very same form of
terminal cancer that had taken his aunt. "Strange, huh?" he remarked, in a
self-mocking tone. He probably would have stopped right there if he had any
idea just how strange the whole situation felt to me at that moment. I was
trying to wrap my mind around the idea of a Jones for a Jones, how even with
9/11 life is vanquished by the banality of disease. Jones went on to explain
that he was "Okay" and that his main problem wasn't "this," glancing over to
his buddies huddled together at the bar, bonding in their sorrow-laced teas-
ing humor. No, it was his 7-year-old kid who was having a problem at school
where they were talking all the time about the disaster. He just didn't know
what to do, and he was worried about his wife, who was left alone to deal

with everything while he had to keep working extra shifts at Ground Zero. Jones made it clear to anyone who would listen that he at least was no hero. He wasn't even there when it happened, arriving by noon, but too late—too late to find his mutual partner.

Despite his disdain for other guys' "taking advantage" of what they called "the free trips and stuff," finally even Jones got an offer he couldn't refuse: a trip to London and a visit with the Queen! With a snicker, he described the trip by describing how "they paraded us around, dinners and photographers." Then he grudgingly admitted, "But we had a good time, the kids liked it." Did Jones finally realize that his refusal to accept help wasn't going to stop people from trying to help, or that his passive aggressive effort to deprive others of a relief he could not personally find did no one any good, or maybe it was simply that all humans have a price? Eventually Jones, like many firefighters, even many men who had been more responsive to the therapy programs, could not get past things in their firehouses that held so much memory. So when his brothers' patience for his mean spiritedness had worn thin and when his pain finally outweighed his loyalty to the firehouse, he asked to be reassigned as far away from Ground Zero as possible, and few said they were sorry to see him go. I do not know what became of him.

The bereft firefighters of New York City 4 months after 9/11 needed to hold onto something, but the only thing they had left to believe in was their own ability to simply keep going. Jones made it clear to anyone who would listen that he at least was no hero.

Shame

In addition to feelings of guilt, many firefighters expressed, always privately, feelings of shame at their failures on 9/11. Spielberg (1993) points out that for men shame is based on their difficulty integrating their emotional needs. In adulthood shame gets integrated through the construction of a heroic identity. Although heroism was negated by the firefighters, the concept served to temper their shame. They both needed it and rejected it.

ENDINGS

Despite all of the ambivalence described, in surveys done in the firehouses that had clinicians, 70% of the firefighters indicated that they felt the program was helpful. Firefighters in others houses asked for the program as well. Clinicians also reported great satisfaction with the program.

Perhaps the clinical vignettes are even more revealing:

RD

I believe some of the men were changed. To quote one of the men who initially came to therapy reluctantly, at his wife's insistence: "Doc, when I talk to you, it is as if I am looking behind a curtain. In my whole life, I never even knew there was a curtain there."

LB

A lieutenant said to me the last day I was officially in the house, "Doc, I did not like your being here at first, but you worked on me, and I think you may have even helped some of the guys. I know you helped me."

SUMMARY

Each of us threw ourselves into an unfamiliar setting with the tools that we have, most importantly that of listener. We bore witness to the experiences of the firefighters. We facilitated the "symbolization" of the experience into language and we offered the opportunity to reflect on the experience, both individually and in the group. We did this in the natural setting in which these men and women live and work. This involved, for us, inserting ourselves into a world and a culture that for the most part was not familiar to us.

As Dori Laub tells us, "The listener to a narrative of trauma actually listens to an event that has not yet been symbolized or recorded." The victim, although fresh from the experience, frequently blocks the recognition of it. As the listener hears it, the trauma is actually being born. The record gets created. (Laub, 1991).

The listener then becomes co-owner of the event; by his listening, he or she experiences the trauma. The listener, the clinician, is therefore in danger of being traumatized as well. (Figley, 1995; Pearlman, 1995; Pearlman & Saakvitne, 1995). One important function of our peer group was to foreclose this possibility.

The fear of trauma occurring again happens when the memory of the trauma becomes clear. As firefighters spoke about the event and the feelings around it, they spoke also about their fears of future terrorist attacks. All of the country was speaking of that anxiety, but for the firefighters it was particularly poignant. Is the act of telling in itself traumatizing? The price of telling may be relief or may be reliving of the experience. This issue is an important debate in the trauma literature.

In Edna Foa's Prolonged Exposure therapy for PTSD, it is postulated that the reliving of the trauma helps the individual organize the trauma memory and therefore helps change the memory schema (Foa & Riggs, 1993). Laub (1992) states that telling of the trauma becomes retraumatizing when the listener is not truly listening. The task of the listener then is to be there, unobtrusive but clearly listening. It is a difficult role but an invaluable one. Perhaps our particular relationship to the men and women in the house, of being there for them but not as regular employees of the department, was especially important. A number of men reported on the importance of that aspect of our role with them.

The losses of 9/11 remind us of our connections to one another. Our personal and cultural tendencies toward narcissism, the isolation of our communities and our refusal to interweave death and mourning into our rituals, move us to forget this. After 9/11 we were all moved to "connect" to others, to connect to our communities. The sacrifices of the firefighters in our community bring us back to this truth. We must remember our own debt to those who perished and to those who survived as well. In this is the beginning of healing.

REFERENCES

Balint, M. (1953). New beginning and the paranoid and depressive syndromes, *Int. J. Psychonol*, 33: 214–224.

Figley, C. (1995). Compassion fatigue: Toward a new understanding of the cost of caring. In B. Hudnall Stamm (Ed.), *Secondary traumatic stress* (pp. 3–28). Lutherville, MD: Sidran Press.

Foa, E.B., & Riggs, D.S. (1993). Post traumatic stress disorder in rape victims. In J. Oldman, M.B. Riba, & A. Tasman (Eds.), *American psychiatric press review of psychiatry* (vol. 12, pp. 273–303). Washington, DC: American Psychiatric Press.

Jacobson, M. (2004, December 20). Firefighters lost their halos. *New York Magazine.*

Laub, D. (1992). Bearing witness or the vicissitudes of change. In S. Felman & D. Laub (Eds.), *Testimony: Crisis of witnessing in literature, analysis and history* (pp. 57–74). New York: Routledge.

Lifton, R.J. (1979). *The broken connections.* New York: Simon & Schuster.

McGiness, J. (1976). *Heroes.* New York: Viking Press.

Pearlman, L.A. (1995). Self care for trauma therapists: Ameliorating vicarious traumatization. In B. Hudnall Stamm (Ed.), *Secondary traumatic stress* (pp. 51–65). Lutherville, MD: Sidran Press.

Pearlman, L.A., & Saakvitne, K. (1995). *Trauma and the therapist.* New York: Norton.

Silver, R. C., Holman, E. A., McIntosh, D. N., Poulin, M., & Gil-Rivas, V. (2002). Nationwide longitudinal study of psychological responses to September 11. *Journal of the American Medical Association, 288*, 1235–1244.

Smith (1971). Identificatory styles in depression and grief. *International Journal of Psychoanalysis, 52,* 259–266.

Sontag, S. (2003). *Regarding the pain of others.* New York: Farrar, Straus, and Giroux.

Spielberg, W. (1993). Why men must be heroic. *Journal of Men's Studies, 2* (2), 173–188.

Taylor,V., & Wolin, S. (2002). *The new normal.* New York: Counseling Service Unit, FDNY.

Wilson, M. (2004, December 8). Firefighters lash out at commissioners, angering Bloomberg. *New York Times, B3.*

Part III

Synthesis

CHAPTER 12

Lessons Learned

What Do We Know About Psychological Interventions for Victims of Crisis?

Robert J. Sternberg

In this volume, prominent psychologists recount their experiences in dealing with victims of crisis, and also describe interventions they have used to help these victims cope with the devastation these crises have caused. In this final chapter, I consider some of the lessons that have been learned from the experiences of the authors and their colleagues. I make no attempt to recount every lesson learned. But I hope that the lessons mentioned here will assist readers who themselves need to aid victims of crisis, who train those who intervene, or who, in the worst of scenarios, themselves undergo the kinds of crises described in this book. My goal in the chapter, then, is to summarize from the book what I believe are the main lessons learned.

1. *Those most in need of help are often those who are most difficult to reach.* In a disaster, some victims are much more accessible than others. The most accessible ones often tend to be those who are salient in the affected community, who in turn are often middle class or somehow part of the visible social structure. But as Mukherjee and Alpert point out, the members of marginalized segments of communities are typically those who are most affected by crises. They are also the ones with the fewest coping resources and the ones who are hardest to reach. Carr worked in Africa with members of communities rarely seen by trained help-givers at all. Dybdahl worked in Bosnia-Herzegovina at

a time that most people would understandably have been afraid to be anywhere near the area. Macomber and Grigorenko note how difficult and dangerous it was to reach those affected by the radiation of the Chernobyl event. Other essays make the same basic point. Those who wish to be helpers in crises often put themselves in harm's way and at substantial risk. This kind of work is not for the faint of heart.

2. *An important role for help-givers is identifying others who, individually or in teams, can be of service.* In a typical psychotherapeutic situation, a single psychotherapist handles the bulk of the professional work. Occasionally, psychiatrists, social workers, or others may have to be brought in, but in the majority of cases, a single therapist is responsible for the results. As pointed out by Dybdahl, the situation is quite different in the treatment of acute distress from disasters, especially when people arrive on the scene of a natural disaster. There are so many different kinds of needs of so many people—psychological, medical, resource-related, and so forth—that typically a single individual could not provide all the help that is needed. Mukherjee and Alpert refer to the mobilization of support networks. Jacobs and Meyer speak of psychological first-aid, most of it administered by nonprofessionals or, at best, by paraprofessionals. In this case, one has to be especially careful in delegating tasks, for there are many tasks for which people who are not professionally trained are not equipped and for which their intervention potentially could do more harm than good. That is why Jacobs and Meyer clearly distinguish psychological first-aid from disaster-based professional mental health interventions. Carr has worked as part of a Mobile Member Care Team. Stamm and Hudnall speak of teams of people who work via telecommuting to help treat victims of disasters. The Firehouse Project of Barbanel and her colleagues was team-based. Dale and Alpert also worked as part of a team in treating victims after 9/11. Disasters almost always require teams of people to meet all the needs that arise.

3. *Working on disaster relief may generate symptoms in help-givers.* Psychotherapy always requires its practitioners to be made of sturdy stuff. But disaster relief requires what comes close to a psychological Kevlar vest. One is working with people who are hurting in grievous ways, and one may oneself be victimized by some of the same forces affecting the people one treats. Carr notes how caregivers in the remote parts of Africa in which she works are subject to a whole variety of hazards, from diseases to street crime to war crimes. Many of them not only treat victims of violence, but become victims of violence themselves.

Dybdahl worked in hazardous areas. Macomber and Grigorenko note the large numbers of people who put themselves at risk trying to help radiation victims. Many of those who braved the radiation seeking to help others themselves later died of acute radiation poisoning. There are physical dangers, there are psychological dangers, and there is the constant wear and tear of dealing with people who are way out on the edge. Perhaps most notable in these cases is just how unpredictable situations of help-giving can be or become. One never knows when "the other shoe" will drop, and the caregiver, like the care-receiver, will become susceptible to trauma. With the exception of telecommuters such as Stamm and Hudnall, caregivers are out there exposing themselves to many of the same dangers as their clients. As Carr notes, many caregivers in Africa, especially church workers, are expected to be on call 24 hours a day. Similarly, when 9/11 struck, there was little rest for the weary. The disaster and its aftermath could not wait for weekend holidays, planned vacations, or even, often, until the next day. Dale and Alpert, or Barbanel and her colleagues, might well have had other tasks that were pressing in their lives. Many of these tasks doubtless had to be put aside. When one chooses to work in disaster relief, one is "out there" in every sense of the word. One hears about things such as, in Carr's work, rapes, disembowelments, people being made to clap and dance as their houses are burned down, and people being buried alive, that one might not hear anywhere else. This kind of work requires tremendous courage and resilience.

4. *There are no easy formulas.* Manualized treatment is becoming something of a rage, at least among some scientists who believe that greater standardization and uniformity of care will result in many outcomes for clients of psychotherapy. Manualized treatment is unlikely to make its way to disaster relief anytime soon. This is not to say that there are no steps that can be codified. On the contrary, there certainly are things one can do in almost any traumatic situation, such as feel empathy and listen to what one's clients have to say. But standardized treatments begin to break down in the face of the vast variety of circumstances that can confront the caregiver in response both to natural and human-generated disasters. Mukherjee and Alpert point out mixed results for cognitive-behavioral therapy (CBT), and suggest that some of the techniques of CBT seem to apply and others do not. Certainly, in the case of the radiation disaster described by Macomber and Grigorenko, much better care should have been taken by authorities to protect caregivers. But, at that point, one can assume that some

of them were not fully cognizant of the risks involved. Cohen has described useful procedures involving play for childhood victims of trauma, but in reading her chapter one cannot help sense how individual each case is, and how much in need each case is of attention to the circumstances of the various particular traumas of terrorism. Staub and Pearlman seem to have devised a program that can be tailored to many of the victims and perpetrators of genocide in Rwanda. It will be interesting to see in the future to what extent it can be applied in diverse circumstances. Their program, like that described by Dybdahl, may provide at least some generality of application in a field in which generality is not easily achieved. Almost certainly, there will not be a uniform drug treatment. As Mukherjee and Alpert note, no one drug treatment is likely to work for all the symptoms that can arise from disasters.

5. *People benefit most if they want to be helped.* Bonanno and Mancini make the point about victims of disasters that applies ultimately to all clients of psychotherapy: Those clients are helped most who want to be helped. Barbanel and her colleagues, too, found some firefighters who were used to and might well have preferred options other than those their team could provide, such as talking to their priest. Part of the therapist's job, especially for victims of tragedy, may be convincing potential clients that something of value is to be offered, and that accepting that something of value is safe. Macomber and Grigorenko report of victims of Chernobyl who did not want to be helped. A substantial number of the afflicted ultimately returned, even illegally, to the areas of contamination. Dealing with such behavior, which can be physically self-destructive for the returnees, is no easy chore. Does one force such people to move again or, because they are adults, let them choose what may be a slow and painful death as a result of radiation poisoning?

6. *Diagnosis is necessary but especially difficult under the circumstances in which people in crisis are found.* As Bonanno and Mancini point out, it is often difficult to distinguish acute grief from chronic depressive episodes among victims of trauma. And there may be a whole host of symptoms among people who have experienced disasters. To ensure good results, one must know what one is treating. Macomber and Grigorenko point out how difficult it was, especially for victims, to identify the extent to which their problems were caused by the events at Chernobyl. Many victims continued to blame the accident for almost anything that went wrong in their lives. Macomber and

Grigorenko quote a poem in which children of Chernobyl refer to themselves as "doomed" and as having "no future." It is hard for the children to figure out what havoc Chernobyl wrought. And some of the people affected, who lived far away from the sight of the disaster but who received wind-borne radiation, will never know that Chernobyl did them in. It will be no easy task for the therapist, any more than for the physician, in such cases to figure out what caused what.

7. *People respond to the same traumas in many different ways.* Cohen notes the ways in which play therapy can be used to understand the variety of different ways in which children respond to trauma. Similarly, in work in Rwanda, Staub and Pearlman found diverse reactions to the same events. The greatest diversity was between perpetrators and victims, who may have perceived the identical situation in completely different ways. In treating both the perpetrators and victims in a group, one of the greatest difficulties facing the therapist attempting to achieve healing may be helping individuals to understand how a given situation looks from a different perspective. As difficult, perhaps, is even getting them to want to achieve an understanding of a different perspective. A similar problem no doubt would be found in the Bosnian tragedy studied by Dybdahl. So much hurt and pain have been experienced by the victims that they may have come to feel that their experiences are the only ones that legitimately bear understanding, and that the experience of those who caused their suffering is not worthy of serious consideration. At present, the same problem no doubt exists among the Israelis Cohen studied, as well as among Palestinians, who may also view themselves as oppressed.

8. *Caregivers going into new cultures must learn to understand the culture to maximize the effectiveness of their interventions.* Carr explicitly points out the need to understand people from cultures radically different from the ones that many of the caregivers themselves were raised in. Similarly, Staub and Pearlman worked in a culture wholly different from their own. Sometimes differences in culture are not transparent but are nevertheless real. For example, in the Firehouse Project, it is clear that the firefighters with whom the therapists worked often thought in terms very different from those of Barbanel and her colleagues. At the very least, they were from a different subculture. To gain their respect and trust was probably no easier, and may have been harder, than would have been the case for individuals from a different land. In telecommuting to disasters, Stamm and Hudnall found it especially important to understand other cultures. In such instances,

one can be working anywhere in the world. One does not have the usual nonverbal and other personal cues associated with helping behavior. So one has to work especially hard to understand one's clients.

9. *Official responses to disasters may be chaotic and potentially harmful and caregivers need to be alert to the quality of information they are given.* Nowhere is this more evident than in the case of Chernobyl as discussed by Macomber and Grigorenko: The attempt of the Soviet government to cover up the extent and severity of the damage only contributed to greater harm being done to innocents. But cover-ups are by no means limited to the former Soviet government. The genocide in Rwanda was initially covered up, the extent of the damage in Bosnia-Herzegovina was initially covered up, the danger of breathing the air near the World Trade Center immediately after the buildings imploded was initially covered up. Caregivers potentially placed themselves in harm's way not only because of the nature of the disasters, but because the extent and severity of the damage that had been caused was busily being hidden. When therapists treat clients, they know they cannot rely fully on the veracity of the information they receive from those clients. The same is true of governmental and nongovernmental organizations alike. One cannot assume they are disseminating one either complete or accurate information. And sometimes the distortions are every bit as deliberate as those of personal clients, or more so.

10. *One must face ethical dilemmas in disaster-relief situations that one may not have faced before.* Dybdahl notes how, when people's survival is at stake, one must question whether scarce resources should be allocated to psychological helping. Often funds are scarce, and even when aid workers volunteer their time, there are potential costs, such as feeding the aid workers or providing them with the resources they need to do their work. We who are psychologically minded may value our work, but others may not value it equally. Cohen reports that there is often a neglect of children's psychological needs in Israeli families and schools. The systems are overwhelmed. In interventions such as that of Staub and Pearlman in Rwanda, the ethical questions might defy even moral philosophers. Is there any understanding of genocide? Should the perpetrators be there together with the victims or should they all be on trial? At what level of responsibility does one have to have been to be tried by a judicial proceeding? How does one deal not only with victims, but with those who have rejected and often

spurned the victims, as Macomber and Grigorenko report happened in the aftermath of the Chernobyl disaster? Psychologists are trained to deal with ethical issues, but perhaps not of the kind that they encounter in some forms of disaster relief. They may need on-the-job training to deal with them, and even that may not be enough.

11. *One may have to be satisfied with, or at least accept, results that ordinarily would not satisfy one.* The goal of treatment typically is to heal a client—to make him or her better, or at least as much better as is feasible. In the case of victims of disaster, one may have to accept a lesser degree of healing than one might be accustomed to. It is not surprising that Bonanno and Mancini report on the difficulty of getting responses to disaster actually to have significant positive therapeutic outcomes. Carr found herself, at times, in need of evacuation. And when she was to be evacuated, it was not easy, and often it was impossible, for all of those for whom she might be caring to be evacuated with her. In the work of Cohen, it is doubtful that children who have experienced the loss of loved ones or substantial physical harm will be quite whole again, at least in the sense they would have been had the terrorist incident not occurred. People who have witnessed rapes and torture, as happened to the clients of both Carr and Dybdahl, may not achieve the kind of recovery a phobic client might back at home. Part of the kind of work described in this volume is an acceptance of what is possible and what is not, when one would have hoped for much more.

12. *The rewards, despite the costs, are incalculable.* Those who treat victims of disaster are changed. That is a theme that emerges throughout the book. Just as the victims were changed by the disasters they experienced, so are their therapists touched by their contact with and willingness to help the victims. Perhaps the most elegant statement of just how touched a therapist can be is to be found in the chapter by Carr: ". . . I went back to the roots of why I was there. I found that those roots were deep and enduring and that I could finally answer the question of whether or not I was cut out to do this work. It wasn't about my strength or energy or will, really. It was about knowing that this was exactly what I was supposed to be doing and what I was made to do. As long as I could do the work with a motivation of love for the people I was helping and joy in doing the work, then I could keep going."

Index

Advances in the Treatment of Posttraumatic Stress Disorder

Cognitive-Behavioral Perspectives

Steven Taylor, PhD, Editor

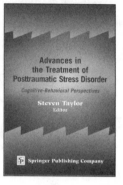

"Steve Taylor...one of the leaders...has brought together an international team of experts to provide us with the very latest in scientifically sound information on the nature and treatment of PTSD. This book is very worthy of the attention of all who work with psychologically traumatized people."

—from the Foreword by **G. Ron Norton,** PhD
Professor Emeritus, Department of
Psychology, University of Winnipeg

Are behavioral and cognitive-behavioral therapies sufficiently broad in their effects on trauma-related psychopathology and related factors? This volume considers many of the complexities in treating PTSD, and emphasizes evidence-based approaches to treatment.

A useful resource for clinicians, trainees, and investigators doing research into the treatment of PTSD.

Partial Contents:

Part I: Introduction • Current Directions and Challenges in the Treatment of Posttraumatic Stress Disorder, *S. Taylor*

Part II: New Developments • Efficacy and Outcome Predictors for Three PTSD Treatments: Exposure Therapy, EMDR, and Relaxation Training, *S. Taylor*

• PTSD and the Social Support of the Interpersonal Environment: The Development of Social Cognitive Behavior Therapy, *N. Tarrier & A.L. Humphreys*

Part III: Treating Special Populations and Problems • Effects of Cognitive-Behavioral Treatments for PTSD on Anger, *S.P. Cahill, S.A. Rauch, E.A. Hembree, & E.B. Foa*

• The Challenge of Treating PTSD in the Context of Chronic Pain, *J. Wald, S. Taylor, & I. C. Federoff*

Part IV: Perspectives on Future Directions • A Glass Half Empty or Half Full? Where We Are and Directions for Future Research in the Treatment of PTSD, *S.P. Cahill & E.B. Foa*

2004   336pp   0-8261-2047-4   Hard

11 West 42nd Street, New York, NY 10036-8002 • Fax: 212-941-7842
Order Toll-Free: 877-687-7476 • Order On-line: www.springerpub.com